Lest We Forget

Lest We Forget

Mandy R. Evans

Andrews University Press Berrien Springs, Michigan

Cover picture, left to right: Rosie, Corrie, Nan, and Mandy

ISBN 0-943872-58-8
Library of Congress Catalog Card Number 91-075695

Printing: 6 5 4 3 2 1   Year: 97 96 95 94 93 92 91

Andrews University Press
Berrien Springs, Michigan 49104

Printed by Patterson Printing Company
Benton Harbor, Michigan

Cover design by Peter Erhard

Color separation and imaging
by LithoMark, Stevensville, MI

October 16, 1991

GUY VANDER JAGT
9TH DISTRICT, MICHIGAN

Dear Mandy:

The true story of Lieske van Kessel and Mandy Evans stretches across two continents, and nearly a half century. From the darkest days of World War II in the Netherlands, to a heartwarming tour of America; from the Oval Office in Washington to Disneyland, in California; this story of courage, heroism, and remembrance reminds us of the personal struggles and sacrifices that provided hope during one of freedom's darkest hours. The message and inspiration of this story reminds us on a personal level what the struggle was all about and demonstrates how a few individuals risked everything to keep the flickering flame of freedom alive then, so that we may all continue to cherish it today.

Like you, I will never forget our time together in the Oval Office with the President of the United States. Your story of courage, heroism, and remembrance is a legacy that I will always remember and cherish. As our nation prepares to mark the 50th anniversary of our entry into World War II, I think that it is only fitting that we pause to remember the many examples of individual heroism that provided inspiration and hope in those dark days of the War.

With best personal wishes,

Sincerely,

Guy Vander Jagt, M.C.

So easy to remember,

Impossible to forget

This story is dedicated to:

*M*y father, for his foresight and love for his family. Few things have ever meant more to me than when he told me how proud he was of me for not having revealed anything following the raid on *De Zwaan.*

My brother, for his determination and courage to follow through on his promise to mama not to end up in the gas chambers at Auschwitz.

My mother, for her endurance and strength.

My sisters Corrie and Rosie, for their will to see it through.

Especially to: Tante Lieske, Oom Twan and Tante Mien, Oom Piet and Tante Annie, Oom Piet and Moeke Zwanns, Jan and Nikki Hornick, and all the others who dared to sacrifice their lives so that we might live.

But foremost to: Oom Kees, my mentor and role model, whom God allowed to finish the task he set out to do. To have known him has been a rare and precious experience granted to only a fortunate few. I still miss him to this day.

All thanks go to God for His incredible miracles. At the time we may not have recognized them, but without them, we would never have survived.

Contents

Preface

 his book not only accounts for the major happenings in the life of the little Jewish girl, Manda, but brings alive all the tastes, sounds, smells and sights of life that are so often overlooked. The humor that she weaves into her memoirs speaks of her rich memory and her love of life. Knowing her as I have for thirty years, I am positive my mother would never neglect such an important survival skill as humor.

The story tells of "Amama" and her woolen-scarf remedy for sore throats—I can attest that the remedy really works.

It reminds me of my grandfather, whom I called "Opa." And though he is no longer living, I again can see and feel his strength, humor, and love in my family. Even at a very young age, I remember believing that Opa was very special.

It reveals my Grandmother "Oma," who at ninety continues to maintain her strong will to survive, who still has her "bag of goodies" for her ten grandchildren and eight great-grandchildren. Oma has never been known for mastering the English language, but I still beg her to tell me stories of the "olden days"; inevitably she shares a humorous story that has us laughing tears.

In all of life, there seems to be a strong desire for order, a sense of balance, a need for equality. During a time when the world seems to go completely mad, the power of good filters through to an evil existence. World War II was yet another historic event that allowed a handful of people to bring true meaning to that often misused word, "hero."

So it was that six years ago I had the opportunity to travel to Europe to meet some of those heroes—heroes who until that time had been only names to me from an earlier manuscript. Looking back now, I realize more than ever what a great privilege was mine to meet and to listen to these truly extraordinary people.

When I met Tante Lieske, she was able to speak only a few English words, but the way she hugged me and smiled made me realize just how natural it was for her to be so selfless and giving.

Tante Mien I found totally enchanting. It was this very pretty, prim and proper elderly Dutch lady who artfully dodged her way past German soldiers to deliver handguns to the underground. To hear the story from her own lips was quite exciting.

But it was Kees who truly was the inspiration for my mother. It is hard to describe the magnitude of emotion that she feels for this man who long ago took the time to bring some joy and education back into her life. He even wrote a poem especially for her.

As I reflect over my own life, I realize I have developed a greater respect and admiration for my mother. Not once can I recall her instilling in my brothers or me a sense of hatred or animosity. Instead, we were told of the unselfish acts of courage, the endurance and perseverance of these individuals and the unconditional love they gave her and many others. I know that that special love has overpowered any bitterness she could have harbored.

And now I feel I have come full circle. I have learned of the atrocities and have felt the sadness; but my mother gave me the gift to remember the good, the kindness, the courage and strength of those who gave so much of themselves. Doesn't it seem ironic that at times of great sadness and human tragedy, it is the smallest of memories that we treasure the most.

— Lorraine Evans Medici
Mandy's daughter

The story you are about to read is an account of the events involving the survival of a Jewish family in the Netherlands during the World War II Nazi occupation.

Although no statistics have been kept in this particular regard, according to the Rijks Instituut voor Oorlogs Documentatie (RIOD), the National Institute of War Documentation in the Netherlands, we may very well be the only Dutch family of that size who survived the Holocaust.

Except for a reasonable amount of artistic license, the places, events and characters are real and, with a few exceptions, names have not been changed.

Mandy R. Evans

Trapped!

ive days had passed and Holland was crushed. The Dutch soldiers, who had so gallantly defended our country, were sent home. The queen and her family had fled to England. Beside the airport, most of Rotterdam and part of the Hague had been bombed, and hundreds of people had been killed. And during all that time, Papa had been waiting for a phone call which never came.

For months, he and his associate, Mijnheer de Jong, had it all very carefully planned. The moment the Germans would invade Holland, the two families would flee to England together. Papa had tried to call him several times, but no one had answered. Something had gone wrong, but what? "We just can't wait any longer. Let's go," Papa told Mama. Thus, he piled the whole family into the car to begin our escape to England via the IJmuiden Harbor. Our baggage was very light. It consisted merely of the clothes on our backs.

German troops were right on our heels. Earlier, in an attempt to stop the enemy, the Dutch had blown up the oil refineries near Ijmuiden and the sky was still aglow. It was a very quiet trip until Corrie suddenly remarked that

Amama was still wearing her black and white plaid velvet slippers. In all the confusion she had forgotten to put her shoes on, and no one had noticed until this moment. Mama shook her head, but Papa couldn't help smiling. Glancing over his shoulder, he said: "Don't worry about it, Mama. I'll buy you a new pair of shoes once we get to England, but first you have to tell me why you're carrying those beans." All eyes went from the slippers to the bag of brown beans hidden in Amama's huge lap.

"You never know when we'll need them. They are very nutritious and they don't take much room."

"That was very good thinking, Mama," Papa commented. He tried to sound very serious. "You always think of everything, don't you?"

Amama smiled proudly. She loved receiving compliments from her son-in-law. Amama, indeed, did think of everything, and she also knew how to bring a ray of light to the darkest of moments.

At last we reached IJmuiden. Just like everywhere else, people were standing around talking about the cowardly invasion. Papa stopped the car and got out to join a group of fishermen. Dressed in their heavy, black, woolen, balloon pants with the silver buttons and their sparkling white shirts, they seemed involved in heavy conversation, while their fishing boats lay idly moored along the cobblestone quay. When Papa reached the men, they stopped talking— but only for a moment—and I watched as Papa shook their hands. There were a lot of gestures. Some of the men shook their heads. After a while, Papa returned to the car. His eyes were filled with concern. Mama tipped her head out of the window. "And?" she asked quizzically.

"I'm afraid we're too late!"

"What do you mean, too late?" she cried.

"The last boat left last night. We're trapped," he mumbled vehemently, crushing his cigarette into the ground. Immediately lighting up another one, he got into the car and started the engine to begin the long, silent ride home.

The beans were left untouched and Amama would never have a chance to buy shoes in England. As for Mijnheer de Jong and his family, they had gotten away in time and had safely arrived in South Africa.

Beginnings

*O*ur family drama, which was to include nearly incredible events after our failed escape attempt in 1940, had started years earlier on a late Sunday afternoon in the fall of 1922, in what seems now a more innocent time.

The platform of the train station in Maastricht was crowded with soccer fans trying to catch their train home. Among them was a young woman returning home from a visit with her cousin. She glanced at her watch. It was nearing five-thirty. Holding her attractive little red hat with her slender, gloved hand, she got on her toes, trying to look over the crowd. What was keeping him? The train would soon be leaving. She was sure she had told him five-thirty before she had left home last week. She hoped he hadn't forgotten. There he was now! She let go of her hat and waved.

"Philip!" she called. He looked in the direction of her voice. He had spotted her. Smiling broadly, he waved back. He had someone with him—a young man. Philip was trying to point her out to him. At last the two men reached her. "*Dag*, Elsa."

"*Dag*, Philip." They embraced.

Then Philip turned to the tanned, dark-haired young man next to him. "Maan, this is my sister, Elsa. Elsa, this is Manus Wynperle, a friend of mine and the best soccer goalie in the country."

"Don't believe a word he says," the young man grinned as he shook her hand.

She returned his smile, then turned to her brother. "I was afraid you had forgotten."

"Of course not," he replied, putting an arm around her shoulder. "It took us a little while to get out of the ball park." He picked up her suitcase and they began boarding the train.

During the short trip to Sittard she learned quite a bit about her brother's friend. He was born and reared in Amsterdam, which didn't totally surprise her. He looks like a city boy, she thought. But what could possibly have brought him to Sittard, the small southern town, hundreds of kilometers away from home? As if he had read her mind, he began telling her how he had lived in Cologne, Germany, for a year while he was playing as a goalie for their local team, K.B.C.

"He won the championship for them," Philip interrupted.

His friend smiled shyly, but she noticed the sparkle in his dark brown eyes when he continued, "After we'd won the championship, Sittard approached me to play for them with a chance to become the trainer—an offer I couldn't refuse. Besides, it was an opportunity to get out of Germany. One year was long enough."

She found herself having more than the normal degree of interest when she asked, "Do you have a job in Sittard?"

He shook his head. "No. I bought a store. Household goods. Dishes, some furniture, carpeting—that sort of thing."

She nodded. "I see. Are your parents living in Amsterdam?"

Again he shook his head. "They are living in Sittard, too. Until his retirement, my father was an officer with the merchant marines. He is not in the best of health. So I decided to move them both out here. That way, I can keep an eye on them."

"How considerate," she thought.

"Didn't you tell me you have brothers and sisters?" Philip asked.

"Two of each. I'm the one in the middle," he grinned, turning to Philip. There was a pause, following which the two men became involved in a heavy discussion about the soccer match they had just seen. Elsa had never been a real soccer fan and she began looking out of the window for a while, not really seeing anything. Why did she feel so ill at ease? With two brothers of her own, she usually didn't have any problems being around men. As a matter of fact, Philip, who had to chaperon her every time she attended any kind of social event, had often called her a "tease and a flirt." But today was different. Now and then she could feel Maan's eyes resting on her. When she turned away from the window, their eyes met briefly. She could feel herself blush. Yes, he was very good looking, indeed.

That evening he stayed for dinner. The next evening he came to visit, and the next . . . and the next. As he told her many years later, he had fallen in love with her little red hat.

On August 14, 1923, relatives and friends gathered in the old synagogue in Sittard to witness the solemn wedding ceremony of Manus Wynperle and his beautiful bride, Elsa, who later became my parents.

All through the service, Philip smiled broadly. He had good reason. After all, it was he who had brought them together.

Upon their return from a honeymoon in Switzerland, the young couple moved into a small house near the store.

Someday they hoped to have saved enough money to buy a house, but for the time being, this was more than adequate. Earlier that year, Papa had become a representative for two large German manufacturers of fine china and crystal, an employment which took him away from home most of the week. Carrying two large suitcases filled with samples, he travelled hundreds of kilometers by train, from one town to the next, to show and sell his merchandise. As a result, the burden of operating the store fell largely on Mama's fragile shoulders—twelve hours a day and often as many as seven days a week. Soon they were making enough money to hire a salesgirl to relieve Mama, especially on Sundays, so she was able to join Papa at the soccer games.

During the quiet evenings alone in the months that followed, Mama often thought of how drastically her life had changed. Her mind wandered back to the modest farm house where she grew up, and the small adjoining store that carried mainly groceries and men's suiting. That store had always been filled with the wonderful, overpowering smell of freshly ground coffee. While her father had visited the outlying farms, using his horse and cart laden with wares, her mother had tended the home and the store.

Except, of course, on the Sabbath. That's when life came to a complete standstill in the orthodox household of Herman and Rosalie Silbernberg. A smile crossed Elsa's lips as some of the memories started to take shape and color. The Friday night dinners, served on a white lace tablecloth; her mother lighting the candles.

Of all the Holy Days, however, she had probably liked Passover best of all. The table never looked more beautiful than on the night of the Seder. The sparkling crystal and the special "Passover" dishes, which, once a year, her brothers helped carry down from the attic, but not until every room in the house had been cleaned from floor to ceiling.

The next day, dressed in their Passover finery, the whole family would go to synagogue together, where they spent most of the day. She had to admit there were times when she truly missed not being able to go to synagogue on the

Sabbath as often as she liked. Oh, she still joined her parents on the Feast days, but it wasn't quite the same.

"It's all a part of growing up," her mother explained. "Remember, things never stay the same. Instead, you should thank God for having married such a good man." Then she had shrugged her shoulders. "So, he'll keep his store open on the Sabbath. It's not his fault that he was raised in an unorthodox home."

In the short time that her mother and her husband had known each other, a deep mutual admiration and affection had developed between them, and she wondered if her mother couldn't be just slightly prejudiced.

She gently stroked her bulging tummy. Soon they would be a real family. They were both looking forward to the event with great anticipation, but until then, there was still a lot that needed to be decided upon. Her main concern was who would look after the store after the baby was born. Would she, like her mother, be able to take care of the baby and the store at the same time? Maybe they should hire another salesgirl, or better yet, a woman to help her take care of the baby. They had to come to a decision pretty soon. She made up her mind that she was going to discuss it this weekend—the moment Manus came home. She was not going to put it off any longer.

The advertisement had called for "a capable woman who likes children." Papa had been quite skeptical of the idea at first. It had taken hours of reasoning on Mama's part before she had finally won him over. In his final argument, needless to say he didn't have the last word, he had determined the qualifications.

The applicants were numerous, but none of them met with Papa's approval. Then, one cold wintry night in late February 1924, a young girl in her late teens, dressed in a dark gray, threadbare coat, appeared on their doorstep. From under her well-worn bonnet came a tuft of carrot-colored hair. As soon as Mama opened the door, the homely, freckled face broke into a wide smile. Mama knew right there and then, this was the right one.

"Are you the lady who is looking for someone to take care of her children?" the girl asked softly.

"Child," Mama corrected her. "Our first one. Come on in. It's too cold to stand out there." The girl followed her into the living room. Mama could think of only one thing. How would she be able to convince Maan that this was the person they had been looking for? She had worried needlessly. For reasons of his own, Papa agreed and Maria was hired.

"And, what do you think?" she asked, after the girl had left.

He shrugged his shoulders and picked up the newspaper. "I couldn't help having *rachmones* with her," he replied.

She couldn't believe her ears. What had happened to his qualifications? Then her face broke into a smile. She should have guessed that her husband would feel sorry for the girl the moment she had walked into the room. She slowly got up from her chair and began carrying the empty teacups to the kitchen.

"I think she'll be with us for a long, long time!" she called from the kitchen.

"What makes you think that?" he asked, while his eyes moved across the sports section of the newspaper.

"I don't know. I just have a feeling that she will."

"Did you hear her say that she knows how to cook?" he commented.

Did she detect some sarcasm? She chuckled. She realized her cooking would never measure up to her mother-in-law's. She dried the cups and put them in the cupboard. In the end, they agreed they had made a wise choice, and a wise choice it turned out to be. Maria stayed for twelve years, just as Mama had predicted. Not only did she become indispensable where it concerned the care of "us," the children, but she emerged as a beacon of strength in times of grief. And there would be plenty of that.

On a beautiful Sunday in the spring of 1924, on Maria's day off, Mama gave birth to a tiny baby girl, while somewhere between two goal posts, Papa scored another victory for his club. As befitted an old and loyal friend, Philip was waiting for him at the train station that night. "It's a girl!" he yelled. They named her Corrie.

Soon after Corrie was born, Mama and Papa decided to move into the apartment above the store. Not only was it very convenient, but it gave them all the space they needed. And so, after a brief recess, Mama returned to her place behind the counter, leaving the baby in Maria's capable hands. The fact that she was the oldest of ten brothers and sisters soon became evident, putting Mama's mind at ease.

Everything was going quite well for the young couple. The store, as well as Papa's wholesale business, prospered and soon they were able to hire another salesgirl. This gave Mama a chance to be with the baby for a day while Maria went home to visit her family. In the meantime, Papa had signed up with another soccer club. He practiced mostly on Saturday; on Sundays he played, either at home or out of town. Occasionally, Mama would go along, but not very often.

Except for their grandparents, neither Mama nor Papa had yet lost someone close to them, so when *Grootvader*, Papa's father, died in December 1925, although not totally unexpected, it came as a serious blow. Mama had grown very fond of her father-in-law in the few short years she had known him, and she took it almost as hard as Papa.

The pain seemed somewhat eased by the arrival of a new baby shortly after. In February 1926, Nan was born. Officially he was called Nathan after his recently departed grandfather. He was a chubby little fellow with a head of thick black hair. Everyone agreed he was the spitting image of his father. With two small children to take care of, Maria's workload was increased considerably, but she never complained, not even on those weekends when she was asked to stay so Mama could go with Papa to watch him play at one of his out-of-town soccer games. At times, however, she must have wondered what she had gotten herself into, especially when in June 1928, another baby arrived—another boy. Unfortunately, very unlike his brother, he was frail and sickly with an undetermined blood disorder. He died at the tender age of three months.

It seemed that after the death of the baby, Papa's and Mama's lives suddenly began to change. The string of events that was to follow would keep only the strongest of families together.

The depression of the late twenties and the early thirties did not bypass their small town. While unemployment increased, business quickly declined, and it wasn't very long before the store began to show a considerable loss. The wholesale business didn't seem to fare much better and Papa began to travel less and less. Two salesgirls were needed no longer. First one was laid off, then the other. But Maria stayed. As the customers grew fewer in number, the bill collectors became more numerous. Standing idly on the stoop in front of the store, Mama was soon able to spot them a mile away. She'd run inside, lock the door, and turn the sign in the window to "CLOSED." Many years later, she'd laugh until the tears would come each time she told us about it, but it wasn't very amusing at the time. After all, she had led—pretty much—a sheltered life, void of any real hardships and tragedies; and at times, it seemed a century ago since that Sunday afternoon at the train station in Maastricht.

Papa was not the type of person to let difficult times get him down. In a final attempt to regain some of his losses, he depleted all of his savings to buy at very competitive prices—and uninsured—a boxcar load of fine china and crystal at the famous Leipziger Messe in Germany. He planned to do very well with it, but he soon learned that all the merchandise had been stolen, and they were left penniless overnight. To save the store, the local bank offered to help them by controlling their finances until all of their bills were paid, and after the initial shock had worn off, they decided to start anew.

During it all, there was also a moment of great joy. In November 1929, Rosalie was born. The chubby little girl began to look more and more like her brother, with her large, dark brown eyes and black, curly hair. She turned out to be not only beautiful but exceptionally bright as well. Without any feelings of resentment from the other children, "*Ikke My*" (I me), as she called herself, became the apple of her father's eye. As young as she was, she possessed the rare talent of winning the hearts of everyone around her—until that dreadful day in October 1932. "Ikke My" suddenly became ill. She had awakened with a fever and wasn't able to stand up by herself. "My leg hurts!" she cried.

The doctor was called, and he had her immediately admitted to the hospital. Fully conscious, "Ikke My" died ten days before her third birthday, but not until she had reminded Papa, who not for a moment had left her bedside, of the new coat and hat he'd promised her for her birthday. Although Mama and Papa stuck to their belief that she had died of polio, the real cause would always remain a mystery.

Through it all, Maria showed her never-ending love and support. When Mama and Papa returned from the funeral, "Ikke My's" bedroom was rearranged and her little white bed, as well as all her clothes and her toys, were quickly and quietly removed from the house.

Many years later, when Mama visited Maria who by then had a family of her own, they had a cup of tea together. Marie suddenly got up and walked over to the large china cabinet that dominated her humble living room. Carefully, she took a small metal Easter egg from one of the shelves. "I kept this for you," she said as she handed her former mistress the precious little toy. For a moment Mama held it between her hands, fighting back the tears. Then she held it up against her ear and shook it gently. Yes, even the peanut that "Ikke My" had put in it was still there.

Ironically it had been Mama who had shown herself to be the strongest. To Papa, the loss of his little girl was cruel and unacceptable. He retreated to a world of his own. For months, he just sat in his chair and stared out the windows.

Once again, the burden of the store, along with all its financial problems, fell on Mama, who was once again pregnant, this time with me. Since time seems to be the healer of all wounds, no matter how slowly, Papa gradually began to pull himself together. In May 1933, it was finally my turn—also a chubby baby, but very blond. I would remember only two grandmothers, as "Apapa," Mama's father, died of a stroke just two months before I was born.

The death of the other two children left a large age gap between Nan and me. But it was only a minor problem that Mama and Papa knew how to solve easily. In June 1935, my playmate was born. Another Rosalie. With this latest addition, we definitely had outgrown the apartment and we moved to a large two-story house on the same street and not far from the store. One person, however, didn't move with us—Maria. After almost twelve years, she was returning to her hometown to get married—and there she is still living to this day. Her sister Nellie came to take her place.

It was the fall of 1937. The evenings were growing longer and colder. Inside, however, the fire filled the room with a soothing warmth. Mama and Papa were occupying their favorite chairs beside the hearth. He was reading the newspaper, and she was mending some of our clothes. The house was very still. We children were tucked safely away in bed, including Corrie and Nan, while Nellie was enjoying a night off. The quiet was broken only by the crackling noise of the flames and the ticking of the Frisian wall clock.

The headlines in the paper were flashing more ominous news of Hitler's fast-growing power. Presently, Papa stopped reading to put out his cigarette in the large, shallow, mother-of-pearl shell with the brass alligator mounted on its edge—a wedding gift, and really too pretty to be used as an ashtray. He briefly glanced at Mama. Then he returned to his paper.

"I have a foreboding feeling," he said, scanning some of the other news stories. She knew all too well what he was referring to. "Me too," she mumbled, trying to break off a thread with her teeth.

"I feel increasingly more uncomfortable living so close to the German border," he said. "What would you say if we moved to Amsterdam?" He sounded almost casual.

A little startled perhaps, but not too surprised, she dropped her sewing in her lap. "And sell the store?" He answered with a nod. She tried to hide her misgivings.

He had lit another cigarette. There was a heavy silence. She took a sock out of the basket and studied the hole.

"What would you be doing?"

"I have been thinking of starting a tire business."

"You have? What made you think of that?"

"A few weeks ago I ran into someone I hadn't seen in years. We had dinner together and he told me that he was planning to start a tire business. I got the impression that he's somewhat short of money, because he's looking for a partner. He asked me if I would be interested."

"What did you tell him?"

"Well, that I would have to give it some thought and I would have to discuss it with you first, of course." He folded the paper and put it on the table next to him.

She had the feeling that he had already decided. "What about Mama?"

He smiled gently. "You don't think for a moment that I would leave her behind?"

"No, of course not," she replied. As so many times before, his love for her mother clearly showed. "What if she doesn't want to come?"

"Don't worry. Just leave it up to me."

A smile crossed her lips. She'd hate to leave the area, especially her brothers. Her sister Sophie had moved to Amsterdam a year earlier. The thought of the big city scared her, but in her heart she knew he was right. Besides, she wouldn't think of interfering with her husband's deep concern for her and the children. She threaded her needle. "When will we be moving?"

"As soon as the store is sold." He looked at her, his dark eyebrows slightly raised. He was very much aware of her reluctance and he had expected a lot more opposition. It made him feel rather guilty. He leaned forward and took her hand. Her eyes rested for a moment on his strong, tanned hands. They always seemed tanned, even in the winter.

"Everything is going to be all right," he said, patting her hand lightly.

She looked up and smiled, "Sure."

More at ease, he let go of her hand and leaned back in his chair. She folded the last garment and put it on top of the basket. "Would you like another cup of tea?"

"I'd love one," he said. It was a long time before she finally went to sleep that night. Alone with her thoughts, she reflected on the past fourteen years. It would be strange without the store. Except for the brief rest after the birth of each of her children and the funerals of two of them, the store had been her life since the day they were married. And during all that time, her children had been in the care of others. Tears welled up in her eyes. Yes, she was looking forward to becoming a full-time mother at long last.

With Mama's approval of course, Papa rented a house in Amstelveen, a small urban community on the outskirts of Amsterdam. And in the early spring of 1938, he loaded his entire family into the car, including our grandmother, or "Amama" as she was lovingly called, and locked the door of the house in Sittard for the very last time. We were on our way to a better and safer place—at least that's what Papa was hoping for.

Chapter 2

Amama's Days

Our new home was situated on a friendly tree-lined street in a middle-class neighborhood with a diversity of religions. In spite of the large number of children of all ages, the neighborhood could definitely be considered as "quiet," except, of course, for the summer months when school was out.

Since only a couple of families on our street owned a car, traffic was almost non-existent. Actually, the busiest times were in the mornings when the usual vendors, with their horses and wagons, would make their daily rounds selling milk and vegetables. The only traffic in the evening was a tall, thin policeman who patrolled the area on his bicycle, which had a very funny-looking seat. It was very small—not much bigger than Papa's hand, and of very hard leather with a very wide groove in the center. When we asked Papa about it, he thought for a moment before he explained that such a seat was good for one's health—especially when that someone rode his bicycle a lot. And with that explanation, our curiosity was satisfied. The policeman seemed very friendly. He smiled as he rode through the street and watched us play. When occasionally a ball would roll his way, he'd take his foot off the pedal and kick the ball back.

Generally, the neighborhood had the appearance of one big family. It wasn't uncommon for Rosie and me to have lunch with some of the neighbors a couple of times a week, while some of the neighbor children sat down to dinner with us.

The house itself was a modest, two-story, brick structure identical to all the other row houses on the street. Downstairs it had a living room, dining room and kitchen. Upstairs were three bedrooms and a bathroom, plus two small rooms in the *zolder* (attic.) Both the kitchen and the dining room gave access to a red-tiled patio and a small fenced-in backyard. Beyond it, surrounded by houses, lay two fenced-in tennis courts. Only a narrow alley separated them from the small, meticulously manicured yards. At each of the corners, the alley branched off to the streets in front. During the summer, the tennis courts were crowded with people, and until late at night, we could hear the monotonous pong, pong, pong as the balls were hit back and forth, back and forth. Although we were able to watch the games from our yard, the box seats, no doubt, were the chairs on the balcony off of Papa and Mama's bedroom.

Papa was indisputedly the head of the household, but in a very loving and caring way. Improper table manners, for instance, were a thorn in Papa's flesh. Consequently, from the moment we were able to hold a spoon in our hands, we were taught to use fork and knife simultaneously, holding the fork in the left hand and the knife in the right. We never could start our meal until we had raised our silverware for inspection. And, of course, we could never start until Mama had taken her place at the dinner table. If one of us occasionally tried, Papa would raise his heavy, dark eyebrows, while his black, piercing eyes sent arrows through the offender's body. "I haven't noticed your Mother sitting down, have you?" he'd ask, and slowly the silverware would be lowered to find its place next to the plate once again.

Once dinner was over, all etiquette was temporarily dismissed. It was time for singing. Conducting us with his index finger, father led us in not only Dutch songs, but English and German tunes as well. One, I especially remember, sounded somewhat like this:

"Has anybody here seen Kelly?
Kelly with the bright green tie?
K. E. double L. Y."
(*Complete with Irish brogue.*)

The only one allowed to make changes without Papa's consent was Amama. With her arrival came the restoration of the Sabbath, undoubtedly more out of respect for her than out of religious conviction, except maybe on Mama's part. On Friday night, Papa would be home early, and while Rosie and I shared the tub as we received our Sabbath baths, Amama would take charge of setting the table. The smell of roast chicken would fill the whole house. Soon the table, covered with the white lace tablecloth, would be overflowing with delicacies—chicken soup with matzo balls, roast potatoes, fresh peas and pear kugel. After dinner, it was time for relaxation and Mama's famous butter cake, so rich, the butter would ooze from between our teeth.

The next morning, Amama would quietly slip out the front door for the short walk to the small synagogue around the corner, while the rest of us were still sound asleep.

I have often wondered why we nicknamed one grandmother *Amama*, while the other, Papa's mother, was simply called *Grootmoeder*. Obviously we were able to pronounce both words equally well, so that couldn't have been the reason. But whatever the origin, it seemed to fit both personalities to perfection. *Amama*, endearing and gentle. *Grootmoeder*, strict and severe. And if Amama was capable of smoothing out any wrinkles, *Grootmoeder* was an expert at putting them back in. I can't—nor do I want to—imagine what life would have been like had *Grootmoeder* been living with us. Her mere visits took a full day of preparation.

First, there was the house. As immaculate as Mama was, she made sure the house was above any criticism. Then, of course, there were we children. We tried very hard to be seen (as little as possible), but not to be heard.

Worse still, were the times when we had to repay her visit. I remember well the sweet, warm smell of freshly baked bread from the bakery below, and how the smell followed us all the way up the stairs to *Grootmoeder's* second-floor apartment. Stiffly seated on her straight, high-backed chairs, we children found the afternoon to be endless. To minimize the chances of our spilling crumbs on the rug, *Grootmoeder* served us a "small" cookie on a plate the size of a dinner plate. All the time while we nervously munched our cookies, she'd watch us from her enormous, grey velvet chair by the window and remind us to chew each bite twenty-nine times for proper digestion. Neither Rosie nor I had any idea what she was talking about, but she definitely had us concerned when, after only five times chewing, the tiny bite was gone.

Our lives seemed to be comprised of an assortment of customs and traditions. Summer meant *nieuwe haring* (new herring.) Each morning, at about eleven o'clock, a small, white push cart would pass through our street. *"VERSE HAAAAARING!! HEERLIJKE VERSE HAAAAARING!"* (Fresh herring!! Delicious fresh herring!) The peddler had arrived; the echo of his voice lingered between the houses. Standing on the stoop, Amama was already waiting for him—her worn, black leather change purse with the silver-colored metal clip clutched between her wrinkled hands. When the cart reached our house, it automatically came to a halt. The peddler knew his steady customers well. He smiled at the elderly lady and chit-chatted with her while fileting the small fish. "This herring will melt in your mouth!" he guaranteed her, as he did each morning. In exchange for a nickel, he handed her the light rose-colored herring, skillfully cleaned, cut into small bite-size pieces and smothered with chopped onion, just the way she liked it. And that's how Rosie and I liked it, too, as seated on the edge of the dining room table, we anxiously awaited Amama's return. When she finally walked into the room, she pulled her chair to the table and began feeding us our "daily treat," one small piece at a time.

Except for the inescapable childhood diseases, we hardly ever had to visit the doctor's office. Rosie and I decided to have the mumps, chicken pox, measles and whooping cough simultaneously. After about four weeks, it had Mama near total exhaustion, but at least it was over and done with. Of course, there was always the common cold, but for that we didn't need the doctor. After all, we had Amama, whose medical treatments were relative to the intensity of the illness.

First, there was the *woolen-scarf* method for scratchy throats and minor coughs. Amama would apply an ice-cold, dripping-wet handkerchief on a very warm throat, and immediately cover it with a one-hundred-percent woolen scarf. The secret was definitely in the "pure" wool. According to Amama, wool kept the heat in. Ninety-percent wool and ten-percent cotton just wouldn't work as well, if at all. Although the remedy was never medically proven, it frequently did stop the cough. At those few times, however, when it didn't, the never-failing *beer porridge* treatment was used. A half bottle of beer in a quart of hot milk would send the patient, within minutes, into a state of total oblivion—a beautiful dream world where coughs were seldom heard.

In the more serious cases, however, when the cold might have settled itself in the chest area, Amama would use the *brown paper and candlewax* method. Using a hot iron, she'd melt candlewax between two sheets of brown paper—any other color wouldn't work—and apply the greasy paper to the patient's chest. Next, she'd cover it with the famous "woolen scarf." Not only would it do away with the congestion, but, in Papa's case, with the hair on his chest as well.

While Amama practiced general medicine, Papa was probably one of the earliest supporters of preventive medicine. Every evening, immediately after dinner, before the food had had a chance to "harm" our systems, Papa would line us up against the dining room wall. Using Mama as his personal Florence Nightingale, he'd order our mouths "open," causing a reflex as we grabbed for our noses. As Mama kept refilling the tablespoon in Papa's hand with the thick, immoveable cod liver oil, Papa slowly poured it down our throats. We gagged, spit and swore never to take it again—at least not until the next evening. Papa's only response was, "Well done." Mama would follow the dose with a candy.

Nan felt that it would be no more than fair for Papa to try—at least once—a little of his own "medicine." One day Nan adequately coated a tablespoon with the cod liver oil and placed it beside Papa's plate. Papa had always loved a bowl of hearty soup. It was one of his favorites, and this night wasn't any different. We could almost see him smile as the vapors penetrated his nostrils. We watched him from the corner of our eyes as he slowly dipped the spoon in the soup, brought it to his mouth, and—there went the spoon, flying through the dining room.

December was the month of spiritual enlightenment, joy and—utter confusion. There was *Sinterklaas*, the feast of Saint Nicolas, essentially a Christian holiday, and there was Channukah, the Jewish Feast of Lights. To complicate matters, they usually followed each other closely. So while in one corner of the room, according to centuries-old tradition, we'd each put one of our shoes in front of the hearth, stuffed with a carrot and stale bread for Sinterklaas' horse, in the other corner Amama would help us light the candles of the menorah. The end result of either celebration was the same—presents.

Next came Christmas, which Rosie and I thought was a somewhat lopsided affair. Although we spent most of our time at the neighbors next door, helping them decorate their Christmas tree, light the candles and sing songs, on December 25 we stayed home, wondering why everybody couldn't have a Christmas tree, matzos, and Easter eggs.

Little Time for Joy . . . Less Time for Tears

*T*he morning of May 10, 1940, didn't seem much different from any other spring morning in the outskirts of Amsterdam, as the early sun filtered through the thin cretonnes, filling the small bedroom with its warmth. Once again, it was that time of year when the streets would soon be bursting with the sound of children playing. I didn't really mind winter all that much; we had plenty of toys to keep us occupied—samples from the store in Sittard—but somehow, everything looked so sad and dreary, especially on rainy days— and there were lots of those. Rosie and I would finally have a chance to try out our new scooters which we had received for Chanukah. Rosie's was red with grey stripes; mine, blue with grey stripes. After all, those were our colors, and whatever gifts we received, Rosie's were always red, mine were always blue. That way, hopefully, there would neither be confusion nor fighting.

Twelve more days and I would be celebrating my seventh birthday. I was getting more excited with each day.

Birthdays were very special at our house. We got to choose our favorite dessert and we had so many relatives visiting, it looked more like a family reunion than a birthday party.

In the other bed across the room, curled up in a ball, Rosie was still sound asleep. All I could see was a tuft of blond hair. She hadn't started school yet and was allowed to sleep in. I jumped out of bed. On my way to the bathroom, I heard voices coming from below—more than the usual morning sounds. As a rule, it was very quiet around the house at this hour. No one wanted to awaken Amama. When I returned to the bedroom, I quickly got dressed in the clothes Mama had laid out for me the night before. I walked over to the window and peeked through the curtains. The tennis courts lay basking in the early morning sun. They looked so pretty with their freshly-rolled, red-clay carpets, trimmed with the sparkling-white lines. They made me think of a new dress. The small, well-kept backyards looked like colorful carpets of flowers, and in the neighbor's chestnut tree, the birds were singing their hearts out. I could have stood there for hours, but I'd better hurry, or I would be late for school.

I turned away from the window and began making my bed. Before leaving the room, I checked one last time to make sure everything looked tidy. My pajamas were put away; everything looked all right. Mama loathed messy rooms, and whenever we left things lying around, she'd make us go back and clean up.

Closing the door softly behind me, I started toward the stairs. I could hear the voices more clearly now. When I reached the bottom of the stairs, I saw Papa and Mama standing in the doorway. Amama, too. I was surprised. She never got up this early. Then I recognized some of our neighbors, Mijnheer and Meurouw Loewenthal and Mijnheer and Mevrouw Verbregge. Before I had a chance to find out what had happened, Papa turned around. He had heard me come down the stairs. His face looked very pale.

"What happened?" I asked.

24

He reached out his hand. I took it. "The war has started," he replied. It sounded like a whisper. Even though Papa and Mama had been talking about "the war" for a long time, I didn't quite understand what it was all about, but I knew, it had to be very bad. "How do you know?"

"The Germans bombed Schiphol last night."

That was another thing I didn't understand, but it wouldn't take long for me to learn. Papa led me across the street. As he pointed his finger in the direction of our airport, I saw dark smoke rise above the houses.

"Will I be able to go to school?"

A smile crossed his lips. "I don't know. We'll find out shortly. But let's go inside and have breakfast first."

The neighbors had begun to leave. Papa waved goodbye as the two of us followed Mama and Amama into the house. Then I realized that I hadn't seen Corrie and Nan. I asked Mama about them, as she walked into the kitchen to fix our breakfast. "Your sister and brother went to see some of their friends." She sounded weary.

I went into the dining room and took my usual place at the table. Amama looked very tired. She looked as if she had been crying. Her eyes were red and swollen.

Mama joined us. Carefully, she put a boiled egg in each of the porcelain egg cups. She buttered a slice of bread and put it on my plate. "Eat your breakfast!" She sounded grumpy. The room was so quiet, the cracking of the eggshell between my fingers seemed disturbing. Everybody was occupied with his or her own thoughts. Amama slowly sipped her tea. Occasionally she wiped her forehead with a handkerchief. It had cologne on it. "4711." I recognized the strong smell. She always used "4711" when she wasn't feeling well. Besides myself, Papa was the only one eating. When he was finished, he lit a cigarette. "Ready?" he asked.

I nodded, quickly swallowing my last piece of bread. Papa took a last sip of his tea and got up. Hurriedly, I ran around the table to kiss Mama and Amama goodbye and followed him out the door. With my hand buried in his, I skipped alongside of him. I had discovered quite some time ago, during our long Sunday-morning walks, that skipping was the only way to keep pace with Papa's long strides.

"What are we going to do now?" I asked between skips.

He hesitated. He raised his eyebrows. "I don't know. We'll have to wait and see." But I knew that Papa had already made up his mind. He was not going to wait. When we reached the school, only a few children were there, most of them accompanied by their parents, whose faces, too, were grim like Papa's. A sign in the window of one of the classrooms read: "SCHOOL CLOSED UNTIL FURTHER NOTICE." My disappointment must have clearly shown as Papa gently squeezed my hand. "I'm sure it won't be for very long." He briefly talked with some of the parents before we turned around to begin our walk back home. Mama and Amama were still sitting at the table—their breakfast untouched.

Five days later, the Dutch army was defeated. It was at this point that Papa decided to try to escape to England with his family. Unfortunately, we had arrived at the harbor too late—the last boat had already left, and we were trapped in Holland.

After the German victory, the country became wrapped in bleakness. Even the sun didn't seem to shine the way it used to. Nevertheless, people tried to put their lives back together again the best they could. School reopened, just as Papa had predicted, and we once again joined our friends in the never-ending games of hopscotch, hide-and-seek and many others. After our unsuccessful escape attempt, however, nothing seemed quite the same.

The changes in our lives started out very subtly and appeared to affect everyone, not just the Jews. Radios were no longer allowed and were to be turned in to the authorities immediately. In spite of the stringent order, however, a great number of people kept one hidden somewhere in the house.

Every evening after dinner, Papa would climb the two flights of stairs to the *zolder* to listen to the latest news bulletins of "Radio Orange" from London, while Corrie and Nan were "sitting watch" on the front door step.

Following the seizure of the radios came the 9 o'clock curfew—8 o'clock for Jews—and the ration coupons. Actually, there was still plenty of food available, but much of it was transported to Germany. Every week, new numbers were published in the newspaper. Mama carefully cut out the ones she needed. Coupons which had expired the previous week, Mama would give to Amama, who would use them to play "store" with Rosie and me. Papa had put our blue lacquered store in the attic. There just wasn't enough room to put it anywhere else. It was almost twice as tall as I. The backboard had shelves and niches displaying tiny jars filled with real staples and candies. From behind the counter, with its toy cash register, we served our customers, of which Amama was our most regular one. We would listen to her heave and cough as she labored to climb the two flights of stairs to visit our store. Occasionally, as in real life, we had to send her back "home" without her groceries because her coupons had "expired." We in no way meant to be cruel— after all, that's the way it was done in the real stores and Amama, as always, understood and played along.

Some Dutch people decided to side with the enemy. They joined an organization called the "N.S.B." We never knew who they were until we were confronted with them. Only one family on our street became N.S.B.ers. Strangely enough, however, they treated us quite nicely, and when their youngest daughter celebrated her birthday, Rosie and I were among the guests. Some people who joined were a real surprise.

One evening, long before curfew, while we were playing ball with some of our friends, our "amicable" policeman came riding by. He stopped. "Whose ball is that?" he asked. He didn't sound as amicable as usual.

"Mine," I replied timidly.

"Don't you know you're not allowed to play ball in the street?" he asked.

Startled, I shrugged my shoulders. "Why?" I thought. "We had always played ball before."

He held out his hand. "Give it to me!"

Carrying the ball carefully with both hands, I handed it to him. The black solid rubber ball had been a gift from Papa when I had had the chicken pox. In horror, I watched the policeman pull a knife out of his pocket and stab the blade deeply into the rubber, tearing the ball to shreds. After he returned to me what was left of it, he got on his bike and rode on.

I stared at the awful gouges, while my tears formed shiny black blotches on the torn rubber. Then I ran into the house. In the dining room, Papa, Mama and Amama were still lingering at the dinner table. When Mama saw me come into the room, she jumped up from her chair. "What happened? Did you hurt yourself?"

I shook my head and held up my ball.

"Who did that?" Papa cried, taking the ball away from me.

"The tall policeman," I sobbed.

"Dirty N.S.B.er," he hissed.

"He never used to get mad at us—for playing ball," I cried.

Papa pulled me onto his lap. "I know, honey. I know." His voice had become gentle again as he tried to explain. "Things are different now."

"I'll buy you a new ball," Amama joined in, trying to make the pain hurt a little less.

"I don't want another ball," I whimpered. "It's not the same." Besides, if I ever would have another black ball, I would always remember the "friendly" policeman. That evening I began to understand a little more. It had been I, and not the ball, that had made the difference.

As the war became more intensified, so became the restrictions. Everyone, sixteen years old and over, had to carry a *persoonsbewijs* (proof of identification), a small grey folder, complete with photograph and thumb print. Although at first glance they may have looked similar, those issued to the Jews had a large "J" stamped on the inside.

To facilitate and speed things up, the German High Command ordered a Jewish Council formed—the so-called *Joodse Raad*—making its leaders, most of them prominent members of the Jewish community, responsible for their own people. One of the council's major tasks was to provide the SS Headquarters with lists of names and addresses. If the Council had hoped for special favors in lieu of their cooperation, they soon would find themselves heinously betrayed. By the end of 1943, most of them had been deported.

By 1941, Jews were barred from restaurants, public parks, public transportation, sports arenas and even stores. We were allowed to shop only at the Jewish markets and certain "Jewish stores," indentified by a sign in the window. But for Rosie and me out of the increasingly limited freedom grew yet another game, carrying the imaginary title of *Mien und Sien.* Dressed up in Mama's clothes, her ostrich-feathered hats and high-heeled shoes, Rosie as *Sien* and I as *Mien* would put on our weekly performance for the rest of the family as we took our make-believe streetcar ride to the Jewish market in the Albert Kuypstraat. Holding tightly to the imaginary leather strap over our heads, we swayed back and forth as the "streetcar" made its turns, grinding its wheels through the tracks. With the ease of professionals, we stepped out of our roles of complaining Jewish housewives into that of the typical Amsterdam streetcar conductor, calling each stop along the way. *"Museumplein!! Ceintuurbaan!! Albert Kuyp!!"* After the performance, Amama would wipe her eyes with her large, white handkerchief. Sometimes I wasn't quite sure if she were laughing or crying. She was probably doing a little of both.

Another birthday had come and gone, but without the usual excitement and fanfare. I was eight years old now. In August of that year, we were barred from all public schools. Nan was transferred to the Jewish high school in Amsterdam. Corrie, who one day hoped to be a pharmaceutical assistant, began taking private lessons with a Doctor of Pharmacy. Meanwhile, Rosie and I were enrolled in the "one-room" Jewish Schoolhouse—that until only a short time ago had been Amama's little synagogue around the corner. Our teacher was a Jewish man in his early twenties. He seemed far more interested in teaching us the finer points of art than the compulsory writing, reading and arithmetic. Except for our daily hour of Hebrew, he spent most of the remaining time teaching us how to draw and *shade* with colors. With our tongues clinched between our teeth, we'd press our colored pencils firmly onto the paper, releasing the pressure gradually as we moved our pencils ever so slowly across the paper. Stars and circles were his favorite designs. When Mama asked what we had learned, the answer was usually the same, "We shaded."

She'd shake her head. "So, what's all this *shading*'?

We shrugged. "Just shading, that's what—stars and circles."

Filled with frustration, she'd raise her eyes to the ceiling. Someday, maybe, her children would be allowed to learn how to read and write like all the others. She'd sigh and continue with her chores. Papa had been very much against the idea of Jewish School and his opposition grew stronger by the day. His children were sitting ducks and he couldn't care less if they'd never learn how to read or write.

One day he made the decision. For Nan, at fifteen, it meant the end of his high-school years; for Rosie and me, it meant the end of *shading*. It would be a very long time before I would see the inside of a classroom again.

Our cousin Guus had been arrested. He was the first one in our family. Guus was the only son of Tante Sophie, Mama's older sister. She and her husband and their three children moved to Amsterdam long before we did. Guus was only a few years older than Corrie. He liked hanging out with her and Nan, and he used to visit our house every Saturday afternoon. Rosie and I would wait patiently for him on the front doorstep, not completely without a reason, I'm afraid. I'm sure Guus was well aware of that. He had gotten into the habit of bringing us each our favorite candy bar—"Tjoklat"—nougat on the inside and a thick layer of milk chocolate on the outside. The moment he appeared around the corner, we'd jump up and run to greet him. He'd grin, holding up the candy bars, one in each hand.

Papa said that the war had made Guus a very angry young man. He was ready to fight the Germans single-handedly and in a way he did. He began printing anti-German pamphlets, handing them out on the streets. Consequently, his defiance and the defiance of so many others led to the infamous "General Strike" which paralyzed transportation and industry in and around Amsterdam. The strike lasted only a few days, when it was viciously suppressed by enemy soldiers. Many of those who took part in the strike were caught and deported to Mauthausen. Guus was one of them. The night of his arrest, at two o'clock in the morning, the Gestapo broke into the house and dragged him out of bed.

A few weeks later, a stranger rang Tante Sophie's doorbell. He had came to deliver a note which had been handed to him from a window of a transport train carrying Jews. On the outside was her address. She immediately recognized the handwriting. Her hands shook as she slowly unfolded the note and read: "Mama, I am fine. Please don't worry about me." It was the last time she ever heard from her son.

Before we knew it, summer had come and gone, and autumn, with its low, swift-flying clouds and dreariness had arrived. Unlike before, Papa was home a lot these days. His office and warehouse in the heart of the Jewish district was no longer considered safe. More and more people disappeared for no apparent reason. Now the click of the mail slot had become one of the highlights of the day for him.

Wiping her hands on her apron, Mama walked into the small vestibule where Papa had just picked up the morning mail. She watched him as he read some official-looking piece of correspondence. She could tell something was wrong. "What is it?"

He didn't answer her. Instead, he kept on reading. Slowly he pulled his fingers through his hair. Speechless, he handed her the letter. Swiftly her eyes ran across the lines. Her hands shook. "Report to the *Sicherheits Dienst* (Security Service)" she read loudly. Her eyes were large with fright.

"The S.D.! Why?"

He shrugged his shoulders. "I don't know."

She handed the letter back to him. "You're not going, are you?" Her voice was choked with emotion.

"Do you realize what would happen if I don't go?" But he didn't give her time to answer. "They would be here in less than an hour to pick up the whole family." She grew hysterical.

He put his arm around her shoulders. "Elsa, please, try to stay calm. Everything will be all right. They just want to talk to me. You'll see." But he didn't sound very convincing. Not even to himself.

"Don't you have any idea at all why they want to see you?" she sobbed.

"I've told you, I don't know. Anyway, for the moment at least, let's try to deal with it as calmly as we can." He put the letter in his pocket and led her into the dining room. "Let's have a cup of tea."

Finally, the day for Papa's appearance before the *Sicherheits Dienst* arrived. He tried to make it seem as if it were just a routine matter. Everyone, including Amama, got up early. Both Mama and Papa looked very tired. Neither one had slept a wink and breakfast was eaten quietly. At last, Papa got up and slowly put on his coat, checking the inside pocket to make sure he had everything he needed with him. He hesitated for a moment, then kissed us all goodbye and quickly walked out of the room, with Mama following right behind. Moments later, we heard the front door shut.

As he rode the streetcar to the *Euterpestraat,* where the S.D. resided, he tried to gather his thoughts. He could only think of one reason why they wanted to see him. He had not registered his business with the German authorities, as all Jews had been ordered. Had he done so, the business would no longer be his. He was sure of that. Someone, however, would have had to expose him, and he had a pretty good idea who it was. His shop foreman hated Jews, even though he had never openly admitted it. Many times he had tried to cause disharmony among the other employees. Now with De Jong gone, and one less Jew to worry about, all he needed to do to make the business his own was to get rid of the other one. The Germans would be only too glad to give it to him in exchange for a Jew. Papa was convinced he was right. As he got closer to his destination, he became more and more unnerved.

When he entered the ominous-looking building, little did he know that, one day, other members of his family would be forced to undertake the same visit. He was led into a large office. The soldier who accompanied him clicked his heels, raised his hand in a *"Sieg Heil,"* presented Papa's name to the officer behind the desk, and left. Motionless, Papa watched the German flip through a stack of papers. "I'm not the only one," he thought. Finally the German pulled a letter from the stack.

Papa listened quietly as the German read his name, address, occupation and place of business.

33

Next, he was ordered to sit down. The interrogation had begun. Contrary to what he had prepared himself for, most questions concerned the whereabouts of his associate, Simon de Jong.

"When did you see your partner last?" Leaning back in his chair, the officer kept blowing long puffs of cigarette smoke in Papa's direction.

"May of last year, I believe."

"You believe!" the German snapped.

"I'm sure it was May."

"Did he tell you where he was going?"

"No. He didn't."

The German grinned. "Your associate just disappears into thin air and leaves you his share of the business. Isn't that what happened?"

Suddenly, Papa became aware of the real reason for the questioning and he felt a terrible weakness coming over him. The German was playing cat and mouse with him. He didn't care about de Jong. He wanted him—and he was looking for a seemingly legitimate excuse.

The German crushed his cigarette in the ash tray. He was getting impatient. "You surely must be sending him his share of the profit."

"I don't . . . I told you . . . I don't know where he is." Papa's voice had grown weak. The German jumped up from his chair and as he leaned across his desk, his cat-like eyes never leaving Papa's face, his hand slowly moved toward the small push button in front of him. "You see this button?" Papa followed every move of the man's hand. "All it takes is one push . . . and you'll be on your way to Mauthausen. Now will you tell me where de Jong is?"

Papa knew the time had come to play his one and only "ace." He reached inside his coat pocket and pulled out a handful of photographs and threw them across the desk. "I don't know where de Jong is!" he cried.

Taken off guard, the German had lost, momentarily, control as he looked at the pictures strewn in front of him.

"What are these?"

"Pictures. Pictures of me and your countrymen when I led them to their championship. Look at them!" The German picked up one of the pictures. "They used to carry me on their shoulders," Papa wept. The German looked up at him, then back at the picture again.

"Der Schwarze Teufel," he muttered.

"That's right. That's me—*der Schwarze Teufel*—the black devil! That's what they used to call me!"

"Take your pictures and get out! Get out of here before I change my mind," the German hissed. Dazed, Papa jumped up, grabbed the photographs, and bolted out of the room.

Drenched in sweat, he stumbled into the house. Mama had been waiting in front of the window. "You're home!" she cried, throwing her arms around him. "What did they say?" Suddenly Papa began to laugh—almost hysterically. Then he burst into tears. Slowly, Mama led him up the stairs and made him lie down on the bed where he lay staring at the ceiling for what seemed hours, until sleep finally took over.

To relieve her stubborn coughing spells due to asthma, Amama religiously carried hard candy to bed with her—*kluemche* she called them. She'd put them on her night stand just in case. First thing in the morning, Rosie and I would softly enter Amama's room, careful not to wake her, to see if there were any *kluemche* left. And, of course, there always were—at least two. I truly believe that Amama would rather have choked than eat the last two.

Nothing seemed different that Saturday morning in November 1941 when I quietly slipped into Amama's bedroom. She had not been feeling too well the last couple of weeks. She had been suffering from a very bad cold. But yesterday the doctor had been to the house to see her again and she seemed a lot better. Mama had made her some good old-fashioned chicken soup and she had eaten every last little bit of it, which, according to Mama, was a sign of restored health.

There were plenty of *kluemche* left, I noticed. I took one, and one, and another one. Amama's head had slid off the pillow. Carefully, not to wake her, I tried to move it back on, but she slid off it again. Something seemed wrong. I touched her face. It felt very cold.

I don't know why, but I suddenly began to scream, "Papa!! Papa!" At the sound of my screams, Papa had jumped out of bed. He stood next to me, "What's wrong?"

"She won't wake up," I cried.

Papa already knew what had happened. Quietly he stared at the motionless body. Then he gently put the pillows under her head. His dark brown eyes shone with tears. "Let's go," he whispered, putting his arm around my shoulders.

Mama was sitting up in bed. She didn't speak.

"She's gone, Els." Papa's voice broke and tears streamed down his face.

The next day, Amama's body was taken by train to Sittard for burial. During the three-hour train ride, Papa never left the side of her casket.

The house had suddenly become very empty. There was a space that no one would ever be able to fill. Who would play with us when it was too cold to play outside? Who would help me with my unfinished knitting project? Who would kiss all our hurts away? And what about the fish peddler? Would he ever again stop at our house? For weeks I'd wake up in the middle of the night, crying. Then it finally stopped. Amama had never really gone away; she had left us with too great a wealth of memories.

Childhood Memories

Papa and Mama's official engagement picture

Papa and Mama on their wedding day

"Grootmoeder" with Corrie

"Amama"

"Ikke My"

Papa and Nan on the occasion of Nan's Barmitzvah

Papa (in white sweater) with his soccer team

Left to right: Rosie, Nan, cousin Roos, Corrie, and me

At a children's party before my birth.
First row center: "Ikke My," and to her right Nan and Corrie.
Only three of these children survived the holocaust.

Our home in Amstelveen from which we were evicted.

Our family's last vacation together in Putten.

The tennis courts behind our house in Amstelveen

Chapter 4

Our Flight Begins

hy had this Sabbath seemed so different from all the others? The fact that we had to start to wear the Star of David, that's why. Made of bright yellow cloth with the word *"JOOD"* ("JEW") in large, black, Hebrew-like letters printed in the center, the star had to be worn on the left side of our outer garments. Early that Sabbath morning we had gone to the house of Mijnheer Heiman, the Jewish tailor, who was in charge of distribution. Each time he had handed one out, he had shaken his head, mumbling something in Yiddish and stealing a brief glance at the recipient. Papa had been visibly upset. He swore he'd never would wear the "thing." I thought they were quite pretty, actually, and I couldn't wait for Mama to sew mine on. As she held up the garment to check if it was sewn on straight, she sighed, "What will they think of next?"

She didn't have to wait very long for the answer. About a week later we received an official notice from the German High Command. We were given 24 hours to vacate our house and report to the bus station on May 5, 1942. We were to take nothing but a change of clothing. After mama read the letter, she broke down. She looked at Papa with tears streaming down her face. "Maan, what are we going to do now?" she cried.

Papa hesitated for a moment. Only God knew how badly he wanted to ignore the German order. He gently put his arm around her shoulders. "I'm afraid we don't have much of a choice, so just let's stay calm." He picked up the notice again and stared at it for a moment. "All it says is that we will be taken to Amsterdam for a physical. There's nothing mentioned about what they're going to do with us afterward. They'll probably just let us go. You'll see." He had difficulty believing his own words, but he realized that his family had always counted on him and would continue to do so. Silently he prayed, "Please God, just a little more time. All I need is a little more time."

"What are we going to do with our furniture and our china?" Mama asked tearfully. Papa looked at her in amazement. "Well, are we going to let them steal everything we have worked so hard for?" Mama continued, crying.

Papa thought he'd never understand this woman! Even under the worst of circumstances, she was thinking about her furniture and china. His impatience showed when he said, "Elsa, all we have is 24 hours. That's all!"

She sighed, "I guess we won't find anything when we return."

During a brief pause a million thoughts must have crossed Papa's mind. "Let me think about it for a while," he replied.

That evening, after dark, all kinds of people silently moved in and out of our house through the back door. Mevrouw Verbregge, our neighbor to the right, took our Sabbath dishes: our neighbor on the left took our good linens. The lady who helped Mama clean house once a week came to get the brass ornaments Mama had collected for years and proudly displayed on a large stand in the vestibule. Finally, the milk man came to replace our dining room set with an old one. And old it was. One of the chairs

44

had only three sound legs. The fourth leg had been temporarily glued on and was ready to come off at any moment.

The next day, an hour or so before we were to leave, two members of the Gestapo arrived. One of them, a short, fat man carrying a pad and a pencil, began inspecting the house, writing everything down as he moved from room to room. He even made note of our toys. When he returned to the dining room, he seated himself at the table. The moment the two men arrived, Nan had seated himself on the three-legged chair, but ever so lightly. The fat Gestapo looked at the pad in front of him and moved his pencil down the lines. "Anything else to report? he inquired while his eyes stayed fixed on the paper.

"Nothing!" Papa replied harshly.

The man looked up, grinning sarcastically. "Well, then I guess it's time to go." he said.

Papa bit his lip as he picked up the small suitcase. The Gestapo followed us down the hall and out the front door. After one of them had secured the door, he took a seal out of his pocket and stuck it to the door.

The neighbors were watching us silently. Some from their doorways, others from behind their curtains. Mrs. Loewenthal was crying. A few raised their hands reluctantly. For a brief moment, our playmates stopped their games to watch us walk away. When I reached the corner, I turned around to wave one last goodbye to my girlfriend, Elsje Verbregge.

The bus station where we ordinarily had taken Bus "H" to Amsterdam looked far from the same. Several buses were waiting and, unlike the usual handful of passengers, a long line of people closely guarded by German soldiers stood quietly alongside the buses. It was a mixed group of men, women and children. Many looked drawn and tired as they clutched a small piece of luggage. Even though most of us knew each other, a whispered greeting or a nod of the head were the only signs of recognition. The unspoken words were in the exchanged glances. I wondered where they were going to take us. Would we ever come back? I had difficulty understanding any of it.

At last we boarded one of the buses. The last ones on were a couple of German soldiers who seated themselves in the front. When we pulled away from the curb, some of the women started to weep. A baby cried. The mother tried to rock it to sleep as she softly hummed a lullaby. Seated by the window, next to Papa, I looked back as the familiar scenery slowly slipped away. Then all that was left were the pictures in my mind.

The bus trip seemed agonizingly long. I recognized some of the streets, but after a while the sights became unfamiliar. For the rest of the world, life seemed to go on as usual: women were on their way to the market, the milkman was scooping milk from a large can and children were playing—little children not yet old enough to be in school. I craned my neck and watched them until they disappeared from sight. It made me feel sad to think that no one noticed us.

We had left the residential area and the houses and apartments were replaced by old, ugly buildings that looked like barracks. We had reached the *Zeeburgerijk*.

The bus slowed down. The man in front of us turned around in his seat. "The *Slachthallen* (the slaughter halls)," he muttered. Was this the end of our trip? The slaughter halls? That's where they killed animals! I winced at the thought.

I looked up at Papa who, until now, had been staring quietly out of the window. "Why do we have to go there?" I asked. I seemed to have awakened him from some deep thoughts.

"Oh, just to see the doctor," he replied. "Nothing to be worried about."

"But why? We're not sick?"

Papa smiled. "I know, but some of the other people might be." Papa always had the answers.

At last the bus came to a stop in front of one of the buildings. The doors were kept closed. There were lots of buses, I noticed, and long lines of people.

Finally the doors opened and we were ordered off the bus and into a line. One after another we passed the doctors. The process was very slow with so many people and only a few doctors. Finally it was my turn. My throat felt dry. A man in a long white coat pulled me toward him. He wore a band with a mirror around his head. "Open your mouth wide!" he ordered. Hesitantly I obeyed, watching Papa from the corner of my eyes. "Say Ahhh!"

"Ahhh!"

"Your tonsils are enlarged. They need to come out."

I started to tremble. Even though I didn't know what he was talking about, he still scared me. I looked at Papa and grabbed his hand. He tried to comfort me. "Not now, honey. The doctor means later—much later."

Papa's words made me feel a little bit better, but I was still scared. Meanwhile, the doctor had taken out his stethoscope. The stethoscope felt cold. He listened to my chest. "You're in good health," he said unsmilingly. "Next!"

After our whole family had finally passed the inspection, we were seen by a German officer. He read our names, glancing intermittently at Papa, as if he were expecting a confirmation.

Papa nodded. "That's right."

"Report to this address." He handed Papa a small card.

Papa looked at it and put it in his pocket. "We will," he replied, as he calmly began to make his way toward the door with the rest of us following closely behind.

"Where are we supposed to go?" Mama asked, once we were outside.

"To the Plotzke's—another Jewish family. What a great way to catch two birds with one stone!" Papa raised his eyebrows. "How stupid do they think we are? A trap that's what it is. A death trap!" He reached in his pocket, took out a cigarette and lit it. "Let's go!" he said. He sounded determined.

"Let's go, where?" Mama wanted to know.

"Mother's."

"Your mother? You know how upset she'll be? All of us in that small apartment?"

But Papa had already started walking in the direction of *Grootmoeder's* house. His mind was made up. He glanced at Mama over his shoulder. "Mother will understand. Anyway, I'm taking Corrie and Nan to Jet for the time being, so it's going to be only you and me and the two little ones." Tante Jet was Papa's younger sister. She was married to Oom Huug, who was not Jewish, and therefore was exempt from all the terrible things we had to go through.

Streetcar after streetcar passed us. They all carried the now-familiar sign in the window: "NO JEWS ALLOWED."

After a while, Rosie became tired and Papa had to carry her the rest of the way. When we arrived at the apartment, Papa rang the bell. Moments later, the door sprang open. *Grootmoeder* was standing at the top of the stairs. "Maan? Els?" She cried out. "What an unexpected visit!." She was obviously in a state of shock.

We began climbing the steep stairs. As usual, we were welcomed by the warmth and the delicious smell coming from the bakery below. It made me realize how hungry I was. We hadn't eaten since we'd left the house, and that had only been a slice of bread with a little jam and a glass of milk—the only food left in the house.

When Papa reached the top of the stairs, he hugged his mother and gently pushed the elderly lady in the direction of the living room. As Papa tried to inform her as calmly and as clearly as possible of what had happened, the rest of us took our usual positions on the straight-backed chairs, our hands neatly folded in our laps.

"Twenty-four hours was all they gave us," Papa stated, as he tried to explain the sudden visit.

Seated in her big chair by the window, *Grootmoeder* actually seemed to have lost her composure. I felt sorry for her.

"How long will you be staying?" she asked. Her voice sounded weak.

"I don't know. Let's hope not for very long. Corrie and Nan will be staying with Jet. Meanwhile I'll be getting in touch with some friends who I know will be able to help us. But until then, we'll have to have a place to stay."

She looked outside, as if the answers to it all were out there somewhere. A light rain had begun to fall. At last, she turned slowly away from the window. Her face had a sympathetic look. "Stay as long as you have to."

"Thank you, Mother." Papa went over to her and kissed her lightly on the forehead. Then he walked over to the window, and with his hands resting on the window sill, he looked down on the shiny, wet street below. The rain made everything look fresh. He glanced up at some of the centuries-old trees arched across the canal. Next his eyes moved to the age-old bridge. Such a peaceful scene. Such a beautiful city. He sighed, turning slowly away from the window. He pulled a chair next to *Grootmoeder's* and took her hand in his. Reluctant to look at her, he said: "There's one other thing we need to discuss, Mother."

"What's that?" She was obviously not ready for any more surprises.

"When we leave here, you'll be leaving too."

Instantly, *Grootmoeder* regained her fighting spirit. "I'm not going anywhere!" she cried. "This is my home."

"I don't think the Germans care, so you may have to reconsider. I promise to find a good and safe place for you."

Turning her head away, she wept softly. "We'll see," she cried.

Gently patting her hand, Papa decided to put the issue to rest, at least for the time being. He knew better than to argue with his mother.

Our stay with *Grootmoeder* wasn't particularly joyful. Once she recuperated from the initial shock, she became her old self again. She kept a close eye on our every move and had a fit when we dropped a crumb on the floor. She continuously argued with Mama, who wasn't allowed to help her in any way, because whatever she did wasn't quite good enough.

Papa went out almost every day without wearing his "star." A week or so after our arrival, he returned home happier than we had seen him in a long, long time. "We're leaving tonight!" he announced, smiling broadly.

He had taken Mama totally by surprise. "Leaving? Where to?"

"To de Vechtstraat!"

"Who do we know in de Vechtstraat?"

"Someone I used to do business with. His wife is Jewish, he isn't. I don't think you have ever met them. It will only be for a short while, because Twan is going to try to find a more permanent, safe place for us." Mama's eyes grew big.

"Twan? When did you see him?"

"This morning." He sounded almost triumphant. Twan Maintz and his wife Mien had been long-time friends of Papa and Mama. They were living in Geleen, a small town on the outskirts of Sittard. I remembered their names, but I couldn't recall what they looked like. Mama and Papa had so many friends, many of whom were either soccer players or ardent fans of Papa. "It's much too risky to talk over the phone," Papa continued, "so we decided to meet in het Vondelpark.

"Are you telling me that he has joined the resistance?"

Papa nodded. He reached across the table and took Mama's hand. "Els, we're going to get help! We are finally going to get help!" And as always, when he became emotional, his nostrils began to quiver.

Later that afternoon, the four of us started out on yet another walk. This time from the Joseph Israelskade to de

Vechtstraat, a pleasant tree-lined street, not too far from Grootmoeder's place. Corrie and Nan were to join us later.

Grootmoeder moved shortly after. Papa had been able to locate a place for her in a Christian Home for Senior Citizens.

Our shelter at de Vechtstraat was a small three-bedroom, first floor apartment. The couple who had so generously offered to share their home with us were about the same ages as Papa and Mama. Like Tante Jet, the woman didn't have to worry about the Germans hurting her because she was married to a non-Jew.[1]

Undoubtedly, our presence not only changed their daily routine but also made their apartment very, very crowded. We four children shared one of the small bedrooms which had two folding, double beds as the only furniture. It allowed us just enough room to climb in and out of bed. During the daytime the beds were folded against the wall. That way we had more room to move around.

The days were long and dreadfully boring. They went by ever so slowly. Each morning I watched from the living room window as the other children left their homes for school. They ran and chased each other. I don't think I ever felt more envious. As soon as they were gone, and the pleasant tree-lined street was quiet once again, my hurt inside would go away—until the next day.

Our apartment was close to one end of the street, where a large field formed a natural borderline. It was literally the end of town. Going the opposite way—toward town—the street became gradually busier—where the shopping district began. Besides the many stores, there was a Jewish market place, one of several around town. Since more and more merchants had begun refusing to serve Jews, the market was one of the few places left for Jews to do their

---

[1] After the war we learned that when the marriage began to fail, the husband chose the least expensive solution—the "final" solution. Instead of divorcing his wife he handed her over to the Gestapo. She was deported and never heard from again.

shopping. Papa called them "death traps," and he was very upset with Mama when he found out that she had gone there to do some shopping, taking Rosie and me along with her. "I don't want to see you near that place!" he had warned her sternly.

Papa himself, however, kept venturing out. He rented a small office in an inconspicuous part of the city. Here, he was able to conduct some business to sustain us, mainly with old and trusted friends. Mama worried herself sick each time he left the house. She realized that their money was running low and that every nickel counted, but was it worth it? She cried each time he walked out the door, and each time he tried to reassure her. "Don't forget, I was born and raised in this town. I know every alley and every back street. They don't! I can get away very quickly, if I have to!"

"I hope you're right," she'd sigh.

That year of 1942 presented us with a beautiful summer, if nothing else. Occasionally we were allowed to play outside as long as we stayed away from the crowds. I considered it a real treat when I was asked to mail a letter in the large red mailbox at the very corner of the street.

Occasionally Rosie and I could walk over to the field. The tall, cool grass felt good. Beyond the field was the *Miranda Bad*, a large public swimming pool. Ironically, it had been named after De Miranda, a well-known Jew who, had he lived, would not have been allowed in since it, too, carried the large white sign with the bold black letters *"VOOR JODEN VERBODEN"* ("NO JEWS ALLOWED").

When our bodies became hot and tired from playing, Rosie and I plopped down into the grass and listened enviously to the laughter and the sound of splashing cool water as they drifted across the walls of the pool.

Indoors, our only toy was the couple's tiny, gray kitten—which Rosie and I had begun to think of as "ours." At night we would sneak it into bed with us and play with it until it finally went to sleep, exhausted. One night we almost lost the kitten. Whoever had pulled out our bed from the wall had not straightened its legs all the way. Suddenly the legs collapsed and the bed crashed to the floor. Ordinarily, it would have been very funny, but not this time. We discovered to our horror that our kitten was caught underneath. It cried so loudly we couldn't stand it and covered our ears to turn off the cries. "Someone help!" we shouted.

We didn't know whether to jump out of the bed or to stay where we were. After a moment of confusion, which seemed to last for hours, someone finally lifted the bed off the floor with Rosie and me still in it. There was our kitten, lying on its side, terribly shaken but, thank God, unhurt.

One day Corrie, Rosie and I decided to take a walk to Amstelveen to visit our friends. We cut across the field to *De Zuidelijke Wandelweg* or *De Wandelweg*, as it was commonly called. Over the years, the age-old trees on either side had formed a natural tunnel of shade. All along the road were numerous soccer fields and lush, green meadows where well-fed cows had once lazily grazed in the shade of the willow trees along the narrow streams. But they were no longer there. They had long since been transported to Germany. To those who were used to visiting the *Wandelweg* on Sundays, when soccer fans from all over the city and surrounding areas came to watch their favorite team play, it hardly looked like the same road. I remembered spending many an afternoon along the sidelines, munching on a large almond cake while Papa watched the game. Afterwards, we would go to Tante Jet's house and she would serve us some refreshments before we started our long walk home. Those had been long, unforgettable walks. That, too, was all over now. Papa never went to the games anymore. This day we only met a few cyclists. One lady raised her hand in a friendly greeting: *"Dag!"*

In spite of our shortcut, it took us almost two hours to get to our destination. Once in a while we rested on one of the many benches along the way, while the sun, filtering through the leaves overhead, created playful shadows all around us. I felt sorry for Nan. He wanted to come along, but he was no longer allowed outside, except when absolutely necessary. His dark complexion made him a real target.

Our house still stood empty, just the way we had left it, with the front door still sealed. Somehow, the street didn't look quite the same. Although we visited some of our friends, we spent most of the day with Mijnheer and Mevrouw Loewenthal. It seemed as if we were no longer part of it all. We were different now, even to those who had once known us. Later that afternoon, we began our walk back to the city. When we reached the corner of our street, we ran into our Nazi neighbor. He seemed very friendly and talked to us for a while. Corrie tried to remind him of our curfew hour and we were quite surprised when he said, "Don't worry. As long as you're with me, you'll be all right." We made it back in time and I was glad to get "home."

It was a beautiful Friday morning. The market was crowded with Jewish shoppers in spite of the fact that in the last several months their number had decreased considerably. Most of the shoppers were women and children. As usual they visited the market on Fridays to buy the freshest fruits and vegetables for their Sabbath dinner. Plump, kosher chickens were scrutinized and pinched for freshness. No one was going to sell them second-rate merchandise, especially not for the most important dinner of the week. While the women shopped and argued with the vendors about the price, the children played between the carts. Occasionally one would try to "sneak" an apple, in which case strict discipline would be enforced with a firm slap on the backside by an apologetic mother. It was a familiar scene, one which had been repeating itself week after week as long as memory could recall.

This Friday didn't seem any different—until suddenly there was the sound of approaching trucks. The hustle and bustle came to an abrupt halt. Confusion and fear ran among the shoppers and merchants alike. Anguished mothers called their children, while old people cried helplessly. Panic erupted as everybody tried to leave the market at the same time. The attempt was futile. It was too late. German soldiers surrounded the area and sealed off every exit. Some tried in vain to break through the German barriers. At last the bedlam subsided. Quietly shoppers and vendors climbed on the backs of the trucks. Papa had been right. The market was indeed a death trap.

We didn't hear about what had happened until Papa returned home shortly after lunch. Apparently he had been near the market when it all happened. By hiding in a stairwell he had escaped the raid.

"We can't stay here any longer," Papa explained. "It's just getting too dangerous around here. We're leaving this afternoon."

"Where to this time?" Mama cried. The situation was beginning to get to her.

"Calm down, Els. Everything is taken care of. Corrie and Nan will be staying with Huug and Jet, and the rest of us are going to the Rokin to stay with Tante Annie and Oom Piet. I have talked to them already and they are expecting us. They told me they're happy to have us. As soon as we're settled, I'll get in touch with Twan."

Who were Tante Annie and Oom Piet? I wondered. I felt as if we had entered a long tunnel which grew darker and darker as we moved along further and further, with neither an end nor a light in sight.

Again we started on another long walk across bridges and along canals—destination: Rokin 101, the center of the city. When we reached the four-story office building, Papa rang the bell. The door swung open immediately. The building was very quiet. All the employees had obviously left for the day. Spooky, I thought, as we climbed the three flights of stairs. The place smelled funny. I couldn't figure out what it was—some sort of an "old" smell. When I looked up, I saw two people leaning across the fourth-floor banister. They were smiling broadly. Kind, wrinkled faces. They belonged to Tante Annie and Oom Piet Sijmonsma, the caretakers of the building.

Our new hiding place turned out to be much more comfortable than the previous one. The large rooms allowed us plenty of breathing space, especially the living room with its large overstuffed chairs. The parquet floor, buffed to a high sheen, was partly covered with a carpet, worn, but still rich in color. In the corner, near one of the windows, were a table and six chairs which served as the dining area. A huge grandfather clock overlooked the total setting. And there was always that "old" smell. It seemed to linger everywhere. Since we were no longer allowed outside, except when we had to travel, I could spend hours peeking through the heavy lace curtains that covered the tall windows watching the traffic and people below. But most of the time, Rosie and I played in the attic. It was quite similar to the one we had at home, except we had neither a "store" nor Amama to play with. As a result we became experts at creating our own games.

Tante Annie and Oom Piet were truly wonderful old people. They were also quite the odd couple. He, thin, quiet, almost serious. She, at least a head taller than her husband, heavy set and bubbling with laughter that filled the whole apartment. Often she would laugh and cry at the same time, and that's when she reminded me of Amama. Mama and Tante Annie really hit it off. If they weren't in the kitchen cooking or baking, they'd be sitting in the living room chatting over a cup of tea. It wasn't my imagination, but Mama seemed much happier than she had been in quite some time. No doubt Tante Annie had something to do with it.

The couple had two sons and one daughter. One son was married, the other a priest. Their only daughter, Zus, was still living at home, even though she was already in her late twenties. Zus was thin, like her father, but tall and outgoing like her mother. Rosie and I became quite fond of her. At night, after all the employees had left for the day, she would take us downstairs to help clean the offices and give us a chance to release our bottled-up energy. There was one odd thing about Zus. Mama had told us that she was a nun, but she didn't wear a habit like other nuns I had seen. Besides, she was wearing a wedding band. I was sure that nuns didn't marry. And if she was married, where was her husband? The whole thing had me thoroughly confused. One evening when we had gone downstairs to clean, I mustered enough courage to ask her why she wasn't wearing a habit. She smiled. "I'm a worldly nun," she explained. "Worldly nuns are not required to wear habits."

"But why are you wearing a wedding band?" I blurted out. "Nuns don't marry"

She laughed heartily. She sounded just like Tante Annie.

"Well, nuns do marry; they marry Jesus."

I must have looked puzzled, because she started to laugh again. I was truly shocked. I had heard about Jesus, but I never knew he had wives. More confused than before, I decided to drop the subject.

Twan, of whom Papa had spoken so often, became a regular visitor at the Rokin, even though he had to travel all the way from his home in Geleen. A few times he brought his wife along. They had been friends with Mama and Papa for a long time, and the four of them seemed to enjoy each other's company very much as they talked about all the good times they had had.

Twan was a big, balding man whose booming laugh seemed to have a contagious effect on those around him. His wife Mien wasn't any less outgoing. I noticed that she had a strange habit of raising her eyebrows whenever she spoke, almost like a nervous twitch. Rosie and I began to look forward to their visits almost as much as Mama and Papa. As a result, we had raised their status of "friends" to that of *Oom and Tante* (Uncle and Aunt).

Both of them were deeply involved in the resistance—a word I had not understood until just recently when Papa explained that the resistance, or underground, was made up of people who tried to save Jews—not just us, but other

Jews as well. He added that if the Germans should catch them, they would no doubt be killed. It was then that I began to feel an even closer kinship with them.

Besides being our benefactor, Oom Twan was also the communication line between us and the rest of the family. This day, especially, Mama was anxious to hear about her brothers. Her youngest brother Oom Ies and his wife and their baby daughter had gone into hiding and, at last, so had her older brother Philip and his family.

When Oom Twan told her about Philip, Mama looked relieved. "Thank God," she whispered.

"That's right. I have been trying to persuade him for I don't know how long, but he kept resisting," Oom Twan said. "He was convinced that they would be much better off if they followed German orders." He shook his head, as he continued. "They would have gone like sheep to the slaughter. . . . " He paused for a moment, staring at the cigarette in his hand. "Can you imagine, he even had special coats made for all of them—fur coats—with wide hems to hold enough money to see them through, just in case." Again he shook his head as if in disbelief.

"Something must have shaken his faith in Hitler," Papa remarked.

"Whatever it is, I'm glad he's come to his senses."

Her eyes brimming with tears, Mama listened quietly. "Twan, how will we ever be able to thank you!" she said in a choked voice.

With a nonchalant motion of his hands, Oom Twan dismissed the words of gratitude. Then he reached into his coat pockets. "I have brought you your false I.D. cards. . . . At least I thought I had . . . . What did I do with them? . . . . Here they are." He looked relieved, as he pulled out two small, grey folders. He quickly checked on the inside to see which one belonged to whom before he handed them over. Mama laughed when she saw her new name. "Tonnie," she read. "It sounds so strange after having been Elsa all my life. I hope I'll get used to it."

"You'd better," Oom Twan reprimanded her gently.

"And who are you?" she chuckled, glancing at Papa's I.D.

"Jaap," Papa said, and his voice seemed to hold an element of cynicism. Mama tried to ignore it. "Oh, well, that's easy to remember, the same name as your brother."

"Did you get one for Corrie and Nan?

"Of course. How else would I have been able to take them to Oldenzaal?" he replied.

"That's right. I'm sorry, I completely forgot."

After a brief stay with Tante Jet, Corrie and Nan had been moved to Oldenzaal, a town in the eastern part of the country and quite close to the German border.

"Corrie is now Lida and Nan is Gerard—Gerard Bolkenstein," Oom Twan laughed. Papa and Mama joined in. I rolled my eyes. Gerard Bolkenstein! It sounded so unlike Nan.

Then Oom Twan pointed at us. "And you two—although you're too young to carry an I.D.—from now on you will be Rosie and Manda De Boer—'*Rotterdammertjes*' (two little orphans from Rotterdam). Your parents were killed in the bombing. It is very important that you remember that. "

We promised. But why "De Boer Rotte?" I wondered. I didn't like it. It didn't sound at all Jewish, but then, neither did Bolkenstein.

In a few days, Rosie and I had to leave het Rokin. The underground felt it no longer safe for two little girls to live above three floors of busy offices.

When Oom Twan arrived that morning in early September 1942, he had come, not to visit, but to take Rosie and me to our next hiding place—Oldenzaal—to join Corrie and Nan.

The station was crowded with German soldiers—some carrying rifles and heavy backpacks. Soon we were swallowed up in a sea of green, black, and brown uniforms as we slowly made our way to the platform. When the train chugged into the station, everybody began pushing and shoving. The brakes squealed, and the train had come to a halt. The moment the doors were opened, people came pouring out, while others tried to get on at the same time, to assure themselves of a seat. I experienced a brief moment of panic when I lost touch with Oom Twan's hand, but finally we made it aboard in one piece. We were even lucky enough to find some seats.

The doors were locked and the train got underway, passing shabby-looking houses and blackened factories. Soon after, the city was left behind as the train rolled through the peaceful countryside. Rain-filled clouds moved along rapidly. A few noisy sea gulls flew by our window, and I envied their freedom.

A conductor came to collect our fares and a fat German officer stopped by to check Oom Twan's I.D. *"Ausweiss, bitte."* Oom Twan reached into his pocket and handed him the little folder. He examined it closely, while over his wire-rimmed glasses, his beady eyes moved quickly from Oom Twan to Rosie and me and back to Oom Twan. Obviously satisfied, he smiled politely and returned the I.D. *"Gute Reise,"* he commented, wishing us a pleasant trip.

"Danke schoen," Oom Twan replied equally polite.

Outside the train station in Oldenzaal, Nan and Corrie were already waiting for us. I was so happy to see them that for a moment I completely forgot the sad goodbyes earlier that day. The last thing I heard was Papa's choked voice: *"Hou je taai* (hang in there)!" Little did I realize that his good-bye would be the first of a long string of good-byes.

I couldn't believe the quietness of Oldenzaal, especially compared to Amsterdam with its continuous noise. Walking along the narrow path through the forest, I could hear only the birds and the sounds of little animals scurrying away. The smell of the pines and the sound of the tiny branches breaking beneath my feet made me think of Putten, the little town in the forest-rich part of Holland called *De Veluwe* where we had spent our last vacation along with our neighbors, Mijnheer and Mevrouw Loewenthal. We had had a wonderful time. I remembered Papa had to rent a bicycle-for-two because Mama didn't know how to ride a bike. One day, Papa had decided we should all go for a long walk. The next thing we knew, we were following our Jewish "pied piper" through the forest. After a half hour or so, Mama and Mevrouw Loewenthall had begun to worry a little, wondering if we were getting lost. But Papa was very sure of himself as a guide, in spite of the fact that the mile markers kept contradicting themselves considerably from one point to the next. After about two and one-half hours, we had at last stepped out of the woods—too tired to move another step, except for Rosie who had been given a piggy-back ride most of the way. Looking back now, I realize we did have a fun time that day, but Papa's image as a guide was slightly tarnished.

The two-story brick house located on a quiet street at the edge of town looked very much like our house in Amstelveen, except our street had been a lot livelier. At the end was a large, open field bordered by yet another forest. "Don't ever go near that field!" Corrie warned.

"Why?" I asked.

"There's a gypsy camp."

"What's a gypsy camp?"

"Never mind. I'll explain later," she said. "Meanwhile, do as I tell you, and never go there!"

We followed Corrie through the narrow alley to the back of the house and into the kitchen. "We're home!" she yelled.

A woman about Mama's age came rushing in. "I'm sorry. I didn't expect you back so soon," she said, while shaking hands with Oom Twan. "Twan, how are you?" Not waiting for his reply she immediately turned to us. "You must be Rosie and Manda. I have heard a lot about you. I'm Mevrouw Van den Heuvel." We shook her hand. "Let me take your coats. Did you have a good trip?" She continued chattering as she piled our coats across her arm.

"We had an excellent trip," Oom Twan replied. It was the first time he had been able to get a word in edgewise.

"Please sit down!" she called over her shoulder, as she carried our coats out of the kitchen. Then we heard her call,

"Tilly! The girls are here!" Corrie and Nan exchanged quick glances, and Oom Twan's face broke into a smile.

Soon after, Mevrouw Van den Heuvel returned. She was a short, plump woman. "Corrie, make Twan a cup of coffee!" she ordered. "I'm sure the girls would also like to drink something," she added, as she joined us at the kitchen table. Watching Corrie, she pointed her finger to one of the cupboards. "The *Ranja* is in the cupboard over the stove."

Ranja? Were we going to have Ranja? I hadn't had any in ages. I loved the thick, syrupy, orange drink, especially if it hadn't been diluted too much.

A young girl in her teens with carrot-colored hair and hundreds of freckles walked into the kitchen. "She must be Tilly," I thought. My eyes were glued to her face. I had never seen anyone like her before. Her face was blue, especially her lips. Rosie noticed it too. The girl must have been aware of our stares, but she dismissed them smilingly, as she greeted us with a handshake. "I'm so glad you're here!"

Later that day when Corrie took us upstairs to show us our bedroom, she explained to us that Tilly had been born with a bad heart. "I don't want you to stare at her. She's a very nice girl. You'll get used to it."

By the end of the day, we had met all the other members of the family— their eldest daughter Loes and their two younger children, Robbie and Greetje, who were about Rosie's and my age.

Oh, and there was Piet—tall and blond, in his early twenties. Although he wasn't Jewish, like us, he, too, was in hiding, trying to elude the work camps in Germany. Last, but not least, we were introduced to Mijnheer van den Heuvel, a big, balding man like Oom Twan, but that's where similarities ended. Seated at the head of the table, dressed in a shiny, black suit which had seen better days, and mashing his already mashed potatoes to near mush, he instilled instant fear in both Rosie and me.

It took me a long time to get to sleep that night. The mashed potatoes, along with a late snack consisting of gooey porridge, weighed heavily on my stomach. Besides, I wasn't used to sleeping with four in one bed. I felt homesick, and our journey had only just begun. There was no turning back. But I shouldn't complain; we still had a bed to sleep in and for us there would be at least another tomorrow.

My first impression of Mijnheer Van den Heuvel had been correct. My fear of him never diminished. I often wondered about his family. Moving through the house, chattering all day, Mevrouw Van den Heuvel became instantly demure the moment her husband set foot in the door after his day's work as a cook at a local penitentiary. Seated at the head of the dinner table, his presence generated very little conversation, if any. The only one who didn't seem to be affected by him was Piet, who in his own jovial manner chose to ignore him. From beneath my brow, I watched Mijnheer Van den Heuvel as he butchered his mashed potatoes, night after night. It never ceased to fascinate me; nor did the shiny, black suit, along with the starched white shirt and the stiff, cardboard-like collar. It appeared to be the only outfit he owned.

The late evening snack of porridge, which had kept me awake for such a very long time that first night, turned out to be a nightly ritual to be repeated at breakfast. Surprisingly, I got used to it, just as I had gotten used to Tilly's blue face.

Corrie was right, Tilly was very nice. Much nicer than her older sister, who spent hours in front of the mirror trying to look beautiful. I thought that she was really trying to make Tilly feel like Cinderella. I felt sorry for her.

Occasionally, we were allowed outside, but school had become merely wishful thinking, and with envy I watched Robbie and Greetje leave the house each morning. Corrie and Nan spent a couple of hours each day with us trying to teach us reading and arithmetic, but it wasn't the same as school. To fill the long, idle hours, we began to cut out paper dolls from old newspapers. Soon we had strings and strings of them.

Although physically we weren't part of a classroom situation, we nevertheless became afflicted with one of its evils—head lice. Once Robbie and Greetje had brought them home, it didn't take very long for Rosie and me to get them. Frantically, Corrie shampooed our heads until the strong soap started to irritate our skin, but the lice kept coming back in increased numbers. It became harder and harder to treat the open sores, until eventually there was no alternative but to shave our heads. We looked awful.

To add to our misery, we found ourselves hungry a lot of the time. The diet of "mashed potatoes and porridge" filled our stomachs, but it left a terrible craving. One day, Corrie, Nan, Rosie and I decided to go for a brief walk. It was a beautiful, crisp, fall day. As we walked down the quiet street, we passed a little bakery. The pastries in the window looked delicious, in spite of the fact that the creamy icing was just a cover-up for the ground peas-and-flour pastry shell underneath. I could hear my stomach growl—or was it Corrie's? Maybe Nan's? I didn't know. Four pairs of eyes were glued to the display in the window. A plan grew, and before we knew it, we were inside the store—without money. And while Corrie and Nan held the clerk's attention, I quickly removed one of the pastries. There wasn't really a whole lot to share, but it tasted delicious.

In late October, Nan left us to join Papa and Mama in Amsterdam.

December 2, 1942, was a bitterly cold day. Dressed in her old coat, a kerchief tied around her head, Mama climbed on the *"D-Zug* (D-Train)" to Oldenzaal. She was glad she'd left the house early, as she was able to find a seat by the window. Through the dust and grime, she watched civilians and soldiers milling about. Some of the soldiers seemed unusually happy, laughing and slapping each other on the back. She suspected they were on their way home for a short leave to celebrate the upcoming holidays. Others stood around waiting quietly, lonely and tired. For the Dutch people, *St. Nikolaas* was rapidly approaching—four more days to be exact.

The ancient feast had more or less become a national holiday, and before the war even some Jewish families had taken part in the annual celebrations. Mama was not ashamed to admit that she and her family had always enjoyed it, along with Channukah, the Feast of Lights. Even now, during these dark days of war, there was an unmistakable feeling of anticipation in the air.

The train was filling up rapidly and soon became very crowded. Then there was a shrill whistle, and the train began to roll out of the station. Her view became momentarily obscured by the steam of the engine. It was still dark outside. Gradually, the train picked up speed and the ugly, blackened factories and rundown houses were left behind and replaced by snow-covered meadows and fields. It looked so desolate at this time of the year, especially without the animals, but peaceful nonetheless.

Mama no longer consciously absorbed the scenery. Her mind once again had become occupied with the worries that had been with her day and night for the last month or so, ever since Nan had returned from Oldenzaal. Ignoring all warnings against the dangerous trip, she had finally decided to go to Oldenzaal to see for herself what exactly was going on. The words that kept creeping into her mind most of the time were "head lice." She shuddered at the thought of her girls having head lice and tears welled up in her eyes.

"*Ausweiss, bitte!*"

The gruff voice startled her. When she looked up, her eyes met those of a German officer. Nervously she searched through her purse for the small folder. There it was. With an unsteady hand, she presented him with the forged I.D. No matter how expertly reproduced, she knew that there was always that small chance that an experienced eye would discover the slightest inaccuracy. Her hands felt sweaty.

65

"*Wo fahren Sie hin?*"

She shrugged her shoulders, pretending not to understand. Why did he want to know where she was going? Had he noticed anything different about the I.D? If she could only stop her heart from throbbing so.

"*Wohin!?*" The officer repeated. He sounded slightly annoyed.

Again she shrugged. By now clearly irritated with the ignorant *Hollaenderin*, he returned the folder. Smiling awkwardly she quickly put it back in her purse, not knowing whether to laugh or cry. She took a deep breath. The worst was over, and with a strange feeling of victory, she listened as the officer's footsteps retreated to the rear of the car, his voice slowly fading away: "*Ausweiss, bitte! . . . Ausweiss, bitte!*"

A gentle snow began falling and for a little while she watched the flakes whirl by the window in a disorganized pattern. She glanced at her watch. It seemed hours since she had stepped onto the train.

The conductor announced the next stop, "Oldenzaal!" Only a few other people besides herself were getting off. Dragging her suitcase behind her, she pushed herself through the crowded aisle toward the exit. Minutes later, she stepped onto the platform of the tiny train station.

"Mama!"

Instinctively she turned around. The girls! Her girls! And the tears which had been held back for so long began to run freely down her face. Locked into each other's arms for what seemed eternity, we laughed and cried at the same time. Mama was the first one to speak. "Your faces feel so cold. Did you have to wait very long?"

Corrie shook her head, "Ten minutes at the most."

"I'd say that is long enough in this cold weather."

Again we hugged and cried. Wiping her tear-stained face, Mama took a step back for a quick inspection. Nan was right, she thought, he had lost quite a bit of weight.

"I can't believe how much you have grown," she said, looking from Rosie to me.

"Especially their feet," Corrie commented.

Mama laughed, but when she glanced at our shabby shoes, there was hurt in her eyes.

"All they do is complain about their shoes being too small," Corrie said.

"I promise to talk to Oom Twan when I get back to Amsterdam. Maybe he'll be able to locate a couple of coupons for us so we can buy you some new shoes," Mama replied. Undoubtedly, Oom Twan would try, but she knew in her heart that the chances of getting new shoes were very slim. Only if someone else was willing to sacrifice coupons for us would we be able to get a new pair, and most people needed them for themselves.

Carefully, Mama began removing our hats. This was the moment she had dreaded the most and her face showed pain and disgust when she saw the sore-looking, shaven heads. She quickly put our hats back on. Exchanging quick glances with Corrie, she hugged us again. Trying to keep it light, she said: "Don't worry. We'll get rid of those lice in no time. But we better get started. It's too cold to be standing here." And with Rosie and me on either side of her, holding her hand tightly, and Corrie carrying the suitcase, the four of us were on our way back to town along the narrow, winding, snow-covered path through the forest, its trees heavily laded with fresh-fallen snow.

"Tell me," Mama said, "what has happened since I saw you last?" All three of us started to talk at once. "One at a time, please!" she laughed. There was so much to talk about, we didn't know where to start, and our voices and laughter echoed through the snow-covered pine trees. For a little while the war seemed very, very far away. We had to stop a few times to give Corrie an opportunity to switch the suitcase from one hand to the other.

"This thing is pretty heavy," she commented. "What's in it?"

"Not a whole lot. Some extra warm clothing and a pair of extra shoes. But why don't you let me carry it if it's too heavy for you?" Mama reached out to take the old valise.

Corrie refused. "It's all right. I can carry it, but you're sure it's only some extra warm clothing, huh?" Her wink didn't escape us.

"Absolutely!" Mama retorted, trying very hard not to smile.

Pursuing the subject a little further, Rosie asked, "Did *St. Nikolaas* bring us something, maybe?"

Mama shook her head. "I'm sorry, but *St. Nikolaas* didn't have any money this year, with the war going on." She sounded very sincere and her face showed real disappointment. "When the war is over we'll make up for it, I promise."

We knew she was not telling the truth about *St. Nikolaas* having no money. Maybe he didn't have a whole lot, but there had always been something, and we were sure there was something else in that suitcase besides clothes. Keeping a secret was not one of Mama's strongest points, so we began to guess. Dolls? Clothes? But she shook her head with every new guess. Soon it became clear that for once she had decided to keep her secret. "Papa and Nan are sending you big hugs," she said, trying to change the delicate subject.

That night after Mama had put us to bed, Rosie and I quietly slipped out of the room and started our search. It didn't take us very long. Mama always had picked easy-to-find hiding places. There were the gifts—unwrapped, of all things—behind some clothes in the hall closet— two coloring books, two boxes of crayons, two brooms and two dust pans. A few more gifts were there, but they were wrapped in plain white paper and had "Corrie" written on them. I recognized Mama's handwriting. We had no doubt that these were our gifts. According to Papa's law of "Nuns of the same order always wear the same habits," Rosie and I always received identical toys. Thus we ended up with two of everything. If Papa had wanted to prove that there was no room for discrimination in his house, he may have been stretching his "law" a little too far at times, but he surely prevented a lot of arguments.

When *St. Nikolaas* morning arrived, we were very surprised and excited, of course, when we opened our packages to find coloring books, crayons, brooms and dustpans.

Mama stayed for two wonderful weeks. When she left, our lice were gone, just as she had promised. Every night she had spread a newspaper out on the dining room table and with our heads bent over the paper, she had very carefully moved a small, black, fine-toothed comb through the stubble on our heads, so not to open the sores. After every stroke, she had checked the comb and the paper, killing each louse with a little "pang" of her fingernail. We not only felt better, but we also looked better. We had gained a few pounds and our hair had started to grow again.

By Christmas, Mama had returned safely to Amsterdam.

January 6, 1943 . . .
Amsterdam

is forehead pressed against the windowpane, Nan watched the people and traffic in the street below.

It was cold. The street and sidewalk were covered with slush from previously fallen snow. A sharp north wind was blowing, keeping the bicycle riders barely in their seats. Those heading south had the wind at their backs and scarcely needed to pedal. Those going north were bent over, barely able to move their bikes against the blistering wind. It was sort of fun to watch them.

It was January 6—the Feast of the Three Wisemen—and most Catholics were taking the day off, which was probably the reason the street wasn't quite as busy as usual.

Nan wished he could go out for a moment to get some fresh air. He had not been outside since he had joined Mama and Papa after leaving Oldenzaal in October. He knew he shouldn't complain, that he should be grateful to be alive. Many of his friends had not been that lucky. Still

71

he felt frustrated. It wasn't easy to be caged like an animal, day after long, boring day.

At times he wished he were back in Oldenzaal with his sisters. He especially missed Corrie. A smile crossed his lips as he thought back at all the mischief the two of them had gotten into, especially at school, driving Mama sometimes to the limit of her endurance. Now, between getting up in the morning and going to bed at night, there was nothing but the passing of time. Occasionally Oom Piet had given him some chores to do, but they were hardly big enough to fill the long empty hours. He had read practically every book and magazine in the house, some of them even twice. But he realized that going outside was out of the question. German restrictions had become tighter by the day and raids across the city were part of the daily order.

His eyes followed the streetcars as they rolled up and down the wide street. In the direction of the Munt Tower, his eyes rested briefly on the large department store of Vroom and Dreesman and the huge golden letters on its storefront. He tried to recall how long it had been since he had wandered through the store. He used to spend hours in the toy department picking and choosing until he had found just the right kit for his woodworking projects.

An idea popped into his mind. What if he would ask Mama to let him go to the store to buy a kit? It would keep him busy for days. He was not at all surprised when she at first refused, but he was not going to give up that easily.

"It's just across the street. I should be back in twenty minutes." She had noticed his weariness, and she had worried a lot about him lately. Unable to resist the sad look in his eyes any longer, she finally gave in.

"Please be careful," she pleaded.

"I promise. I'll be right back. You'll see."

He gave her a hurried peck on the cheek, grabbed his coat, and quickly walked out of the room, afraid she'd change her mind. Carefully, he went down the four flights of stairs, hoping that he wouldn't meet anybody. This was the hardest part. When he shut the heavy front door behind him, he stopped for a second to draw a deep breath of fresh air. Feeling happy and exhilarated, he crossed the street in the direction of the department store. Occasionally he glanced in some of the store windows along the way, without stopping or slowing down.

People were quietly sliding by, their heads bent to protect themselves from the icy wind. No one was paying any attention to him. Mama's worries had been unfounded. She was a worrier by nature and he doubted if she'd ever change.

The sound of a motorcycle pulling up along the sidewalk beside him made him turn his head. The bike had come to a halt. Instinctively, he began to walk a little faster, but he did hear the question.

"Are you Manus Wijnperle's son?"

This question was to become branded into his mind for the rest of his life. His body stiffened, but he kept walking.

"Stop! Turn around!"

Hesitantly he complied and looked into the pale eyes of a man dressed in a long brown leather coat. Someone else, dressed identically, was seated in the sidecar. The man who had asked the question came walking slowly toward him, carefully removing his large brown leather gloves. He stood so close that Nan could feel and smell the man's foul breath.

"You haven't answered me. Are you Manus Wijnperle's son?"

"Yes." His reply was almost inaudible.

"I thought so." A smile crossed the man's lips. There had never been any doubt in his mind; the boy's resemblance to his father was unmistakable.

"It isn't very wise for you Jews to lie but you know that of course," the man continued sarcastically. Again there was that scornful smile.

Nan nodded.

"My name is Abraham Puls. Your father and I have known each other for quite a long time."

At the mention of the name, flashes of stories began to cross Nan's mind. Yes, he had heard about Abraham Puls, the small-time operator of an unprofitable moving business. He had spent a lot of time in the ghetto where Papa had had his warehouse. Too poor to buy tires for his old truck, he had come to Papa, who was the only one who would extend him credit. When the Germans had walked into Holland, Puls had immediately recognized the opportunity to improve his miserable lifestyle and had offered his services to the enemy. After all, he knew where many of the Jews were living. According to German orders, he would move the belongings of those who had been transported to concentration camps to Germany, but not until he had first removed any valuable objects for himself. The real money, however, was in finding hidden Jews, for which he was being paid "per head." Officially, he had no authority to make arrests, but that was only a minor problem and very easily solved. The Germans teamed him up with a Dutch policeman by the name of Meyer, also a Nazi sympathizer, so the two of them would drive around the city looking for innocent victims. It was this team that made January 6, 1943, the most remembered day in our lives.

Meyer had gotten out of the sidecar to join his partner. Puls started to put his gloves back on in the same deliberate manner as he had taken them off. "We've got him. Let's go and find the rest of them," he said, never letting his eyes leave his victim's face.

They parked their motorbike on the sidewalk and with Nan between them, they walked the short distance to the Singel where they took him into a small dimly lit ground-floor office. It was sparingly furnished with a desk, a couple of kitchen chairs, and a telephone.

"Sit down!" Meyer ordered, as he pushed Nan in the direction of the chair next to the desk. Puls seated himself behind the desk and reached for the telephone. Nan's eyes quickly wandered around the room. Meyer sat in a corner, leafing through some papers. Then his eyes fell on the door:

it was ajar. For a split second, he considered his odds. It was his only chance.

He lurched toward the door and ran out into the street. Gasping, his heart throbbing, stumbling at times, he ran into an alley connecting the Singel with the Kalverstraat, with Puls and Meyer in pursuit.

"Stop!" He heard their shouts, but he kept running.

"Stop that Jew!" Puls yelled.

Someone jumped in front of him. He tripped and fell to the ground.

"Please, please, let me go, please?" When he looked up, there was a grin on the stranger's face.

"Thank you, we'll take it from here." It was Puls's voice. A small crowd had gathered. Someone jerked him to his feet. It was a policeman. "N.S.B.er-traitor!" Nan thought.

"Remove his belt!" Puls ordered. Meyer pulled the belt out of the loops of Nan's pants. He had lost a lot of weight in the last year, and he had to hold onto his trousers so as not to lose them. He had never felt so humiliated. He trembled. He could hear some of the spectators laugh and tears of rage sprang into his eyes.

"Let's go and visit the rest of your family!" Puls said, grabbing his victim by the arm. Silently the small party started out toward the Rokin. The policeman, no longer needed, stayed behind.

They walked Nan straight to the building and up the stairs. Nan realized that he had been followed from the moment he had left the house that morning.

Mama was helping Tante Annie clean off the breakfast table. Papa and Oom Piet had gone down to the cellar early that morning to repair the furnace. Except for the clatter of dishes, it was strangely quiet around the house. A few times Mama had walked over to the window. Almost an hour had passed since Nan had left and he had not yet returned. She was worried. "He probably has forgotten all about the time," she tried to calm herself; after all, he was still a boy, and she knew how he liked to roam through the store.

Suddenly she heard unusually heavy footsteps coming up the stairs. Heavy—like boots. Her heart skipped. Tante Annie came running from the kitchen.

"Who do you think it is?" she asked, drying her hands on her apron.

"I don't know."

The footsteps were coming closer. The living room door flew open and in horror the women watched as two men dragged Nan into the living room.

"Oh no, dear God, no!" Mama cried. Then she collapsed.

Papa had never been a person who had particularly enjoyed fixing things around the house, but lately he had welcomed some of the little chores Oom Piet had shared with him. Dressed in a pair of old coveralls, wearing a large cap, and carrying a toolbox, he had followed the old man to the cellar to work on the furnace. It had been fairly early and only a few office workers had passed them on their way down. None had paid much attention to the two "janitors." As he handed Oom Piet the tools, he reflected on how his life had changed in the past year or so. Probably the hardest thing to accept was the total lack of freedom. Until recently, he had occasionally ventured out to visit his "one-room warehouse," but that had become practically impossible. The German net had tightened itself more and more, and the "warehouse" was left abandoned. They just had to make do with whatever money was left.

A smile crossed his lips as he recalled the time he had traded some tires for a jute sack full of live eel. Surely he had realized that they weren't kosher, but he had never been very particular about that, except when Amama had been around. And as much as he loved eel, he had been only too happy to trade. Walking home that evening, he had spotted a German patrol just ahead of him. Quickly he had turned into an alley, but he had tripped, the sack had dropped out of his hand, and the eel went slithering all over the ground. He had hesitated, but not for very long, before getting on his hands and knees to salvage most of the delicacy. The next day they had laughed all through the meal as he had repeated the story in every minute detail.

Then there had been the time when he had watched from a safe distance as a fairly large crowd had gathered on one of the bridges. More than the usual number of Germans had been there, and his first impulse was to turn into the next street and disappear, but curiosity had drawn him closer to the bridge. "What's going on?" he had asked one of the spectators.

"A little boy has fallen into the water."

"Is anyone trying to get him out?"

The man had shrugged his shoulders, "I don't think so."

Without another word, he had pushed himself through the crowd, removed his coat and shoes and dived off the bridge into the icy water. He had had to make several attempts, but finally he had surfaced, holding a limp, motionless body above the water. Finally, with the help of some of the bystanders, he had brought the child to safety. Dripping wet and shivering, he had applied first aid, forgetting the danger he had put himself in.

"He's breathing!" he had whispered, mainly to himself, and his eyes had been fogged by tears.

When the ambulance had at last arrived, and he had handed the ashen-faced child over to the attendants, reality had struck him. Quickly he had forced his way in the direction of the spot where he had left his shoes and coat.

"Jewboy!" It had sounded like a whisper.

He had stopped dead in his tracks. Slowly turning his head, he had looked into the face of a young woman. She wore a lot of makeup and smelled strongly of cheap perfume. She was, undoubtedly, of questionable reputation.

"Hurry up, let's get out of here! Let's get you into some dry clothes!"

"What about my shoes?" he had argued, visibly surprised by the unexpected offer.

"Never mind your shoes. Hurry! Don't you see? The place is crawling with *krauts*."

"Where do you live?" he had asked, staring at his bare feet.

"Just across the bridge, less than a minute walk. Let's go!"

Reluctantly, but without further protest, he had followed the woman through the crowd.

When he had arrived home, that afternoon, in a somewhat ill-fitting suit, there had been some explaining to do.

"I know you'll never believe this," he had laughed, "but. . . ."

Of course Mama had believed him. After all, it wasn't the first time he had prevented a child from drowning, and she knew that nothing, not even the war, could have stopped him. She had hugged him. She was proud of him and glad to have him home safely.

"Isn't it ironic?" she had said. "You saved the little boy's life and in turn the prostitute saved yours, all on the same day."

He had agreed. It had been a good day for a change.

Oom Piet had begun to clean up his tools. "Why don't you go on upstairs?" he suggested. "The women are probably waiting with the coffee. Tell them I'll be right up."

"All right."

Papa had to admit he was ready for his mid-morning cup of *ersatz* coffee. At first the dark-looking substitute had tasted terrible, but as with so many things these days, he had gotten used to it.

When he reached the last flight of stairs he suddenly stopped. A man's voice! He cocked his head. Who was up there? Then he heard the pleas and cries.

"Take me with you if you want to, but please don't take my son, please?"

"Elsa!" He gasped. What in the world had happened? He carefully took another step.

"Where is Manus?" the voice shouted.

"Manus?"

"Yes, Manus. Your husband!"

There was a long pause.

"Answer me!"

The voice sounded familiar. Papa tried to remember when and where he had heard it before.

Then he heard her sob, "Manus was arrested along with our daughters. We have not heard from them since."

"Good answer!" he thought.

"You're lying; but don't worry, we'll find him before this day is over along with your daughters."

Puls! That's whose voice it was. It was Puls! He clenched his fists. He wanted to run upstairs and kill him. The girls! What if Elsa broke under pressure? Torn, he tried to gather his thoughts. He had to let the girls know, now! There was no time to lose.

Blinded by tears of anger and frustration, and forgetting about his own safety, Papa turned around and ran down the stairs into the street to the nearest telephone booth. His hands trembled so badly, he was barely able to dial the number. It was ringing! Hurry up! Answer!

"Hello?"

"Twan?"

"Yes."

"This is Jaap. Tonny and Gerard are sick. Please contact the girls!"

There was a click. Oom Twan had hung up. He had understood the coded message. For a moment Papa rested his head against the cold metal of the telephone. In what was only a matter of minutes his whole life had been shattered. His wife and son were gone, and nothing he could do would get them back. He felt like a coward for not having gone upstairs to help them.

"I've failed them. They counted on me and I failed them!" he cried.

Then he realized the futility of his grief. He had the girls to think about. He left the telephone booth for an unknown destination—a broken man.

Meanwhile, back in the apartment, Mama's pleas didn't touch Puls in the least. He had heard them all before. He walked over to the telephone and started to dial.

"Hello? This is Abraham Puls. I need a truck, right away. Rokin 101 . . . fourth floor. Just two, that's all." He set the phone down. At the mention of his name, Mama had brought her hands to her face. She looked at Nan, who stood motionless in a corner next to the window. Their eyes met briefly. "He knows," she thought. "He, too, must have remembered Abraham Puls."

"Where are you taking us?" she asked with an unsteady voice that was hardly audible.

"The S.D. will decide that!" Again the sinister smile appeared which had so frequently crossed the sadistic face.

Mama bit her lower lip. The S.D.! She realized it was too late for Nan and herself, but what about Tante Annie? She had to try to save her.

"If you take us, will you please not take this old lady? She meant well," she begged. Puls glanced contemptuously at Tante Annie as if he had only just now noticed her, but he didn't answer. Instead, he turned around and walked across the room toward the window, observing the street below. After a while, having moved the curtain aside, he fixed his eyes on the oncoming traffic, impatiently tapping the large leather gloves against his long coat. Suddenly, his expression relaxed. He turned around at once.

"The truck is here! Let's go!" Pointing at Tante Annie, he ordered: "Get their coats!"

Crying softly, the old lady obeyed. She helped Mama into her coat. "Here, Elsa, don't forget your purse," she whimpered, handing Mama her worn brown leather bag.

"Thank you, Tante Annie."

80

"Let's go!" he shouted this time.

Weeping uncontrollably, the three clung to each other.

"I'll pray for you. I know God will listen."

"Thank you, Tante Annie. Thank you for everything."

Meyer, who had been guarding the living room door, began pulling them apart, shoving Mama out of the door first.

With one final hug for Tante Annie, Nan quietly followed, his head dropped to his chest. Puls was the last one to leave the room. He slammed the door behind him, leaving the old woman behind, unharmed, but heartbroken.

And Oom Piet? Realizing what was happening, he left the building while Zus, who had been cleaning the bedrooms across the hall at the time of the raid, had quietly slipped down the stairs, carrying a small cash box containing Papa's meager savings.

The green trucks had become a familiar sight around the city and drew a crowd wherever they were parked. This time was no different. A small group of curious onlookers watched as Mama and Nan were loaded into the back of the truck, followed by two German guards. Slowly the truck pulled away from the curb with Meyer at the wheel and Puls seated next to him.

Their first stop was a small office at the *Ceintuurbaan.* Here, Mama and Nan were searched for any valuables before being handed over to their captors' superiors. All they got (stole) were a couple of watches. Mama was allowed to keep her golden wedding band.

Next, they were taken to Police Headquarters where they spent the night.

The following morning, they were taken to the Euterpestraat—Headquarters of the S.D.—the same place where Papa had once been interrogated. Flanked by two guards, they were led into the interrogation room. It was large with very little furniture. Behind a desk sat a German officer who evidently had been expecting them.

"Sit down!" he ordered, motioning toward the two chairs in front of him.

They obeyed, their eyes lowered to the floor.

"Look at me!" the officer shouted.

Startled by the sudden outburst, they lifted their heads.

"Remember, I can make this very unpleasant for you!" Slowly he slipped a cigarette from a silver case and lit it.

"You Jews are such fools! Don't you realize how much better off you would be if you would obey the Fuehrer's orders? Don't you?" he sneered. There was a long pause, during which his eyes never left his victims. Slowly he rose to his feet. He seated himself on the edge of his desk, making his overweight body in the ill-fitting suit even more noticeable.

"So what can you tell me about the rest of your family?" he grinned, carefully studying his immaculately manicured fingernails. There was no answer. He raised his head, his eyes fixed on the two people in front of him.

"Speak!" he shouted. "Where is your family?"

Frightened, Mama whispered, "My husband and our daughters were arrested. We have not heard from them since."

"I see." Agitated, he flung his cigarette to the floor and squashed it with his boot. He got up and walked over to her. Motionless, he stood in front of her, his hands folded behind his back. Then he grabbed her purse out of her hands and returned to his chair. Slowly, he emptied the contents in front of him. The first thing he picked up was a photograph. It was quite large, almost too large to fit into a purse. For a brief moment he studied the picture of the beautiful little girl with the large, dark brown eyes and the black curly hair.

"*Sehr schoen,*" he muttered to himself. "Who is this?" Mama's lips trembled, unable to speak.

Nan took over. "That's my little sister," he scornfully retorted. "She died a long time ago. She was only three years old."

"A very beautiful Jewess, indeed," the German commented. Then, seemingly no longer interested, he tore it into tiny pieces.

"No-oh, no!" Mama screamed while jumping up from her chair trying to stop him.

"Sit down!" he yelled. Slowly she sank back, burying her face in her hands. "It was the only picture I had left of her," she sobbed.

"You won't have any use for it anymore. I promise you."

"Swine. Filthy swine!" Nan thought while looking at Mama from the corner of his eyes, trying to fight back his own tears.

When she looked up, she watched the German deliberately drop the tiny fragments in the wastebasket beside his desk. Suddenly there were no more tears to cry. Despair had turned into hate, a hate so great, the likes of which she never would have thought herself capable.

Meanwhile, the officer continued carefully to search through the rest of the contents, as if nothing had happened. He picked up a small piece of paper. It had something written on it. It looked like an address. He read it silently. Oldenzaal. "Where is Oldenzaal?" he wondered.

They watched him read the note. Nan glanced at Mama. Her eyes had become large with fear. She remembered the note. She had forgotten to destroy it after her visit to Oldenzaal.

Slowly, the officer pushed the buzzer in front of him, then he leaned back in his chair.

"You have been very helpful. Very helpful indeed," he grinned.

The doors behind them flung open. Heels clicked. "Heil Hitler!"

"Heil Hitler! Take them away!"

Once again they were loaded on the truck, tired and numb in body and spirit.

Their next stop was the prison at the Amstelveenseweg. They were allowed a brief goodbye. They embraced each other, their faces wet with tears.

"Goodbye, darling. Please, do as they tell you," she cried.

"I will. I will. Don't worry about me." Then, through his sobs, she heard him whisper, "Mama, we may end up dead in Holland, but you'll never see Germany, never! I promise you."

Not understanding, she looked into his soft brown eyes. So young and so full of courage and hope, even now, she thought.

Then they were led away, each in a different direction.

Chapter 6

January 6, 1943 . . .
Meanwhile, in Odenzaal

On the other side of the country, everybody was sleeping in. It was the Feast of the Three Wisemen and everybody was staying home from school and work, including, unfortunately, Mijnheer Van den Heuvel. Sad to say, I had to admit that I had begun to dislike him more and more.

Winter had come to Holland and it was bitterly cold. With a thick layer of frost on the windows, it felt good to be able to crawl back under the warm blankets. I wondered how much longer we would have to stay with the Van den Heuvels. Not too long, I hoped. Maybe at the next place I would be able to go back to school. I had tried to quit thinking about school, but it wasn't easy. Soon I would be ten years old and, thus far, I had had less than two years of school, counting the time we had spent in Jewish school. I probably would never be able to catch up with the rest of the class once the war was over.

I heard someone going down the stairs. Probably Mrs. Van den Heuvel, who was always the first one up, no matter what day it was. I could feel Rosie stir next to me. Corrie was still sleeping like a log. As far as our sleeping habits were concerned, nothing had changed. Corrie was still the last one to wake up. At home, after calling her several times, Papa would take a wet sponge and squeeze it out over her head. She'd scream and holler, but it always worked.

Gradually, more noises began to fill the house. Soon the whole family would be gathered around the breakfast table for the daily ritual of porridge and bread, after which it was off to church. I guessed it was time to get up.

It was almost as cold inside the church as it was outside. Seated next to Corrie, I kept my hands tightly clamped between my knees to keep them warm. While waiting for the service to start, I let my eyes wander around the building. The colorful stained-glass windows, the many statues, were all so different from our "shul," the small unpretentious building that later had served as a one-room schoolhouse. Of one thing I was sure: it had to be much more difficult to be a Catholic than a Jew. In our shul, all one had to do was sit down and listen; the women on one side and the men on the other. Here one had to know when to kneel, when to stand up, when to sing, when not to sing. Rosie and I had been very confused at first and had done everything completely opposite. We had knelt when we shouldn't have, and we had gotten up when everybody else had knelt. To suppress our snickering, we had stuffed our mittens in our mouths. Very upset, Corrie had had a long talk with us explaining how important it was to behave ourselves and to try and do everything right. "Some people may no longer believe that we are orphans from Rotterdam," she had warned. "Just watch the people sitting in front of you and copy what they do." We had gradually gotten better at it.

The altar boys in white, freshly-starched, lace-trimmed tops over their red frocks had begun to light the candles. The boys in our shul had worn a "talles," a beautiful white silk prayer shawl with black stripes and long white fringes.

The priest approached the altar. He looked very stately in his red and gold robe. We all got up; the service had finally begun—in a cloud of sweet incense, which I didn't particularly like.

Behind me, I could hear the plate being passed—*clang, clang,* went the coins. The priest had moved the large missal from one side of the altar to the other, and I knew that the service would soon come to an end. My feet were freezing. I could hardly feel my toes any more, and I was wondering if I would be able to walk the long way home. "Amen." Quietly, people started leaving their pews, kneeling one last time.

The wind was blowing even harder than before. It went straight through my coat, and the 15-minute walk home seemed twice as long. My legs felt numb. The old woolen stockings, mended over and over again, were beginning to wear pretty thin. I noticed that Rosie was about to cry. Corrie had put her arm tightly around her shoulders, trying to protect her from the biting wind. I felt sorry for her. At home, she had been quite spoiled, perhaps because she was the youngest, but with Mr. Van den Heuvel around, she didn't dare to complain. She was scared to death of him, especially after the beating she had received a few nights earlier.

One of the Van den Heuvel's house rules was that the younger children had to get ready for bed before dinner. That way, as soon as dinner was over, we were sent upstairs. I don't think Mijnheer Van den Heuvel liked having us around. About a week or so before, after we had been sent upstairs to get into our pajamas, Rosie had climbed onto the bed, dressed only in a little undershirt. "Watch me!" she had laughed, using the mattress for a trampoline, jumping higher and higher, and watching herself fly by in the dresser mirror. We had laughed so hard, we hadn't heard Mr. Van den Heuvel come up the stairs. Suddenly there he was, his huge frame planted in the doorway. I had never seen him look so mean. While grabbing for her pajamas, Rosie had quickly jumped off the bed, but it had been too late. In two steps, he had been across the room, his belt in his hand. He had beaten her so hard I was hardly able to stand it, but she refused to cry, which had made him even madder. Papa had never, ever beaten us.

Sometimes I wondered why the Van den Heuvel's were hiding us. One time, I had overheard Nan talking to Corrie. He had told her that Mijnheer Van den Heuvel was only helping us for the money and that Papa was paying him two hundred guilders per month. Lately, Mevrouw Van den Heuvel had been wearing Corrie's fur coat every time she went out. It was not a new coat—actually, it was quite old. Mama had given it to Corrie so she would keep nice and warm.

"I just love your coat, Corrie," Mevrouw Van den Heuvel had said. "You don't mind if I wear it so once in a while, do you?" Once in a while? Every day was more like it. Afraid to say no, Corrie had reluctantly agreed.

When we finally arrived home everybody, except Mevrouw Van den Heuvel, who had gone into the kitchen to fix the "special" dinner, ran for the hearth to warm their chilled bones. Soon the whole house was filled with a delicious aroma of roast rabbit, the one thing I had really come to like. It was a welcome change from the daily "mashed potatoes."

After dinner, Mijnheer Van den Heuvel, newspaper in hand, retreated to his big chair beside the hearth. Not long after that, we heard him softly snore, while the paper lay discarded on the floor next to his chair. Corrie and the two older girls had gone to the kitchen to help with the dishes, while Robbie and Greetje had joined Rosie and me at the dining room table to help us cut paper dolls. We had rows and rows of them and we were ready to tackle the next project—houses for our dolls. We didn't know how yet, but with nothing much else to play with, we would find a way.

Soon everybody had gathered in the living room. Piet had put more coal on the hearth, and the orange flames jumped wildly behind the tiny mica windows. I liked Piet a lot. I could tell he really liked Corrie, but Corrie was "in love" with Paul, who lived in town. I guess he was rich because she had told us that he owned horses. She had met him one day while taking one of our occasional walks through the woods. After that, she didn't care much for having Rosie and me tag along, but she knew she was not supposed to be hanging around with him. It was too dangerous. Poor Piet had to stay in the house most of the time because if the Germans got hold of him, they would send him to a labor camp in Germany.

For the moment, the house seemed strangely peaceful. The sound of Mevrouw Van den Heuvel's knitting needles, the ticking of the old wall clock, the turning of a page—it felt good to be inside, while the wind howled across the fields.

Twilight came early. Mevrouw Van den Heuvel laid down her knitting and got up to turn on the light. "Children, I want you to clean up and get into your pajamas," she said. At the sound of her voice, Mijnheer Van den Heuvel woke up. After we had neatly folded our newspapers and gathered our dolls into the large shoe box, we climbed the stairs. On other days, with Mijnheer Van den Heuvel still at work, we would push and shove, trying to beat each other to the top of the stairs, but not today. Today we were trying to act like perfect little children, so as not to upset the peace and quiet. So far so good.

We had almost finished our evening meal of oatmeal and bread, when the doorbell rang. It was so unexpected, it startled everybody. "Who could that possibly be . . . and in this weather?" Mevrouw Van den Heuvel wondered aloud, as she got up to answer the door. Peeking through the small window, she saw a young boy standing on the doorstep, his hands buried deep in his pockets, vigorously stomping his feet trying to keep them warm. She opened the door slightly.

"Telegram, ma'am," the boy mumbled, pulling an envelope from one of his pockets, and without another word he turned around, jumped on his bike, and rode off through the cold, dark night.

Mevrouw Van den Heuvel slowly closed the door, glancing at the envelope. Her hands shook as she tried to open it. Her heart stopped when she read the coded message. She understood. When she came back into the dining room, her face had a blank look. "It's for you," she said, handing Corrie the telegram.

Corrie took it out of her hand and began reading the message. Her eyes became large with fear.

"Mama is sick," she gasped. Her heart sank. She, too, knew what the message meant.

Covering her mouth with her hands, Mevrouw Van den Heuvel began to cry. Mijnheer Van den Heuvel reached across the table.

"Let me read it," he said, annoyed by his wife's loss of control. Corrie handed him the telegram. Suddenly the peaceful day had turned into a nightmare. Orders were flying back and forth.

"Girls, clear off the table—quickly—get the dishes in the sink! Corrie go upstairs and check the room! Don't forget the pictures on the mantel!" Mevrouw Van den Heuvel cautioned. With tears running down her face, Corrie began to remove Mama's and Papa's photographs which they had allowed us to put up. "Piet, get your bicycle out of the shed! Have it ready . . . you may need it!" Mijnheer Van den Heuvel warned. Piet nodded and got up. Seconds later we heard the kitchen door open and shut.

I still had no idea what was going on. Except for Rosie, Robbie, Greetje and myself, everybody had left the table. When I saw Corrie go upstairs, I got up and followed her.

"Who sent the telegram?" I asked, watching her as she checked closets and drawers.

"Oom Twan, I guess."

"Is Mama in the hospital?"

"I don't know. It didn't say," she replied tearfully. I couldn't understand what she was so upset about. After all, Mama had been sick before.

"I want you and Rosie to stay real close. You hear?" she said, busily putting away our clothes.

"Why?"

She hesitated for a moment, searching for the right answer. "We may have to go back to Amsterdam."

"Tonight?"

"Maybe. I don't know. We'll see."

I followed her back downstairs.

During all this time, Rosie had been playing quietly with her food. For once, Mijnheer Van den Heuvel hadn't had time to get mad at her.

"What happened?" she whispered when I returned to the table.

"Corrie says that we may have to go back to Amsterdam."

"Tonight?" There was a hint of excitement in her voice.

"I don't know. Maybe. Corrie wants us to stay real close."

"Why?"

"I've told you. I don't know why! Just do as you're told!" Rosie was always asking questions. "Why?" "Why?"

Piet had returned to the living room. "Listen!" he said.

Off in the distance we could hear the vague sound of a motorcar. "A car!" Mijnheer Van den Heuvel said.

"Quickly! Get out—quickly!"

Carrying our coats, Mevrouw Van den Heuvel pushed us toward the kitchen door. "Here, put your coats on! Hurry!"

Seconds later we were standing in the snow, our coats unbuttoned, with only our pajamas underneath them, and just a pair of slippers to cover our feet.

I saw Piet grab his bicycle and disappear into the alley. The sound of the motorcar became stronger. Holding hands, we ran across the patio, then underneath the barbed wire, dividing the neighbor's fields from that of the Van den Heuvel's, and onto the neighbor's patio. With our backs tightly pressed against the dividing brick wall, we heard the car turn into the street. It came to a halt. Doors slammed, rifle butts pounded the front door.

"Wo sind die Jude?" (Where are the Jews?)

Moments later, the kitchen door flew open and searchlights threw their beams across the fields to the left of us. Suddenly, though I thought I had forgotten everything Papa had told us to do "just in case," subconsciously I understood. One move, the slightest noise, and it would be all over. Motionless we stood against the wall, holding each others hands so tightly, it hurt.

Then there were footsteps—boots. They were coming closer through the neighbor's alley. The small gate swung open—the silhouette of a man. We recognized the neighbor's son. He stopped for a moment and looked at us, then he continued toward the kitchen and entered the house, closing the door quietly behind him.

After what seemed hours, the searchlights were turned off, the shouting stopped, doors were slammed angrily, and a car sped off into the quiet of the night without its wanted cargo. Safe! Once again, we were safe!

Unable to move, we stood against the wall. We heard the kitchen door open. Someone came walking across the frozen snow.

"They're gone," Mevrouw Van den Heuvel whispered, as she stuck her head around the corner of the wall. She helped us inside, as we were barely able to walk. Mijnheer Van den Heuvel was talking on the telephone.

"Mulder? This is Van den Heuvel. I am going to send one of my children over for a liter of milk. . . . About half an hour. . . . Yes. . . . Thank you." He hung up, mopping his brow with his large white handkerchief.

A short time later, Piet walked in. When he saw us, his face broke out in a big smile. "Thank God!" was all he said as he put his arms around us.

"They can't stay here," Mijnheer Van den Heuvel interrupted. "Farmer Mulder is expecting them. Piet, will you take them?"

"Of course!"

We got dressed quickly and in less than fifteen minutes we left the house in Oldenzaal for the last time. With Rosie and me seated on the back of Piet's bicycle and Corrie and Piet walking alongside it, we began the half hour walk across the dark, icy fields to Farmer Mulder's, a haven for Jews in transit.

Wadded in her hand, Corrie held twenty guilders, which Mijnheer Van den Heuvel had given her—a "generous" share of the two hundred guilders he had received only a few days earlier. The fur coat also stayed behind.

When we reached the old farm house, a dim light was burning in one of the windows.

"Hold it," Piet said, handing Corrie the old, rusty bike. Rosie and I almost slid off as it tipped heavily to one side, while Corrie desperately tried to keep it straight on the icy surface.

Piet knocked on the barn door. There was the sound of fast-approaching footsteps.

"Who's there?" came a voice from within.

"It's us, Piet and Corrie!"

A bolt was being removed and the door opened. "Come in quickly, and bring in your bike," came the voice of a man. I assumed he was Farmer Mulder.

After Piet helped us down, we were hardly able to move. Our legs were frozen. Inside the barn, cows were lined up on either side; some were lying down, others were munching on the hay piled in front of them. A few were looking curiously over their shoulders, lowing softly as we stumbled by.

"You couldn't have picked a worse night," the farmer remarked as we followed him across the barn and into the living room. For a moment I wondered if we would be able to smell the cows from inside the house.

When we entered the room, a tall, heavy-set lady with rosy cheeks and thick blond braids circled around her head had gotten up from her chair to welcome us.

"Come in!" she said, reaching out. Tears were in her eyes as she took Corrie's hands between hers. No words were needed; there was unspoken compassion in her gentle blue eyes. Mevrouw Mulder knew Corrie from the times when Mevrouw Van den Heuvel had sent her over for milk and eggs.

"And these must be your little sisters," she said, turning to Rosie and me.

Corrie nodded, "Manda and Rosie." We awkwardly shook hands. She smiled.

"Let's take off your coats. You must be frozen to the bone. Poor kids!" the woman groaned as she helped us with our coats. Then pointing in the direction of the two over-stuffed chairs beside the hearth, she said, "Sit over there where it's nice and warm. Meanwhile, I'll go and make you all a cup of hot chocolate." She quickly left the room.

"Coffee for me!" the farmer called after her.

"I know! . . . I know!" came the answer from the kitchen.

"Sit down!" Farmer Mulder said, pulling a couple of chairs away from the dining room table.

The room was cozy. A brisk fire was burning in the polished stove, coloring the mica windows bright red. I rubbed my frozen legs. The tall grandfather clock chimed eight times. Farmer Mulder leaned back in his chair, slowly sucking on his pipe. He was a stockily built man with a rugged, but gentle expression.

Mevrouw Mulder returned from the kitchen carrying a tray with mugs of steaming hot chocolate for us and coffee for Mijnheer Mulder. Smiling broadly, she put two mugs and a large platter with cookies on a little table in front of us. "Drink this, it will do you good! And make sure you eat all those cookies!" *Lick cookies!* (Cafe Noires, Mama used to call them). How long had it been since we had last seen those? They had been one of our favorites. Covered on one side with a coffee-flavored glaze, we would lick them until all the glaze was gone, hence the name *lick cookies*. The cocoa tasted delicious, not at all like Mevrouw Van den Heuvel's. Hers had been just like water. This was made with real milk, thick and creamy. I could feel my body beginning to thaw.

Sipping the warm drink, I looked around the room. My eyes rested on the large, ornate china cabinet full of pretty things. Mama had had one almost exactly like it, but the Germans had taken it away. A huge cross hung between the two windows. Catholic, I thought. It seemed that everybody we had met thus far had been Catholic. The many colors in the thick velvety carpet were dancing in front of my eyes.

I looked over at Rosie. Her face was beet red. "Is my face red?" I whispered. She looked up, her eyes half closed. She nodded. "Yours, too," I said. Slowly she brought one hand to her face. She was tired, too. I don't know why, but I always felt sorry for her. I knew she was very homesick.

Mevrouw Mulder had joined the others at the dining room table. "I hope no one saw you coming out this way." Her voice sounded concerned.

Piet shook his head. "We came across the fields."

"That's good, because you never know who your friends are these days."

"Now tell us exactly what happened," Farmer Mulder said. Occasionally sipping their cocoa, Corrie and Piet gave a detailed account of the raid earlier that evening, while the farmer and his wife listened intently to every word.

"Do you have any idea how they found out?" Farmer Mulder asked.

There was a long pause as Corrie glanced at Rosie and me, and then at Piet. There was hesitation in her voice, when she said, "I don't know. I really don't know."

Farmer Mulder was sure that Corrie hadn't told him everything, but he didn't want to probe.

Mevrouw Mulder had pulled out a large red handkerchief and dabbed her eyes. "The good Lord was with you."

"He sure was," Farmer Mulder agreed, and as he looked at the young girl sitting across from him, he wondered where she found the courage and strength to go on. She was still so very young. "Where are you going from here?" he asked.

"I'm leaving early tomorrow morning for Hilversum. I'm planning to see a friend of Papa's. From there I'll try to get in touch with the underground."

"Are you certain you can trust him? I mean this friend of your father's."

Corrie nodded. "I'm positive." Then she added, "I'm more concerned about calling the underground from here so soon after the raid. They're probably tapping all the phones in the area."

"You're probably right," Piet said, taking a long, slow puff from his hand-rolled cigarette.

"I'm so grateful that you let us come here," Corrie said, "but I wonder if I could ask for one more favor?"

"What's that?" Mevrouw Mulder inquired.

"Would it be all right if Manda and Rosie stayed here with you? I am sure someone will be in touch with you shortly to take them somewhere else."

"Of course," the woman replied cheerfully, putting her hand on Corrie's arm. "We will take very good care of them, won't we, Papa?"

Farmer Mulder nodded. "Sure, no problem."

Rosie's eyes met mine. I noticed panic! We'd never been left on our own before.

"And how about you, Piet, what are you going to do?" Farmer Mulder asked.

"I'm returning to the house tomorrow morning. I doubt that they'll be back." He crushed his cigarette butt in the large brass ashtray.

"Let's hope you're right," the older man replied, and he slowly got up from his chair. He emptied his pipe and hung it back in the rack with the others.

The clock chimed again. Mevrouw Mulder looked up. "Nine thirty. That late already! We better get to bed. Tomorrow is going to be another long day." She got up and began clearing the table.

"I hope you don't mind spending the night in the loft?" the farmer laughed, putting his red, calloused hand on Piet's shoulder.

The young man smiled. "To tell you the truth, I could go to sleep on this floor, right now."

Mevrouw Mulder left the room with a tray full of dirty cups and returned with a stack of blankets and a pillow. "Here, Piet, take these. I'm sure they'll keep you warm."

"Oh, thank you very much."

"You're welcome."

"Well, good night, everybody!"

"Good night!" The two men disappeared into the barn.

"Corrie, you will sleep in the guest room and the girls will be sleeping in this room." Mevrouw Mulder explained.

This room? Where were the beds? I wondered. The woman must have read my mind as she walked to the other side of the room and opened a set of double doors, about a foot off the floor.

"Is that a bed?" I asked.

"It sure is," Mevrouw Mulder chuckled. "It's called an alcove."

"My grandmother used to have one just like it," Corrie remembered.

All I could think of was "a box." Once in "the box," I closed the doors. Rosie had a fit. "Hush up! Do you want everybody to see us when they get up in the morning?"

"I don't care," she whimpered. "It's too dark!" We finally compromised, and with the doors ajar, we dropped off to a deep sleep.

Chapter 7

Return To Amsterdam

$\mathcal{O}$ur stay with Farmer Mulder was short lived. A few days after our arrival, the underground got in touch with us, just as Corrie had predicted, by means of Mevrouw Van den Heuvel, who came to pick up her weekly supply of milk and fresh eggs. Farmer Mulder had been told that someone called "Roel" would be coming to get us the following Sunday.

The first couple of days without Corrie were very frightening, especially that Sunday morning immediately following our escape. Rosie and I had been left by ourselves while the farmer and his wife went to church. Looking through the kitchen window, down the snow-covered path leading into the dark, wintry forest, I was consumed by loneliness and self pity. We were just like Hansel and Gretel —except there was nothing out there on the path to show us how to get back home.

The next few days, for the most part, were spent helping Mevrouw Mulder bake cookies and following the farmer around as he milked the cows and churned the milk. We began to like it better and better. We had wonderful breakfasts of fried eggs and home-baked bread—no porridge, and no mashed potatoes, thank God. Rosie had gotten used to "the box," and even the smell of the cows on the other side of the living room wall had become familiar and good. I wished that we could stay longer, until the end of the war maybe, but it was not to be.

When Sunday rolled around, our shopping bag was packed and we were ready to move on. Roel arrived shortly after dinner. He visited briefly. Then it was time to go.

At the edge of the walk, we turned around to wave goodbye one last time to the two familiar figures in the doorway. Mevrouw Mulder, bundled up in her large black crocheted wrap, pressed a red-colored handkerchief against her face; Farmer Mulder had his arm around his wife's shoulders.

With Roel carrying the shopping bag, we were on our way to the train station to continue our "exodus" without a destination—at least that's how it seemed to us. Our lives became a pattern of "hellos" and "goodbyes" in rapid succession. I felt lonely, tossed to and fro, and I tried to push back the tears. To make matters worse, my toes were hurting worse than ever in my darned shoe. I guess Mama hadn't been able to get a coupon for new shoes after all.

It was beautiful out-of-doors, just like the day when Mama had come to visit. The snow on the tree branches glittered in the sunlight. It was very still. Nothing seemed to move.

The tall, thin man walking between Rosie and me seemed very nice, but he was still a stranger, a nice stranger, and I didn't know how to start a conversation with him.

Roel was the first one to speak. He asked, "Did *Sinterklaas* visit you this year?"

We nodded.

"What did he bring?"

"A dustpan and a broom and lots of candy," I replied hurriedly.

He looked down at Rosie, "And how about you?"

"The same . . . we always get the same."

"Hmm. How come?"

"Because Papa says that if we get the same, we won't fight."

"I see. But how can you tell which toys are yours and which are hers?"

"Because mine are always red and hers are always blue," she explained.

"You know, I think that's a very good idea. Your father must be a very smart man."

We agreed.

"Do you have children?" Rosie asked, feeling a little more at ease.

"No, not yet, but some day when we do, we'll buy them all the same toys—in different colors, of course." We laughed. I had guessed right; Roel was very nice.

We were early and the train station was all but deserted. When the train finally arrived, it was crowded, as usual, and there were no empty seats left. Standing in the crowded aisle, hanging on to Roel's coat, we tried to keep our balance as the train swayed along the tracks.

After a while, some people got off and we were able to get a seat.

"Where are we going?" I asked.

"Back to Amsterdam," Roel replied.

Amsterdam? My heart skipped a beat, and in a hushed voice, I said, "I didn't know we were going back to Amsterdam."

He smiled.

I could hardly wait to get there. The rest of the trip was quick and uneventful. No one even came by to check Roel's *persoonsbewijs*.

When we left the train station, it was snowing gently. The sidewalks were slushy and dirty. We crossed the street to catch a streetcar. It was virtually empty, as was typical for late Sunday afternoon. I noticed that the sign "NO JEWS ALLOWED" was still in the window, but was now slightly discolored.

When we got off the streetcar, we crossed the street, turned a corner, crossed another street and continued until we reached a small traffic circle surrounded by apartment houses with small stores beneath them.

Roel began searching for his keys. "We must be almost there," I thought.

"Here it is!" He sounded joyful as he stopped in front of one of the apartments and opened the door. "Very quiet, okay?" We nodded. In front of us loomed a tall, steep staircase. I immediately noticed the thin cord, parallel with the banister. *Grootmoeder* had had one just like it, except hers had had a basket at the end of it. That way, when the delivery men came at the door, all they had to do was put the merchandise in it. In turn, *Grootmoeder* had pulled up the basket and put the money in it. Most of the time, however, the cord was only used for opening the door.

"Go ahead," Roel whispered as he gently pushed us up the stairs. A woman was waiting for us at the top.

"Hello, girls," she said in a barely audible voice. "Come in." She quickly kissed Roel on the cheek and we followed her inside the apartment.

"When I heard someone come up the stairs, I thought it was you," she said. "How are you, girls?"

"Fine," I answered politely.

"Fine," Rosie echoed.

"I'm Lena, Roel's wife"— as if we hadn't guessed already.

"And let me guess. Your names are Manda and Rosie."

We nodded. "How come everyone knows our names?" I wondered.

"Let me take your coats."

Then she turned to Roel. "How was your trip?"

"Excellent. No problems whatsoever."

"You know, girls, Roel and I have a surprise for you, but you have to promise to be quiet when we show you." Rosie and I looked at each other, puzzled. "Come on," she gestured. We followed her across the room where she opened another door.

"Look who's here," she said. We peeked inside a bedroom.

Papa! We were stunned—unable to move. The next thing we knew, Papa had his arms tightly wrapped around us in a tearful reunion. "Why didn't he tell us?" I sobbed, referring to Roel who, with Lena, was standing in the doorway watching us.

"Because it wouldn't have been a surprise, now, would it?" Roel laughed.

"That's right," Lena added.

"You have grown so much I hardly recognize you," Papa said tearfully. Stooped down with his arms still around us, he kept looking at us, in disbelief.

Rosie looked around the room. "Where's Mama?" she asked.

"She's not here. She's still in the hospital." His voice shook as he exchanged glances with Lena and Roel.

"Let's go into the living room," Lena said, changing the subject. "I'll make you something to eat." Holding onto Papa's hand, we went back into the other room.

Later that evening, Rosie was taken to Lena's sister Dien, who owned a cafe at the Thorbeckeplein. She cried and cried when she was told that she couldn't stay, but when she found out that she would be with Corrie, she calmed down. I would miss her.

When I went to bed that night and Papa tucked me in, we both cried, each for our own reasons.

In another part of town, Nan was hunched in the corner of a dingy prison cell, his legs drawn against his chest, and eyes slowly running across the mildewed walls around him. In the gloomy light of a single bulb, he tried to unravel the messages of hope and despair. He wondered what had happened to all of the people who had left their names etched into the broken plaster as a testimony. No doubt, some of them had sat where he was sitting now.

Then his eyes moved to his cell mates. There were seven of them, all of them older than he. Together they shared a space hardly large enough to accommodate half their number. He felt ashamed when he thought of how he had laughed at them that time when they had returned from the barber. Only when one of them handed him a small mirror had he angrily realized the disgrace and the humiliation. That's exactly what they are trying to accomplish, he thought—to humiliate us. As far as he was concerned, they had succeeded.

He suddenly felt very tired. The steady diet of oatmeal that looked and tasted like glue, and the limp, cooked cabbage leaves, along with a lack of sleep, had gradually exhausted his strength. He slid down to a more comfortable position to where he was partly lying down, his knees pulled up to leave room for the others. With his hands folded behind his head, he stared at the ceiling. He felt nauseated. How much longer would he be able to bear the horrible stench of human excrement? He felt like throwing up. How long had he been here? A week? Maybe longer. He couldn't remember. He had lost track of time. He thought about Mama and the promise he had made to her. He hoped she wouldn't remember because there was no way he would be able to keep it. Why had he even mentioned it?

"Raus! Schnell!" The shouting of the guards made him jump up. "What's happening?" one of the prisoners asked.

"Who knows?" another replied, and he laughed bitterly.

Keys rattled. He could hear doors being opened and slammed shut. Their cell door swung wide open.

"Raus!"

For a moment they hesitated, bewildered by the sudden hysterics.

"Schnell!"

The guards started pushing them into the corridor. As more doors were being opened, more prisoners streamed into the already congested corridors, exchanging looks of terror. At last the procession began moving slowly forward through the long corridors into the courtyard.

Out in the wintry night, Nan's teeth chattered. He didn't know whether it was the cold or the fear. His heart pounded in his chest. He could hear some of the women cry, but their cries were quickly silenced. Standing on his toes, he craned his neck in search of Mama, but he didn't see her. Most of the women had their heads covered with big scarves and in the dark, he doubted if he would recognize her anyway. He tried to talk himself into believing that she could still be among them.

The guards began passing out cards with a large red 'S' printed on them. They were ordered to pin them on their coats. He wondered what the 'S' meant. Eventually, he would find out, but not until several weeks later.

After what seemed an eternity, the gates of the courtyard opened. A long line of trucks was already waiting for them, and while Amsterdam slept, the convoy rolled through its dark, quiet streets in the direction of Centraal Station, where a train was waiting to carry still more of the city's approximately 80,000 Jewish citizens to their deaths.

It was still dark when they reached their destination. A whisper passed among the captives. "Where are we?"

"Vught!"

"Vught?"

"Yes, Vught!"

The Dutch concentration camp, erected by the Germans, had begun to serve primarily as a "transit camp" for Jews until the ovens of Auschwitz had a chance to catch up.

Through the snow, they began their silent march, some carrying a few belongings wrapped in a pillow case, others with only the clothes on their backs.

Nan's mind was numb. Hungry and weak, he trudged along with the other prisoners. He had had nothing to eat since lunch time. After a while, the barbed wire surrounding the first buildings became visible. Inside the camp, there was much pushing and shoving as they waited to be assigned to their barracks. The process took the rest of the night and most of the following day.

When Nan arrived at his barrack, he threw himself on the first available cot. Physically and emotionally drained, he fell into an exhausted sleep.

The next moment—or so it seemed—he felt someone shaking him. "It's time to get up! Roll call will be soon!"

He opened his eyes and looked into the gaunt face of an old man.

"Roll call? Where am I?"

The old man smiled weakly. "You are in Vught, my son. You'd better get up or the guards will punish you."

Slowly Nan's memory returned as he arose from his straw mattress to face his first day in a concentration camp.

Chapter 8

Our Flight Continues

he few days I spent with Papa were very happy ones, although frustrating and boring at times. I was given very explicit instructions.

"Don't talk out loud. Don't walk around the apartment unless you have to use the bathroom. When you do, tiptoe. And never, ever flush the toilet. We'll take care of it when we get home." Roel smiled when he noticed my concerned look. "We don't know our downstairs' neighbors very well, and we have to assume that they don't know that anyone is upstairs while Lena and I are gone," he explained. "Do you understand?"

I nodded, but I wasn't all that sure yet about not flushing the toilet and, except for one time, I didn't use it until they came home.

It was evident that Lena and Roel weren't prepared for young house guests—probably because they didn't have any children of their own. A few decks of cards were all that there was to play with in the house. As a result, Papa and I played "Solitaire" most of the time. It was an easy game, but not very exciting.

When I wanted to ask a question, Papa, who was virtually deaf in one ear as a result of a diving accident, would lean across the table, cupping his "good" ear, while I whispered as loudly as I could. It made conversation very tiresome.

At noon, we'd briefly interrupt our game to eat the sandwiches that Lena had prepared for us before she left for work. When it was too dark to play cards any longer, we sat by the window to watch the people until Roel and Lena came home.

And so it was this afternoon, my last day. Oom Twan and Tante Mien were due to arrive shortly to take Rosie and me on the next stage of our journey. Where to this time? We didn't know. We never knew until we got there.

Seated on a footstool beside Papa's big armchair, I watched through the narrow gap between the drapes, as the people trudged through the dirty snow, their faces wrapped in large colorful scarves, their heads covered with all sorts of different headgear. A few of the shopkeepers had turned on their lights. It reminded me of *Sinterklaas* when we had gone shopping at night, admiring the pretty displays and toys in the windows.

Last night had been fun. There was so little fun left in my life, I treasured every pleasant experience. Soon after returning from work, Lena had quietly smuggled me down the stairs to take me to her weekly exercise classes. Before we left, she instructed me: "You are my niece, should anyone ask.

I nodded, anxious to get going.

"Don't forget!"

"I won't."

The cold air felt great and I filled my lungs with enough air to last a year, or so I thought. But the best part was that I was able to talk for a while and hear my own voice again. From one of the benches in the gym I watched Lena do her exercises. Once in a while, some of the other women went over to talk to her, glancing at me sideways, smiling. Lena turned around and winked at me. I smiled back. I knew they were talking about me. Afterward, we had to hurry to get home by curfew.

As my thoughts came back to the present, I noticed that the line of people waiting for the streetcar had grown longer and longer as one car after another went by. Bursting at the seams with people, the cars cling-clanged their bells as they rolled by without so much as slowing down. Still, I recognized the sign in the window, "NO JEWS ALLOWED." I put my head on Papa's lap. He gently stroked my hair. The butterflies were back in my stomach. I didn't want to leave, even though it was boring. Not yet, anyway.

I thought of some of the things that had happened. How long had it been since I had last gone to school? A year? I was sure it was longer than that. Would I ever be able to catch up with my friends? I doubted it, but I really didn't care. Since our narrow escape in Oldenzaal, it didn't seem to matter that much any more. Everything had changed and the war had suddenly become very real to me. I had done a lot of growing up in a very short time. Most importantly, I had come to understand one thing: I was a Jew and I was fighting for my life.

And all the time the Germans were pulling their net tighter and tighter. It was almost impossible to get through any more. Jews were being rounded up across the city and across the country. Sadly, *Grootmoeder* had been among them. For a while, the underground had been able to place her in a home for senior citizens, but, not unlike *Grootmoeder*, she had become discontented with her surroundings and had insisted on being taken back to her apartment. Through the underground grapevine, we learned that she had been arrested only a few days later. I wondered what had happened to her, where they had taken her. Would we ever see her again? She had not been my favorite grandmother, but now I suddenly missed her.

"It's been a terrible winter," Papa whispered, combing his fingers through his hair. It sounded as if he were talking to himself.

"We had a lot of snow in Oldenzaal, too." I tried to sit up so he could hear me better. "That night when the Germans came to. . . ."

"I know. I know. Corrie told me," he interrupted. Tapping his knee, he suggested that I put my head back down again.

I had tried to tell him about the raid once before, but he wouldn't let me finish. Papa had changed a lot. He wasn't as happy as he used to be. Even at Tante Annie's place, he had joked around, but since I'd been here, I had seen him smile only once or twice. He was a lot thinner, too. The dark shadows under his eyes told me that he wasn't sleeping very well. He was probably worried about Mama, and about the rest of us. Mama had been in the hospital for quite some time now. When I had asked him about her, he seemed very evasive.

"I don't know when she'll be home. As soon as she feels better, I guess." His voice had trembled. One thing I did find out. Nan was no longer at Oom Piet and Tante Annie's, but nobody would tell me where he was.

Meanwhile, the room had become completely dark. The clock on the mantle struck five. Shortly after, we heard footsteps coming up the stairs. A key was put in the door. It opened, and Lena and Roel walked into. Without a word, Lena walked over to the window, pulled the heavy black shades, and drew the drapes tightly across so no light would escape to the outside. Then she reached for the wall switch and flicked on the light. It took my eyes a few moments to adjust to the sudden brightness. It was the same nightly ritual.

"How was your day?" she asked, handing Roel her coat.

"Fine," Papa replied. "We have been sitting here very quietly, watching what's going on outside. Is it as cold as it looks?"

"Yes, it's bitter," Roel confirmed. "We better make sure the girls are dressed very warm when they go out tonight." He handed Papa part of the newspaper.

"There are a couple of mufflers in the closet they can use," Lena said, tying the apron strings behind her back. "But we'll worry about that later. Let's have dinner first.

Twan and Mien should be here any minute." Hurriedly, she went into the kitchen. The butterflies were getting worse.

Soon we were all seated around the dinner table. The silence was oppressive. The soup smelled delicious, but I wasn't hungry. I wanted so much to cry, and everyone around me became a blur.

Dien and Rosie arrived exactly on time. Oom Twan and Tante Mien followed shortly after. I realized that the inevitable—the time to say good-bye—had come once again. Sometimes I would pretend that it was only a bad dream. But the hugs and the tears were as real as the trembling hands trying to button my coat and tying the large scarf around my neck and my face, leaving only my eyes uncovered. When I raised my head, I saw Papa's dark eyes, sad and glistening with tears. I noticed how his nostrils quivered, as they always did when he was about to cry. A final embrace, a gentle push. "Let's go, girls, it's getting late." Moments later, we were outside, swallowed up by the darkness.

There had been a time when the darkness frightened me. How I hated it when Mama sent me upstairs to the attic for one thing or another. Reluctantly, I would tiptoe up the stairs, listening intently for strange noises. But coming back down, I'd run, combining the last four or five steps into one giant leap, landing with a thunderous crash right above the living room where Mama was peacefully mending our stockings. As I would calmly enter the room, she would look at me, smilingly, from the corner of her eyes. Surprising now how darkness had become a friend, one of our closest allies.

Roel had not exaggerated. It was indeed bitter cold. Except for a few German patrols, the streets were nearly deserted. Our footsteps sounded like an echo each time we passed one of the deep stairwells leading to the apartment houses. I clung tightly to Oom Twan's hand. In his other, he carried the familiar black shopping bag with the bright-colored flowers. It was far less suspicious-looking than a

111

suitcase. "It's the only permanent thing left in our lives," I thought. "It goes wherever we go."

Suddenly a loud cry ripped the stillness of the frosty night. "*Licht Aus!*"

Startled, my eyes followed the beam of a flashlight as it pointed directly into one of the windows above me. Someone had accidentally let some light get through. Invisible hands were making quick adjustments. The flashlight was turned off and everything became quiet once again. I looked behind me. Tante Mien and Rosie had fallen behind. There was almost a block between us. Poor Rosie. I bet the German had scared her, too. I was surprised that he hadn't stopped us and asked Oom Twan for his *persoonsbewijs*. He had probably thought we were just a family on our way home.

The already sharp northeast wind had notably increased. I was so cold, my whole body felt numb. My legs were too stiff to skip and I had to take at least two steps for every one of Oom Twan's to keep up with him. My side was aching terribly. I pressed it firmly as I tried to stop the sharp pain. I wondered where they were taking us, and if we were ever going to get there. I couldn't remember how many bridges we had crossed? Two? Maybe more. Neither did I recognize any of the streets. One thing was sure! This wasn't where Papa used to take me for walks on Sunday morning.

The black-shaded windows seemed to stare at me like lifeless eyes. Behind them were children, like Rosie and me, sound asleep in their warm beds. I felt a pang of jealousy, but I quickly tried to forget it. After all, I was not like them any more. Some day I would sleep in my own bed again, but I would always remember this night. Until then, I had to be a "big girl," as Papa put it.

Then, out of nowhere, I distinguished the faint silhouettes of barges straight in front of me. The harbor! Were they taking us on a barge? I felt a strange sense of excitement. When we reached the quay, Oom Twan slowed down to give Tante Mien and Rosie a chance to catch up. When they finally reached us, we walked together beside the many barges, moored side by side.

"This is it," Oom Twan said as he stopped at one of the gangplanks. "Be very quiet and watch your step. Those planks are very slippery." In single file, holding hands, we climbed the narrow plank, crossing each barge, one by one, until we finally reached the last one. It was under tow and ready to leave the harbor.

Putt . . . putt . . . putt. The sound of the engine of the tugboat was eerie as it drifted across the cold, dark water of the quiet harbor. Still holding onto each other, we followed Oom Twan along the gangway to the rear of the barge, which was loaded with cargo. It was so low in the water that I probably could have touched it. When we reached the cabin, Oom Twan knocked at the door, three short knocks and one long one—the first four notes of Beethoven's Fifth Symphony, now adopted by the underground as "the sign of a friend."

We could hear someone inside climb the stairs. A bald man, wearing glasses, opened the door. "Come in! We have been waiting for you." Backwards, we followed each other down the narrow staircase with Oom Twan leading the way. I was barely able to move my frozen legs from one step to the next. About halfway down the stairs, I heard Oom Twan's voice say, *"Dag,* Ies. *Dag,* Greta. How are you?"

Mama's younger brother and his wife? Here? On the boat? When I reached the floor, I turned around in disbelief. Rosie reacted the same way. Seeing the puzzled looks on our faces, Oom Ies started to laugh. He stretched out his arms. "Doesn't your old uncle get a hug? How about it, eh?" The next moment, we were all embracing each other.

"Why are you here?" I asked.

"For the same reason you are!" Tante Greta replied smilingly, while she tried to unbutton our wet coats.

I heard Oom Twan introducing us to the man who had let us in a few minutes earlier.

"Why don't I take your coats and you can all sit down," the man said.

"Thank you, Frans," Oom Twan replied, "but we can only stay a short while." He glanced at his watch to check the time.

"Long enough for a quick cup of coffee, I hope."

"A quick one."

Frans disappeared into the kitchen. Soon, everybody was seated around the small room.

"May I borrow a cigarette?" Oom Twan asked, vigorously rubbing his cold hands together. Oom Ies offered him one of his hand-rolled cigarettes. Turning it around between his fingers, Oom Twan inspected it carefully. "I have to say, you're doing a good job."

Oom Ies grinned. "As many as I have rolled, I should be an expert at it by now." He struck a match and leaned forward to light Oom Twan's cigarette.

"You picked the worst night of the year," Tante Greta remarked.

Tante Mien agreed.

"Those are the best nights to transport illegal cargo," Oom Twan added. They all began to laugh. It almost seemed like a family get-together. Like a birthday party, I thought, and the dreaded feeling of loneliness slowly ebbed away.

Frans returned from the kitchen carrying a tray with cups of steaming hot drinks. "The hot milk is for the girls," he explained, passing the tray around. I assumed Frans was the skipper of the barge. He seemed very nice and I wondered if he was married. Tante Greta was apparently the only woman aboard.

Frans took a chair next to Oom Twans's. "You're not going back to Geleen tonight, are you?"

Oom Twan shook his head. "We're staying at a hotel near Centraal Station. We're leaving early in the morning."

"Have you seen Lida lately?" Tante Greta asked. Her voice shook. I had forgotten all about Lida, their baby daughter. The last time I had seen her was a couple of years ago, when they had visited us in Amstelveen. Lida had been only a few months old.

Tante Mien put her cup down. "We saw her a couple of weeks ago," she said. "She is doing fine."

Tante Greta's eyes glistened with tears. "I miss her so!" she cried. Tante Mien put an arm around her. "I understand, but be thankful, Greta. She couldn't be in better hands."

"Does she still suck on her blanket?" Tante Greta inquired.

"She sure does," Tante Mien replied gently.

"Kees and Lieske are spoiling her rotten. You won't know what to do with her when you get her back," Oom Twan interrupted jokingly, but he immediately realized the cold comfort of his words. Tante Greta smiled.

Oom Ies ran a hand through his hair. I've told her over and over again not to worry, but what good does it do? He made a gesture of despair.

Oom Twan glanced at the wall clock. "Mien, we have to get going."

She caught his glance. "I guess so!" She quickly got up from her chair. "I wish they would do away with that curfew."

"I'm afraid we may have to wait a while, yet," Oom Ies replied.

Frans handed them their coats.

"When we came aboard, I thought I heard the tugboat," Oom Twan commented as he reached for his coat.

Frans nodded. "We're planning to leave within the hour."

Again, there were embraces and hand shakes. I watched them as they disappeared through the small door into the cold, winter night, followed by Frans.

Tante Greta began gathering the empty cups. The hot milk had made me sleepy. I could feel myself drift in and out of a state of semi-consciousness.

"You girls must be awfully tired," Tante Greta re-marked. I nodded. She put the tray with the empty cups down. "Let me show you your room first. I can wash those cups later. Did you bring a suitcase?" I pointed at the shopping bag.

She smiled and picked it up. "Let's go."

We followed her to the end of a short, narrow corridor. "This is your room." The gas lamp in the room flickered as she opened the door. It had an alcove just like the one at Farmer Mulder's. I must have shown a glimmer of recogni-tion, when she asked, "Will you be able to climb in by yourselves?" We nodded our heads simultaneously. "Big girls, eh?" she laughed.

"We slept in one before," I explained.

"I see. Call me if you need any help." I nodded. She kissed us goodnight. "See you tomorrow." When she got to the door, she turned around. "I'll leave the hall light on for you, just in case you have to get up. The W.C. (bathroom) is next door." She waved and walked out, closing the door softly behind her.

I pulled our pajamas out of the bag. It didn't take us long to get ready for the alcove. The bed looked as if it hadn't been made. What was worse, however, were the sheets. Even in the dim light of the gaslit lamp, I could tell that they hadn't been washed in quite some time. "It stinks," Rosie remarked.

"I know. But what can we do?"

"Nothing," she decided, and we climbed into the bed. The stench was awful, but fortunately we were saved by our exhaustion, and in no time we had dropped off into a deep sleep.

It seemed as if we had only just gone to sleep when I was awakened by a noise. When I peeked out of the alcove, I saw a dark-haired man. I quickly lay back down again, wonder-ing who he was. Staring at the ceiling of the dark alcove, I listened to the noises. A drawer was being opened . . . then shut. He's getting his clothes, I thought. I wondered if he knew that I was in the alcove? I peeked again. He was walking toward the door. He was leaving. I let out a sigh of relief.

I tried to wake Rosie. "Let's get up. It's morning!"

"I'm tired," she grunted. I shook my head. Just like at home. I decided not to wait for her. I washed my face over the small sink, and dried it with a towel which was flung across the only chair in the room. It, too, was dirty. Compared to the sheets, however, it was hardly worth getting upset about. It was amazing how quickly we seemed to adjust these days. I could feel myself growing up faster and faster.

When I walked into the living room, I saw Tante Greta standing in the kitchen. She had heard me come in. "Good morning! Feel better?" she called over her shoulder.

"Yes."

"How about some breakfast?"

"Thank you!"

The room looked quite different from the night before, but it still was very small. It reminded me very much of a doll house. The kitchen was a couple of steps up from the living room, which I hadn't noticed before—probably because I had been so tired. There was another door. It was closed. A bedroom, perhaps.

Tante Greta came down the steps with a bowl of hot porridge. "It isn't very sweet, I'm afraid. We have just about run out of sugar." She sounded apologetic.

"That's all right." It had to taste better than Mijnheer Van der Huevel's, even without the sugar.

"Where's Rosie?"

"She's still asleep."

"So is your Oom Ies. He's getting lazier by the day," she chuckled.

"Where are you going?" I asked.

"We don't know yet." I wondered if she really didn't know or whether she didn't want to tell me.

"Do you know where Rosie and I are going?"

"Geertruideberg."

"Where's that?"

"Not very far. Two to three days sailing."

"Are we sailing now?"

"Yes, we are. We have been since last night."

"How come I didn't notice?"

"You're not supposed to notice." She reached across the table and gently tapped my hand. Then, she quietly watched me as I finished my porridge.

"Who was that man in our room?" I asked.

Her face had a puzzled look. "Man?"

"Yes, a man. I saw him when I woke up."

"Oh, that was probably Henk. He's the deck hand. That's his room you're sleeping in.

"I see." That explained the dirty sheets, I thought.

"When we need extra beds, he sleeps in *Het Vooronder*," she added.

"Where's that?"

"In the bow."

The door opened and Frans came climbing down the stairs. "Where's my coffee?" he called.

Tante Greta smiled. "It's ready and waiting." She went up into the kitchen to pour him a cup.

Frans sat down on the couch. "Did you sleep well?"

I nodded.

"Did you hear us leave the harbor last night?"

I shook my head.

"How would you like to steer the barge?"

"Me?"

"Yes, you! I knew you hadn't lost your tongue," he laughed.

"I don't know how to steer."

"As soon as you're finished with your breakfast I'll take you up on the deck and teach you."

"I'm finished."

"You are, eh? Well, get your coat on, and don't forget to wear a hat or a scarf. It's very cold." He finished his coffee, and moments later I was up in the steering hut, protected by windows from the blistering wind. Threatening dark clouds were rushing overhead. The tall grass along the river banks bent wildly low with the wind.

"Stand right here." The skipper pulled me gently between him and the large steering wheel. "Put your hands here."

I grabbed two of the large prongs that were part of the wheel. Putting his large hands on mine, he moved the wheel one way, then back the other way, ever so slightly, keeping the barge in a straight line, as it carved its way through the choppy, grey waters.

Suddenly he let go of my hands. Somewhat frightened, I turned my head to look at him. "Go ahead. You're doing fine," he said.

"I can steer!" I cried. I was elated.

"Sure you can. I told you. Nothing to it."

I liked the skipper.

The first day turned out to be just wonderful. At dinner, we met the deck hand. He, too, seemed very nice.

The next day we passed through some locks. While we hid inside, we could hear Frans cheerfully joke with the patrolling German soldiers, hoping that his jovial manner would keep them from searching the barge. They were anxious moments. What if they decided to come aboard? We would all be lost. But we passed through the locks safely. Frans had rolled the dice and, once again, our lucky number had come up.

After three days we dropped anchor in Geertruidenberg. Our journey had come to an end.

Ashore, a man wearing a grey raincoat and a floppy, grey hat was waiting for us. Frans put the narrow gang plank in place and returned to the cabin.

"This is where you girls get off," he said. For a fleeting moment, I thought there was sadness in his eyes, but maybe it was just my imagination. "A good friend of mine is out there to take you home with him. He is a very nice man," he added, trying to reassure us. Then he looked at Tante Greta. "Is this their bag?" pointing at the shopping bag. She nodded. Except for a few things, we had never even gotten unpacked. "Button up your coats and cover your faces with those scarves," Oom Ies warned. "You still have a long, cold ride ahead of you."

I wanted to ask where we were going, but somehow I was afraid to. It really didn't matter. It wouldn't change anything anyway.

We said goodbye to Tante Greta and Oom Ies.

"We'll see you soon," Oom Ies said. His voice sounded hoarse.

"Be very careful," Tante Greta cried as we began climbing the narrow stairs. When I reached the top, I turned around to wave goodbye, one last time. My eyes were stinging. Holding onto Frans's hands, we bucked the wind as we walked across the deck. Oom Ies had been right. It was very cold. The wind hadn't let up at all. I noticed that the man in the grey coat needed both hands to keep his bicycle steady while, occasionally, he had to grab onto his hat. When we reached the end of the gang plank, the two men shook hands.

"*Dag*, Piet."

"*Dag*, Frans."

"Here is your cargo," Frans joked.

The man smiled. "Let me guess. Manda and Rosie. Right?"

I wondered how he knew. He took the bag from Frans and hung it on the handlebar of his bicycle. Then he lifted Rosie off the ground and put her on the crossbar in front of him. He looked at me. "You sit on the back," he said, "but wait until I get on first. I guess we are all set." The exchange had taken but a few minutes.

Frans waved. *"Dag,* girls. God bless you!"

We raised our hands, awkwardly, in a gesture of good-bye. I know that our eyes were begging him to take us back aboard. He swiftly turned around and walked away, pulling the collar of his coat closer around his face. Slowly, the bicycle was set in motion. When I turned around, I saw the skipper wave goodbye one last time before disappearing behind the cabin. We moved further along—into the dark tunnel of the unknown.

The ride that followed was very cold. Practically all during the trip I kept my face hidden close behind the man's back, away from the icy, biting wind. It was a typical January day. The bitter northeast wind had made the temperature drop rapidly, causing the rivers and canals to freeze solid. Still, only a very few people would brave the cold to go skating.

I was worried about Rosie seated on the crossbar. "That wind must just about go right through her," I thought. I hoped that she kept the muffler wrapped around her face. I raised my head slightly to see where we were. There was nothing to see but desolate snow-covered fields with here and there an old farm house. At times, the howling wind turned the snow into a blinding, white mist.

Although the man pedaled as hard as he could, we hardly seemed to move. The man was quite old—at least he looked old—and I couldn't help feeling sorry for him. Occasionally, he would use only one hand to steer while he held his hat with the other, making the bicycle sway dangerously to one side.

At last we reached a more populated area. We crossed a drawbridge and, after what had seemed an endless journey, the man turned into a driveway which led to a very large, red brick corner house. Later we discovered, that it was actually two houses attached to one another. The man stopped and slowly brought his feet to the ground. "We're home," he sighed. After he had helped us get off, he looked at us compassionately. "I'm Oom Piet," he said. "You're now in *Oosterhout*." He stepped off the bicycle and put it in the shed.

Holding our hands, he led us into the house. "Let's go inside where it's nice and warm." We had entered a large, square kitchen. "We're home!" Oom Piet's voice echoed through the house. We heard someone come running down the stairs. A moment later, a pretty young woman with long blond hair appeared in the doorway.

"Let me guess! Manda and Rosie!" Her smile revealed her beautiful, white teeth. "*Welkom!* I'm Janneke." We shook her hand. "You must be frozen," she continued mournfully while helping us with our coats.

"It's bitter out there," Oom Piet commented. He had taken off his coat and was trying to light a cigar. "Janneke, why don't you make the girls something hot to drink."

"What would you like?" she asked. "Hot cocoa or hot milk?"

"Hot cocoa, please." I replied demurely.

"How about you, Rosie? Would you like cocoa, too?"

"Yes, please."

Moments later we were sipping the delicious warm drink and I could feel my body starting to warm up right away. Janneke reached into one of the cupboards and took out a colorful cookie tin. She opened it and put it in front of us. "Here, take some. It will be a little while until dinner." Then she turned to her father.

"What would you like. I'm sure you could use something to drink as well."

"Did you make tea?"

Janneke nodded. "I just made some for *Moeke*."

"Good. Pour me a cup, will you?"

While enjoying his cigar, Oom Piet watched us savor our hot cocoa. "Maybe Janneke will make you some of her famous fudge. She makes the best fudge in the world."

Janneke seemed to ignore the compliment. "When you're finished with your cocoa, I'll introduce you to my mother," she said. "She's very anxious to meet you." A short while later we followed Janneke through the dining room into the living room. My eyes could hardly believe all the beautiful furniture. I had a sneaking suspicion that these were rich people this time, and it made me feel ill at ease.

Seated in the bay window was an elderly lady, quietly looking outside, her hands folded in her lap. Her grey hair looked very soft. On the small table next to her sat an empty porcelain tea cup.

"*Moeke,* our guests are here."

The woman turned her head. Her face broke out into a radiant smile. "How wonderful!" she replied softly.

Janneke led us to her, "Meet my mother. *Moeke,* meet the girls." Unsteadily, the woman reached out and took our hands between hers.

"We're very happy to have you stay with us." Her voice sounded quiet and gentle. Then she pulled us really close to her. "We hope you're going to like it here."

"*Moeke* doesn't see very well," Janneke explained. That's when I noticed the woman's eyes. There was no sparkle in them. A feeling of sadness came over me. She seemed such a sweet lady and I couldn't imagine not being able to see the things around me.

"Did you make them something to drink?" she asked, dismissing her daughter's statement.

"Yes. They just had some."

"How about some of your fudge?"

"*Moeke,* not you, too," Janneke laughed.

"What do you mean?"

"*Vader* told them the same thing."

"He did? I'm not surprised. Nobody can make fudge like you."

Janneke shook her head.

"Hello there!" We turned around. Another young woman had entered the room.

"I'm Trees, Janneke's older sister." We shook hands politely. *"Welkom* to Oosterhout! It must have been awfully cold, riding on that bicycle. Brrr!" she said, shivering.

We smiled. Then she turned to her mother. *"Moeke,* I've finished the laundry. Is there anything else you'd like me to do?"

The older woman shook her head. "No, thank you, Trees. I want you to take a rest now."

A frown appeared on the girl's face. "All right."

That night, seated at the huge dinner table, which perfectly befitted the large living room with all its ornamental furniture, we met Harry and Tonny. Tonny was married and lived in Dongen. She had come to visit her mother for a couple of days. She was different from her sisters—more reserved—maybe because she was older. Her dark hair and her dark-rimmed glasses accentuated her fair complexion. I found myself fascinated by her hairdo. It was arranged in an impeccable roll all around her head, with not a hair out of place. It must have taken her hours to fix it. Harry, the youngest brother, was very nice, too.

There were a lot more brothers and sisters—ten in all— and some day we would meet every single one of them.

After dinner, we joined Janneke in the kitchen to watch her make fudge. There seemed to be an endless amount of stirring needed to get it just right. Finally, she dropped a tablespoon of the syrup-like stuff on the counter where she let it cool for a moment before gently touching it with her finger. "Almost done," she mumbled to herself. Where did they get all the sugar from, I wondered. They had to be rich. Nobody else had any!

At last, Janneke carried a large plate with fudge to the table.

"Try a piece," she said, licking her fingers. "But be careful, it may still be hot." It tasted wonderful.

"Like it?" she asked.

We nodded together. "It's delicious," I emphasized.

"Good. I'm glad," and she handed us the pot and a sticky wooden spoon. "Go ahead. Lick these clean," she laughed.

At last it was time for bed. Rosie and I shared a small bedroom with a double bed. The sheets felt crisp and clean—unlike those in the alcove on the barge. Our first day in Oosterhout had turned out much better than we had expected, and soon we were off to a restful sleep.

The following day we met Annie, the second oldest daughter. She with her husband and their two young children, a little girl and a little boy, lived in the house next door. The children were quite a bit younger than Rosie and I. They were nice, but rather spoiled, I thought.

As the weeks passed, we gradually became acquainted with the other members of the family—all except their son Kees and his wife Lieske. Their names somehow rang a bell. I had heard them mentioned before, but I couldn't quite remember when or where. Suddenly, it came to me. On the barge! Oom Twan and Tante Mien had talked about them that night on the barge. It had something to do with Lida—Lida being in good hands with Kees and Lieske.

Of course, that was it. I had been too tired that night to pay much attention to what was being said. Suddenly it all came together. Lida was staying with Kees, Janneke's brother. That meant he was with the underground, and that's how he knew Oom Twan and Tante Mien. I wanted to ask Janneke about it, but I was afraid to.

As I walked into the dining room one day, Janneke was sitting on the floor across from the radio, her back against one of the chairs. She was checking off her favorite programs in the weekly radio guide. It was her favorite pastime. She had the radio turned on full blast. I sat down on a chair next to her. She looked up. "Do you like The Ramblers?" she shouted.

I shrugged my shoulders. "Who are they?" I yelled back.

She pointed at the radio. "You're listening to them."

"Oh. I don't know. All right, I guess."

She smiled. "I think they're great. They're coming to Dongen next month. I'm going to see them," she bellowed, tapping her foot and snapping her fingers to the rhythm of the music. "Would you like to come?"

I shrugged again. "I don't know."

"I'll take you," she said.

"When is Kees coming to visit?" I suddenly ventured to ask. Seemingly surprised, she looked at me.

"Kees? Soon, I hope. We don't see him very often. He and Lieske are very busy. He's my favorite brother, you know."

"Where does he live?"

"In Born, a small town in Limburg. Actually, he is not living in town, but in a nearby harbor. He and Lieske own a houseboat. You should see it. It's beautiful." There was a pause. Then she continued, "Remember my brother Jan and his wife Almy?" I nodded. "They live not too far from Kees, just a few kilometers.

For a while I sat silent while the music grew louder and louder. I could hardly wait to meet Kees. It would be a while, however, before that day would come.

Chapter 9

A Promise Fulfilled

*I*t had been almost six weeks since Nan's arrival at the camp. He had been assigned mainly to outdoor duties. It was arduous work, but it kept him busy and away from the foul-smelling barracks, at least during the day. The snow had been replaced by rain, and he knew that spring couldn't be too far off. Trainloads of new prisoners arrived daily"—old people, children, mothers with small babies—but he still hadn't been able to locate Mama. He tried to look for her whenever he had a chance to get near the barbed-wire fence separating the men from the women. He wondered if she were sick. Could she still be in Amsterdam?

The barracks had become so crowded that there weren't enough cots to go around. Some people shared their mattresses; while others fell asleep on the stone floor, too exhausted to care. Nan was one of them. After only a few hours of sleep, he would be awakened by the constant gnawing hunger pains caused by the meager diet—mainly potato peelings. Unable to get back to sleep, he would lie awake staring at the ceiling until roll call. Always his thoughts returned to that fateful day in January. If he could only undo it. "Has anyone ever been able to escape from this place?" he wondered. He had pretty much abandoned the idea of ever finding Mama again, and his promise to her turned into a mere dream, while the probability of death became more and more a reality. Nonetheless, he wanted to believe that he would survive. He had to.

Suddenly, at the end of the sixth week, panic broke out among some of the prisoners. A rumor rippled through the camp that all "S" card holders were going to be put on a special "penal" transport to Auschwitz. As long as they were in Vught, their own country, there was still a glimpse of hope. Now this hope quickly began to fade.

"Why all the people with an "S" card?" Nan asked one of the other prisoners.

"Because we were caught hiding," the man answered. "The "S" stands for *Straffe*—punishment." If only he hadn't gone outside that day.

Orders were blaring through the speakers. "All "S" card holders assemble in front of your barracks!" It was late in the afternoon. A cold mist hung over the camp. There was a brief roll call. Then, four abreast, they began marching to the train station, accompanied by a large number of SS guards. This was the same way they had come six weeks earlier.

When they reached the tiny station, the trains were already waiting, and the platform soon became a sea of prisoners. Some distance away, to his right, Nan noticed a group of ragged-looking women. Carefully he moved toward them, his eyes searching, searching. They, too, were wearing "S" cards. Then he spotted the kerchief. It looked familiar. He moved yet a little closer.

"Mama!" he whispered as loud as he could without attracting attention, keeping his eye specifically on the one woman. Instinctively, several of the women turned their heads.

Mama! It was Mama! Her eyes grew large with disbelief. She covered her mouth with her hands, while tears filled her eyes. She started to say something, but he quickly put his finger against his lips, motioning her to be quiet. Carefully, he moved towards her—just a little further. . . . "Mama!" He gently touched her arm. Not able to speak, she put her hand over his, while tears rolled down her face. Instictinvely, she began to remove her scarf and handed it to him, gesturing to tie it around his head. For a moment he hesitated, but knowing that it would please her, he obeyed. His bald head was obviously worrying her. Without exchanging any further glances, they stayed next to each other.

A shrill whistle split the air. *"Einsteigen!"*

There was mass confusion as the SS guards tried to keep the men and the women separated, but all Nan was concerned about was to stay close to Mama. A couple of times she turned her head to see if he was still there. He motioned for her to get on. He was not going to leave her. Not this time. Never more than one step removed, they found themselves in the same compartment, along with several other women. He quickly went for the window seat and pulled Mama down beside him. He was stunned. He couldn't believe it. It had all been too easy. The kerchief . . . it had fooled them. They must have thought he was one of the women.

It seemed hours before all the prisoners were finally herded aboard. A Dutch conductor, accompanied by an SS officer, began securing the doors. Nan pushed his knee lightly against the door, applying just enough pressure to keep the latch from catching. When they reached his door, he watched as a "long" key was put in the keyhole . . . then turned . . . slowly. He could hear his heart pound. The conductor looked up. He caught Nan's eye. Did Nan notice a slight wink of cognizance? "He knows! He knows!" Nan thought as he watched the man pull out the key . . . straight . . . slowly . . . and move on to the next compartment.

Nan took a deep breath. Would he be able to keep his promise after all? He squeezed Mama's hand gently. "She looks awful!" he thought. "So thin. So pale."

The train began to pull out of the station. By now, it had turned totally dark outside and inside as well. Nobody spoke. He wanted to tell Mama something, but he thought better of it. His mind was going a mile a minute without a set plan.

Suddenly the train came to a halt. Some of the women fell to the floor. "What in the world is happening now?" one of them cried.

Nan looked out of the window. "I don't know," he mumbled. He watched as guards jumped off the train shining their flashlights underneath the cars and into the windows. Thoughts tumbled around in his mind. He was nervous. If only it were possible. Once the guards had satisfied themselves that everything was all right, the flashlights were turned off and the guards climbed back on the train. Slowly it pulled ahead in a huge cloud of steam.

This was it! Dead or alive, just as he had promised! Gradually the train increased its speed. Grabbing Mama's hand, he jumped up, pulling her along. The door flew open. He jumped. He tried to hold on to her hand, but he was not able to. She was standing on the tailboard, afraid to jump. The train was gaining speed. Out of breath, gasping, he tried to keep up. Off and on, the steam caused him to lose sight of her. She tried to reach for his hand. Jump! he motioned. He watched as she tumbled alongside the tracks.

As if paralyzed, they lay in the damp grass along the tracks as they watched the train move farther and farther away from them in the direction of Auschwitz. Their faces were wet with tears.

Nan pulled Mama gently to her feet. "Let's go, Mama, We are alive in Holland, but we still have a ways to go."

They probed their way through the dark, across the muddy fields until they reached a road. In one direction they saw some distant lights, in the other there was nothing but complete darkness. They debated for a moment. "Let's go that way," Nan suggested, pointing toward the lights. "It's probably some small town."

Side by side, they walked in silence. Mama shivered.

"Are you cold?" Nan asked.

"A little. How about you?"

"Not too bad. Here—take your scarf." He began untying the kerchief.

"No! You keep it! You know, you really do look like a little girl," she laughed. He didn't answer. "I've probably embarrassed him," she thought. She still couldn't believe what had happend—that she was actually walking right beside him. They passed a few farm houses, shrouded in darkness. Suddenly, there was the sound of slowly approaching footsteps which gradually grew louder.

Mama held out her arm. "Stand back!" she whispered. "Your head, remember?"

A silhouette emerged from the dark. It was an old man, bent over by age, his hands folded behind his back.

"Goede avond," he greeted in passing.

"Goede avond," Mama replied softly. "Excuse me, could you please tell me how I get to the next town?"

The man stopped walking. He didn't immediately answer her. He looked at her curiously. "You're going the wrong way. Those lights belong to a German army camp. Town is the other way," he said, pointing in the direction he was going. "About a half hour walk."

"What's the name?" Mama asked.

"Dieren."

"Thank you! Thank you very much."

The man tipped his cap, folded his hands behind his back and continued on his way.

Nan stepped back onto the road. "Did you hear that? Those lights are a *moffen* (kraut) camp," Mama whispered.

He nodded. "Luck is on our side, Mama."

They turned around and started walking toward Dieren, leaving a considerable distance between them and the old man, until he disappeared into one of the farm houses.

The small town of Dieren was virtually deserted, its streets sparingly lit.

"Where are we going now?" Nan asked.

"Let's find a church," Mama suggested. "We'll call on the priest or the pastor."

Soon they came to a large Catholic church. The parsonage was right next door. Hesitantly, Mama rang the bell. It echoed loudly through the large old home. On the other side, someone was approaching. Slowly the door opened.

"Goede avond, Mijnheer Pastoor."

"Goede avond," the priest replied. "What can I do for you?"

"My son and I, we just escaped from the train to Auschwitz. We're Jews. We need help."

A frown appeared on the priest's forehead, but his eyes expressed compassion.

"Step inside," he said. He quickly closed the door behind them. "I wish I could help you, but I'm under suspicion myself. My brother was with the underground. He was recently arrested. But let me think. . . ." Placing his index finger against his pursed lips, he paused for a moment. "Yes, as a matter of fact, I do know someone who may be able to help you. His name is Mijnheer Cats. He is Jewish, but his wife isn't. They own a small restaurant just a few blocks from here. Why don't you go and see him?" He gave them the directions.

"Thank you, Father."

The priest laid a hand on Mama's bony shoulder. "Good luck and God be with you."

When they stepped outside, they noticed that it had started to rain. They had no trouble finding the restaurant.

"You stay here. I'll go inside," Mama said. Slowly she opened the door, adjusting her eyes to the light. She noticed only a couple, seated at one of the tables toward the back, while the waiter stood idly behind the counter. He came to life the moment Mama walked in and went up to him.

"Goede avond."

"Goede avond," the waiter responded with a probing glance.

"I would like to talk to Mijnheer or Mevrouw Cats," Mama said.

The look in the waiter's eyes had changed to one of recognition. "They're not here tonight. They're having a birthday party."

"Could you tell me where I can find them?"

"Surely." The waiter drew a map on a small piece of paper and handed it to her.

"Thank you."

"You're welcome." he smiled.

She quickly left the restaurant.

They thought they had been following the map accurately, but somewhere along the way they had turned into the wrong street and became hopelessly lost. It was raining quite hard now. Just ahead, someone was leaving a house.

"Hello!" Mama called softly, yet in the stillness of the evening, it sounded hollow and loud. The young man had heard her. They hurried toward him.

"We seem to have lost our way. Could you tell us how we may get to this address?" She pointed at the map on the wet piece of paper. The man looked at it under the dim street light.

"That's right on my way," he said. "If you like, I'll be glad to take you there."

With Nan staying a few paces behind, they began following the young man while the rain continued to drench their clothing. At last, they reached their destination. Mama thanked the young man and began climbing the steps to the Cats' residence. Voices could be heard from within. Mama rang the bell. A woman answered the door. Her eyes grew large when she saw the two pitiful-looking strangers on her door step.

"Is Mijnheer Cats home?" Mama asked. Her voice sounded very weak.

"I'm Mevrouw Cats, who are you?"

"The priest sent us to see you. My son and I escaped. . . ."

"Come in. Come in," the woman interrupted as she seized Mama's arm. Several people had gathered in the hallway.

"What's going on?" a man asked.

"They have escaped," the woman called. "The priest sent them." There was joy in her eyes and her voice.

A man came up to greet them. "I'm Cats. Please, let me help you with your coats."

Moments later they were sitting in the warm living room where the birthday party had turned into a celebration for the two lucky escapees. Some of the guests left, only to return a short while later with warm clothing.

Mama was smart. All she ate was a roll and a glass of milk. Nan, however, ate everything in sight.

Mijnheer Cats had seated himself beside Mama. "You must be exhausted," he said, after listening to her tale about their ordeal.

Mama nodded. "It's been quite a day—an unbelievable day."

"In a little while I'll take you to the apartment above my art gallery down the street. It's a lot safer there. I have it rented out to a man and his wife—caretakers of sorts. So you won't be by yourselves."

"Thank you," Mama whispered.

In the middle of the night, Nan became violently ill. His stomach, which had adjusted to the diet of cooked potato peelings, had not been able to handle the rich food of that evening. A doctor was called in. By morning, Nan's condition was greatly improved.

Meanwhile, the underground in Dieren got in touch with Oom Twan. He received the news with mixed feelings. What if it were a trap? He immediately travelled to Amsterdam to tell Papa, who broke down at the news.

"Just let's hope it's true, Maan."

"How about their I.D.'s?" Papa asked. He sounded troubled.

Oom Twan shrugged. "I'm sure they've been taken away from them. Let's hope they won't check. Just remember, if I'm not back by nine o'clock tomorrow evening, I want you to leave the apartment immediately. Go to Dien for a while." Then he set out to find Mama and Nan.

Peeking through the curtains, Mama and Nan watched as Oom Twan climbed the steps to the gallery, his hand tightly gripping a handgun in his coat pocket. He rang the door bell while he blurted in the "Limbur" dialect, "Elsa, are you inside?" If it were a trap, he would soon find out. But from the room came the response he had hoped for, in the same dialect, "Twan, it's safe." In a few moments, the caretaker's wife answered the door.

"Thank God," thought Twan as he entered the house. A moment later, he held two sobbing people returned to his safekeeping.

Getting the two escaped prisoners back to Amsterdam became one of Oom Twan's greatest challenges. As he had anticipated, neither one any longer owned an I.D. He prayed they would get through the maze safely. The doctor who had treated Nan the previous night returned—this time to bandage Nan's head, making him look as if he had been in a serious accident. At the train station, Oom Twan bought each of them *"Het Volk en Vaderland"*—a Nazi newspaper—to hide behind. On the train, Mama spent quite a bit of time in the bathroom. They got off in Arnhem to transfer to the train for Amsterdam. The train was delayed. They knew they would never make it to Papa's hiding place by nine. When they finally did, Papa was still there, waiting. At the first sight of his wife and son, everything around him suddenly turned dark.

Chapter 10

Kees

$\mathcal{R}$osie and I gradually became part of the Zwaans family's routine. Each Sunday we attended church together—fortunately only in the morning. The church itself was very old, but quite beautiful. The one thing I didn't care about was the nauseating smell of incense. It made me sick to my stomach. Besides, it reminded me too much of Oldenzaal.

Spring arrived. The early rains softened the ground and the first crocuses popped up everywhere. During the weeks that followed, we not only went to see "The Ramblers" in real life, but we also saw our first movie. One Saturday afternoon, Trees decided to take us to see *"Rumpelsteelske."* We had a wonderful time. Trees was so nice to us. At times I felt sorry for her. She was born with some sort of heart problem and she had to be very careful.

As the weather grew milder, we were more frequently sent to play outside with Annie's children. We would much rather have stayed inside, but we were afraid to ask. It was still quite damp out, and the few dresses we owned were not particularly suitable for the time of the year. Seated on the swing, I slowly pushed myself back and forth, back and forth, feeling very disheartened. I couldn't dismiss the idea that Rosie and I had become a burden to so many other people, yet, in my heart, I knew they cared very much. Otherwise, why would they try to save our lives? Still, we were not *real* family, not like Annie's children. Through a mist of tears, I stared at the muddy ground beneath my feet. The rain had made it very slippery. I was homesick—terribly homesick. I tried to fight it. Wiping my eyes with the sleeve of my cardigan, I tried to think of pleasant things, but none came to mind. My depression grew deeper and deeper, and I began to wonder if the war would ever end.

Rosie must have felt the same way. Her problem was most evident at meals. She had begun to fuss again during dinner time. When she was little, she used to have terrible eating habits and Mama often fed her before everybody else sat down to dinner. Mama's excuse had been that she wanted peace and quiet at dinner time. Reluctantly, Papa had agreed. At times, however, Rosie had wanted to eat in the cellar, at the bottom of the stairs, with all the lights off, so no one could see her. To this, Papa never would have agreed, and Mama wisely had chosen not to tell him.

Gradually, however, Rosie's eating habits had improved—until now. At meals I watched her from the corner of my eye as she listlessly moved her food back and forth across her plate. Oom Piet noticed it, too, and his annoyance clearly showed. Trying to escape his glance, Rosie turned her head and looked at me for help. I sensed her desperation, but I didn't know what to do. Oom Piet was very strict; so different from *Moeke*, his gentle soft-spoken wife. One hardly knew that she was around. The clattering of silverware suddenly interrupted my thoughts. Oom Piet had dropped his fork and knife. "Stop playing with your food and eat!" he said, pointing his finger at Rosie's plate. He sounded very angry.

Rosie eyes were brimming with tears. Her lower lip trembled. "I can't," she whispered. It sounded like a cry for help. I felt sorry for her, but I was mad at her at the same time for not trying harder.

"Maybe we should take her into the forest and leave her there," Harry butted in.

"How mean," I thought. Trees didn't think it was very funny either, and she gave her brother a disdainful look. Then she reached across the table and took Rosie's plate, moving half of the food onto her own plate. "Here, I'm sure you can eat that much," she spoke quietly. Rosie's eyes clung to her with gratitude as she took her plate back. I knew I would always remember Trees—always.

Meanwhile, Oom Piet had picked up his silverware and continued his meal. The remainder of the dinner went by in heavy silence.

That night Rosie cried herself to sleep. "You really think they'll take me to the forest?"

"Of course not!" I tried to sound casual. "Grownups always say things like that.

"Papa and Mama never did," she sobbed.

"That's different. Harry did it just to scare you."

"You're sure?"

"I'm sure. He's nothing but a tease. Just go to sleep." Snuggling up to me, she finally fell asleep.

But that was not the end of our problems. One night I was awakened by something that felt strangely warm. Slowly, I moved my hands along my legs from where the warmth seemed to be coming. My hands felt wet. What in the world? Still half asleep, I tried to figure out what possibly could have happened? Then, it suddenly all came to me. Rosie had wet the bed! I knew it wasn't me! Again I felt around under the blankets. Yuk! Everything was wet—the sheet, the mattress—a huge spot. I sat up, trying to think of what to do next. I had to think this one out carefully. Covering my face with my hands, I tried not to panic. Suddenly I had an idea. I wasn't sure if it would work, but it was worth trying anyway.

"Rosie!" I poked her gently. She moaned and groaned. "Rosie! Wake up! You've wet the bed!"

"I didn't," she muttered.

"Yes, you did. Wake up, please!"

She began to cry.

"Quiet! You'll wake up the others!"

"What are we going to do?" she wept.

"Just do as I tell you! Take off your pajama bottoms and sit on that chair." I pointed my finger somewhere into the darkness where I knew there was a chair.

"For sure they'll take me to the forest now!" Rosie moaned.

"No, they won't! Be quiet!" Carefully feeling my way around in the dark, I pulled the wet sheet off the bed and folded it once . . . twice . . . three times. Then I put it under my pillow. Next, I folded the top sheet the same way. Fortunately it didn't get wet, and I put it on top of the wet spot in the mattress. Finally, after I had rearranged the bed, I hung Rosie's pajama bottoms across the back of the chair.

"We can go back to bed now," I whispered. The woolen blanket felt itchy without the sheet. I tried not to think of what would happen if my idea didn't work.

"You won't tell anyone, will you?" Rosie begged.

"Of course not."

"Not even Trees?"

"Not even Trees. Go to sleep!"

The following morning we made our bed as usual. The sheets were still slightly damp. The thought that someone might be changing the sheets and discover the yellow rings never occurred to me.

It was late March when Kees and Lieske wrote that they were coming to visit. The whole family was in a state of excitement—even *Moeke*. She was continuously giving the girls orders not to forget this or that, especially when it concerned Kees's favorite dishes. Consequently, Trees and Janneke spent the better part of the day in the kitchen cooking and baking, including lots of Janneke's fudge. I got the impression that Kees was very special.

"They're here!" Janneke shouted as she ran for the front door. The short, wiry man was almost knocked off his feet by his sister's wild embrace. His wife stood in the doorway, smiling broadly. It was one of those rare occasions when the whole family got together. All of them were crowded in the hallway to greet the anxiously awaited guests. Rosie and I were watching curiously from a distance. At last, it was our turn to shake hands. We didn't need much of an introduction. They seemed to know a lot about us already, and it pretty much confirmed my earlier suspicion that they were members of the resistance. I hadn't quite figured out yet how they fitted into the picture, but I was sure that they did. Kees probably had a lot to do with our staying at his parents' house.

All during the dinner, I felt myself staring at both of them, especially Kees. He looked different from his brothers and sisters—the high forehead, the brown, curly hair, the rugged complexion. Maybe that's what it was—his rugged appearance. I noticed that when he smiled, his lips would curl upward and a gentle glow would appear in his blue eyes. I don't know why, but I felt an inexplicable kinship. The dining room was humming. Everybody seemed to be talking at the same time. Occasionally, someone would say something funny, and the sound of thunderous laughter would fill the room.

After dinner, the women disappeared into the kitchen, while the men retired to the living room. Kees excused himself. "I'll be right with you. I want to talk to the girls for a moment." He took us into the sun room and seated himself between us. "Tell me, how do you like it here?"

"Fine," I lied. How could I possibly tell him about all our problems?

"Have you been doing any schoolwork?"

I shook my head.

"How come?"

141

I shrugged my shoulders. "I don't know."

"Well, I think we'll have to do something about that." Wrinkling his brow, he thought for a moment. "I've got it. I bet Janneke would make a good teacher," he laughed, ruffling our hair playfully. "I'll talk to her, and we'll talk some more later." With that he got up and left the room to join the others.

Rosie and I looked at each other. "He's nice," Rosie stated.

I nodded. "Very."

That evening Lieske put us to bed. "She's very pretty," I thought, as I watched her check some of our clothes. Her warm brown eyes perfectly matched her dark curly hair, which bounced on her shoulders with each move she made. "You could use some new clothes," she remarked, holding some of our dresses up against the light. "They look pretty worn. Do any of them still fit you?"

"Some," I replied.

She turned around and looked at us with a mournful look. "Did you brush your teeth?" We nodded. She kissed us good night. "I'll see you tomorrow." She turned off the light and closed the door softly behind her.

Kees and Lieske were able to stay only a couple of days, but they promised to be back in a few weeks. After their departure, I never felt quite the same. I missed them. It was strange to miss two people that much after having known them for such a short time. I was glad that a "few weeks" wasn't all that long.

Rosie was doing much better at mealtime, especially after Trees started to take her under her wing. She served her only very small portions and Oom Piet hardly ever got mad at her anymore. She only occasionally wet the bed, probably because Harry quit teasing her about the forest.

One day Janneke came back from town with several school books. Soon after, we started our first class.

In spite of all the pleasant things that were happening, I still wasn't able to fight off homesickness. I had been homesick before when I went to visit Tante Sophie in Amsterdam, but never like this. And it wasn't until one Sunday afternoon that I began to realize what was really happening to me.

The weather was sunny but cool and, as usual, we had been sent outside to play. Fluffy white clouds rapidly scudded overhead. I didn't feel like playing. Instead, I sat down on a little tricycle, which was parked idly on the sidewalk. I guess I rather expected the owner to start screaming at any moment, but she didn't. And I wanted a place to sit and think. Leaning across the handlebars, my head resting on my arms, I watched the ripples in the water of the *Wilhelmina Kanaal.* The ripples were moving fast just like the clouds. My eyes followed them until they disappeared beneath the bridge, the same bridge we had crossed the first day we arrived.

Rosie and the other children were playing in the field around the corner, across from the house. Their laughter floated through the air. The field, the laughter—somehow they made me think of our hiding place at the Vechtstraat. Everything lately seemed to remind me of one place or another. We had been in so many places in such a short time!—like the fluffy, little clouds, I felt I, too, had been aimlessly scudding along. None of the places, however, had ever reminded me of home. Home—it seemed ages since we'd left it together. Papa, Mama, Nan, Corrie—where were they now? Would we ever see them again? Tears filled my eyes as I buried my face in the crook of my arm. Where had those awful thoughts come from? I had never had them before. I had changed. Unconsciously, very gradually, I had moved into a state of awareness.

"I want my tricycle!" The sound of a little girl's voice woke me from my thoughts. I quickly wiped my tears. She was only a little girl, but I resented her, nevertheless—probably, because I envied her.

"Here! Take it!" I snapped. For a moment I thought she was going to cry. Her lip trembled. "I'm sorry," I said. She grabbed her tricycle and wheeled away.

Once again Rosie and I faced a new experience. A friend of the Zwaan family, a young woman in her early thirties, had died. A Requiem Mass was to be held and everybody was to attend, including Rosie and me. On the way to church, Trees tried to explain the Requiem Mass to us. As I understood it, we had to pray for the dead woman's soul which had now gone to heaven.

I didn't think Jews went to heaven. No one had ever mentioned it when Amama had died. I wondered if I should ask Trees. She seemed to know so much about God. Well, I decided, it really didn't matter.

The church was crowded with sad-looking people. The priest prayed for a very long time and, occasionally, the congregation responded in unison. When the service ended, we went over to the home of the dead woman. I was terrified. Inside the narrow hallway, people waited their turn to go inside the living room to have one last look at her. The house smelled of incense, just like the church. Rosie was holding my hand. I could feel her grip tighten as we got closer to the room. I knew she was scared, too.

"I have to go to the bathroom," she whispered.

"You can't go now. You have to wait."

"How long?"

"I don't know." She probably didn't have to go at all. She probably just wanted to go and stay there until it was time to go home.

When we had reached the living room, people were crying and moaning around the casket. Inside the casket, everything looked white—the white mask-like face, the thin, lifeless, white hands entwined with a light blue rosary, the white dress—everything was white.

That night, neither us was able to sleep. Trying to chase away the scary pictures of the dead woman, we began thinking of fun things, such as our *"Mien and Sien"* act—an improvisation of two Jewish housewives on their way to the Jewish market place and, of course, the unorthodox way Papa used to put us to bed. First, he would carry us up the stairs, one on his back, the other in his arms. Then he would take us, one at a time, into his strong arms and rock us slowly back and forth, uttering the silly words of *"een . . . snee . . . witte brood . . . "* (one . . . slice . . . of white bread). With each word he would rock us a little higher. When he reached the word *witte brood,* he threw us high up into the air and watched us come bouncing down on the mattress. Occasionally, we were allowed an encore, but not very often.

As soon as we ran out of funny things to think about, the dead woman's face instantly reappeared. When Harry walked in to turn off the light, Rosie started to whimper, "Please, leave the light on? I'm scared."

"Scared of what?"

"The dead woman."

"We can't sleep," I added.

Harry smiled. "Just a minute. I'll be right back." We heard him run down the stairs. Rosie and I looked at each other wondering what was he up to. A few minutes later he returned, carrying a thick book. "This will make you go to sleep," he said, and he pulled the chair close to our bed.

"What is that?" Rosie asked.

"A story book," he replied. "Which one do you want me to read? Any favorites?"

I shrugged.

"How about you, Rosie? You're so scared, which one would you like me to read to you?"

"I don't care." Her voice sounded tearful.

"All right. I'll pick one out myself." Harry began reading. His voice was very soothing and for a while I followed the story word for word. After a while some of the words were lost. Then there were just fragments—words. Next, it was time to wake up. Neither one of us remembered hearing the end of the story, but we agreed that Harry was actually quite nice.

Almost four weeks after their visit, Kees and Lieske returned. They brought us new socks and each a new blouse. "How's your school work coming?" Kees inquired.

"They're doing just fine." Janneke yelled from the kitchen. She obviously had overheard his question. Wiping her hands on her apron, she handed him a folder with our papers. Carefully, he checked every sheet of paper. He had a very serious look on his face, one that I had not yet seen. When, at last he closed the folder, his face broke into the familiar, upturned smile, "I think you both did very well. How about a reward?"

I shrugged, wondering what it could be.

"How would you like to visit your Mama and Papa?"

Rosie and I looked at each other in disbelief. The scene on the tricycle a few weeks ago flashed in front of my eyes.

"Today?" I asked.

Kees grinned. "How about tomorrow?"

"Tomorrow?" Our two voices sounded like one. Kees nodded his head. We could hear Janneke's laugh coming from the kitchen.

"But you have to promise me that you'll be in bed early." Then, in a spooky voice, he whispered: "We'll have to get up at three o'clock in the morning."

"It will still be dark!" Rosie remarked.

"I know. Now you go ahead and see Lieske."

We jumped up and ran out of the room to look for Lieske.

"I believe she's upstairs," Kees hollered after us.

When we entered our bedroom, we found Lieske talking to herself. "Blouse, skirt, socks. Hi, girls!" she interrupted herself, as she continued checking our clothes.

"We're going to visit Mama and Papa!" we cried.

She laughed. "He's told you, eh? I'm just sorting out your clothes. I want you to look your very best. I'll put them on that chair, right there," she pointed, "so you won't have to search for them when you get up. Did he tell you what time you'll have to get up?"

We nodded. "Awfully early, isn't it?" she laughed. Again we nodded.

We went to bed right after supper. I couldn't sleep. Besides being excited, I was also worried that Rosie might wet the bed. When sleep finally came, it seemed as though it was just about time to get up.

Somewhere in the town of Helmond, two other people hadn't been able to sleep either. Shortly after their escape, Mama and Nan had joined Papa in Amsterdam. The three of them had been moved out of the city to the small town of Helmond, which was about 55 kilometers east of Oosterhout. They were hiding in a couple of second-floor rooms in the home of a retired chief of police and his wife. Neither Papa nor Mama had slept a wink as they awaited our visit.

The alarm went off exactly at three o'clock. I was wide awake when Lieske quietly entered our room. She shook me gently. "It's time to wake up," she whispered.

"I'm awake," I replied.

"Wake up Rosie and get dressed." She flicked on the light and closed the door behind her.

"Rosie! Rosie, wake up!" I whispered, shaking her gently.

"Why?" she moaned.

"We're going to visit Mama and Papa, remember?" Like a flash, she jumped out of bed. "Don't make noise!" I warned. I was so happy she hadn't wet her bed, I wanted to hug her. We dressed quickly. My hands shook as I tried to button my new blouse. I liked it. It felt so nice and soft.

In the bathroom, Lieske wiped our faces with a wet cloth and combed our hair. I looked at myself in the mirror as she fixed my bow. She made sure there were no wrinkles in it. When she was through, she put a finger under my chin and lifted up my head, giving me one of those funny looks where she would purse her lips, but her eyes would sparkle with laughter. "You look very pretty," she said, making one final adjustment to the bow in my hair. "I guess we're ready." She thought for a moment. "Not yet. You forgot to brush your teeth." She watched us as we brushed vigorously, taking turns spitting the toothpaste in the sink.

"Now, we're ready. Let's go!"

She turned the light off and the three of us tiptoed down the stairs where Kees was already waiting for us, our coats draped over his arm.

"All set?" he asked in a low voice.

"Yes," Lieske whispered.

Before we walked out the door, Kees turned around to give his final instructions. "Should anyone ask you where you're going, the answer is 'Grandmother's,'" and he repeated: "You're going to visit your grandmother."

The next minute we were on our way to the train station. I wasn't afraid of the dark any longer, but there was still something eerie about traveling in the wee hours of the morning.

When we walked onto the platform, only a few people were waiting. Some of them were soldiers. The train arrived on time and Kees and Lieske helped us climb aboard. Plenty of seats were available and Rosie and I both plopped down by the window. The lights inside the train were turned low. I peered outside and watched the people seated inside the little coffee shop. A few were reading. Others were slowly sipping their coffee or tea as they stared at the waiting train. I thought, "Maybe they're looking at me—wondering where I'm going at this time of the night." As soon as the train began to move, Kees got up and pulled the shades.

"Try to get some sleep," he said. "It will be a little while before we get there."

I hardly slept, but I didn't feel the least bit tired. Yet, I wanted very much to please Kees, so I shut my eyes lightly. I tried to remember how long it had been since we had seen everybody. The last time we had seen Papa was in January, just before we had gone on the barge. That's when Mama had been in the hospital. We hadn't seen her since she had come to visit us in Oldenzaal. Oddly enough, no one had ever told us that she had come home from the hospital. As a matter of fact, no one had told us anything. I was really excited about seeing Nan again. We hadn't seen him in ages, it seemed. Kees probably thought I was sleeping. The butterflies were starting up again; that meant we would soon be there.

"Helmond! Next stop, Helmond!" The sudden sound of the conductor's voice ringing through the almost empty train made me jump up in my seat.

Kees smiled. "We're almost there," he said. The train ride had been uneventful. No one had asked any questions. Nobody had even been around to check the I.D.'s. The train came to a halt. Outside the station daylight had broken.

"Let's walk," Kees suggested. "It's not very far."

The house was a typical row house with a small fenced-in front yard and flower boxes in the windows. Kees rang the bell. An elderly man opened the door. *"Dag, Kees!"* he greeted.

"Goede Morgen," Kees replied.

"Dag!" Lieske echoed.

"Come on in. They have been waiting for you for quite some time."

Kees pushed us gently ahead. When I looked up, I saw Papa and Mama standing at the top of the stairs, while Nan was leaning across the banister, waving at us. We flew up the stairs to be caught in their embrace. Mama cried softly and, as always, Papa's nostrils quivered. Nan seemed so much taller. I had to put my head way back to look at his face.

Mama kept wiping her tears. "Let's go inside," she said. "Your breakfast is waiting."

We followed her into "their room," where a simple table was set. "It's not very much," she apologized. "But food is so scarce these days." I noticed how she and Papa exchanged quick glances.

149

All during breakfast there was a reserved joy, unlike the cheerfulness we had known at home. I felt more like a guest than family. My eyes met Mama's. She smiled awkwardly. There was so much catching up to do and so little time in which to do it. The day went by fast, much too fast. Just when we started to feel more comfortable, Kees announced it was time to return to Oosterhout. Surprisingly, the parting was easier than I had expected. There were hugs and kisses. Mama's voice was choked with tears. She said, "We'll see you again soon!" Papa didn't speak. His expression was sorrowful.

"*Dag,* Nan!"

We hugged. "*Dag,*" he whispered.

At the bottom of the stairs, we waved one last goodbye. Our visit had come to an end.

Not very long after our visit with Mama and Papa, I had to leave Oosterhout quite unexpectedly. Oom Twan came to take me with him to his home in Geleen. It seemed ironic that after wandering around the country for more than a year to dodge the Germans, I would return to the same spot we had left in 1938 to escape them in the first place.

Rosie stayed behind, but Oom Twan promised that she would join me soon. To ease the transition, Corrie was brought to Oosterhout from Breda, a town about ten kilometers south of Oosterhout. Following the raid in Oldenzaal, she had found shelter with a family consisting mainly of priests—two brothers and several cousins.

Shortly after my departure, the Zwaans family met with a terrible tragedy. Tonny's husband had come up to visit one day. When he left the house to return home, darkness had already set in. It was very foggy and there was a steady drizzle. Late that night the phone rang at the Zwaans home. It was Tonny. She sounded very worried. Her husband wasn't home yet, shouldn't he be? Silently, they agreed, but they tried to calm her down. Maybe he had stopped off somewhere? If he had, she argued, wouldn't he have called her? He was not the type of person to worry anyone needlessly, especially not his wife, and certainly not at a time when she was expecting their first baby!

Tonny's husband never returned home. The next day, his body and his bicycle were pulled from the waters of the *Wilhelmina Kanaal*, almost directly across from the Zwaans's house. The skipper of one of the barges remembered hearing a distant splash as though something large had fallen into the water, but the darkness and poor visibility had kept him from seeing what it was. After a moment or two, he had gone inside, shrugging it off as "probably nothing."

When Rosie joined me a few weeks later, she told me all about it, not leaving out a single detail. I shivered. I was glad I hadn't been there.

Oom Twan and Tante Mien had three children: Wies, their eldest girl; next, another daughter, Gertie, and last, but not least, Joe, their son who at fourteen could at times be a real pest. Oom Twan was home very little. He was a supervisor at the *Maurits* coal mine and he often worked nights. When he worked days, he would frequently leave right after dinner without explaining where he was going. As a result, Tante Mien was pretty much in charge of the household.

I don't quite know how or why, but soon after Rosie arrived, two "friendly teams" emerged: Gertie and Rosie versus Wies and me. Joe wasn't invited to join either team.

Like Janneke, Wies and Gertie loved to make fudge. Unfortunately, however, sugar wasn't quite as plentiful as in the Zwaans family. Most of the time there was a shortage, and when Tante Mien finally was able to lay her hands on some, she would carefully hide it, but never quite carefully enough. One of the "teams" would always know where to find it and, in great secrecy, make a fine batch of fudge and hide it, to be eaten afterwards under the same shroud of secrecy—usually in the bedroom. The real challenge was to try and find each other's fudge. Poor Tante Mien—when she discovered that most of her sugar was gone, she'd fly into a rage, and would be just about ready to tear the whole house apart in a fruitless attempt to find it. That was one of the main reasons why we kept Joe out of it. He would undoubtedly have told on us.

I don't think Joe liked us very much. That was not a total surprise, because at that stage of his life, he didn't seem to like anyone. One of his favorite pastimes was trying to lock us out of the house.

One day while Tante Mien had gone to the store, Wies, Gertie, Rosie, and I had gone into the garden to pick vegetables for dinner. When we tried to get back into the house, we found all the doors locked. Behind the sliding doors of the dining room stood Joe, grinning. Wies banged on the kitchen door, her green eyes flashing.

"Let us in!" she hollered. Joe threw his head back and laughed.

"Wait 'till I tell Mam!" Gertie threatened.

But Joe didn't frighten easily. He turned around and walked away. Moments later, he stepped out the door onto the flat roof above the kitchen carrying a small cigar box, which I recognized immediately. It was Rosie's and mine. We used it to save our cigar bands, which we had begun collecting when staying in Oosterhout. Most of them were given to us by Oom Piet, and some of them were very beautiful. I couldn't believe we were about to lose them. "He is just trying to scare us," I told myself. But in horror I watched him raise the lid, ever so slowly.

"Wies! Tell him not to!" Rosie cried.

Wies's face turned beet red. "Don't you dare!" she screamed. But Joe didn't listen. He kept raising the lid as we stood by helplessly, watching the first bands fly out of the box, quickly followed by the rest of them. They sailed through the air. A few of them returned to the earth, but most of them floated farther and farther away on the light summer breeze, until they were no longer visible. Rosie cried hysterically. I was in shock. Meanwhile, Wies and Gertie began chasing some of the bands in an effort to save them.

Gertie, her dark eyes narrowed, shook her fist at her brother. "Wait 'till Mam gets home, she'll tell Pap, I know she will."

Joe grinned as he brushed his wind-swept hair away from his forehead. "I'll open the door for you!" he called down. Then he went inside, taking the empty cigar box with him.

When Tante Mien returned home, she immediately sensed that something had happened. When she asked, the girls told her. For a moment or so she seemed to be debating with herself, trying to control her anger.

Her eyebrows raised, she finally spoke. Her voice sounded quite calm. "I'll have your father take care of you," she told Joe.

I had never seen Oom Twan angry until that evening. Joe neither appeared at the dinner table, nor did he show up afterwards. For the remainder of the evening, there was peace and quiet, but our cigar bands were gone, nonetheless. Surprisingly, in later years, Joe turned out to be a very good husband and a wonderful father to his family.

It had been quite a while since Rosie and I had had new dresses, and we were ecstatic when Tante Mien returned home from shopping one afternoon with enough material for a dress for each of us. The material was white with tiny red dots. Very pretty.

"You like it?" she asked.

"I do!" Rosie cried.

I gently stroked the material. It felt very soft and silky. "It's beautiful!" I said.

Tante Mien smiled broadly. She felt very pleased with herself. Wies had taken the material and draped it around herself. Shaking her blond curls, she looked at herself in the round mirror over the buffet. "I wouldn't mind having one like this myself," she remarked.

"Never mind, you've enough dresses," Tante Mien laughed, and she quickly took the material away from her daughter.

"By the way, where are Gertie and Joe?" she asked.

"They're not home from school yet," Wies replied.

Tante Mien shook her head. "Those two. They better not have gotten themselves in any trouble!" Then she turned her attention once again to the dress material in front of her. "I thought I had some lace somewhere. I bet that would look really nice along the collar? And maybe a red velvet sash? What do you think?"

Rosie and I nodded in unison.

"That will be very pretty, Mam," Wies agreed.

We could hardly wait until our dresses were finished. Tante Mien seemed very pleased as she watched us try on our new dresses, twirling around in front of the mirror.

The following Sunday, she took us to the park so we could show them off. The weather turned out just right with a sunny, blue sky. I felt very pretty and was sure that everybody was watching us.

"Let's go and feed the ducks," Tante Mien said. Carrying a sack with stale bread, we walked across the grass towards the pond which was surrounded by a wire fence. The moment we reached into the sack the ducks came rushing towards us. It was funny to watch them try to steal the bread away from each other. When it was all gone, they would quickly swim away, showing a total lack of appreciation.

"It's time to go!" Tante Mien said.

As I turned around, there was suddenly the most awful sound, as of something tearing. Alarmed, I looked down.

"My dress!" I cried.

Tante Mien came rushing over, a deep frown on her forehead.

"What do you mean, your dress?" I tried to tell her, but the words wouldn't come. Then she saw it, too, a large tear, where my dress had caught on the fence. I looked at her. Her frown had disappeared. All I saw was compassion. "Stop crying," she said. "It was an accident. I'll fix it."

Rosie took my hand. "I'm sorry," she whispered. It made me cry even more. Nothing could make me feel better. Nothing! I just wanted to go home.

Early one morning while it was still dark, I dragged my eyes open with an uneasy feeling. Why had I awakened so early? Then I remembered. Tante Mien had told me we had to be up and away very early today. When I reached the foot of the stairs, a suitcase sat waiting in the hallway. I paused briefly before I continued on to the kitchen.

Tante Mien was pouring milk into a glass. She looked up when she heard me enter.

"I have made us some breakfast," she whispered. I took my place at the kitchen table and stared at the boiled egg in front of me. I wasn't the least bit hungry. I looked up at the wall clock. Quarter after four. It was just too early for breakfast. I tried to listen for noises, but there weren't any. Everybody was still asleep, except Oom Twan. He was on night shift and wouldn't be home for a while yet. Tante Mien was sitting across the table from me. I noticed her staring at me over the rim of her coffee cup.

"Tired?"

I nodded.

She smiled gently. "I promise to let you have a nap as soon as we get back, but now I want you to eat something." She pointed at my plate. I picked up the egg and carefully broke the shell. My stomach felt queasy the minute I took the first bite. I thought about the suitcase in the hall.

"Dangerous" was the word Tante Mien had used when she had called me into her bedroom a few days earlier. Seated beside me on the edge of her bed, she had stroked my straight, flaxen hair.

"You're getting to be quite a young lady," she had said, a faint smile crossing her lips, but her eyes had remained serious.

What was she leading up to? Was she going to talk to me about "grown-up" stuff? I hoped not. I hated it.

There had been a long pause, as if she was trying to gather her thoughts. "In a few days I'll have to run a very special errand. I'd like you to come with me."

"Me?" It wasn't exactly what I had expected.

She nodded.

"Why?"

"Oom Twan thinks I'll look less suspicious traveling with a child. It will be less dangerous."

My heart beat wildly. My throat turned dry. I wasn't able to speak. Tante Mien had patted my hand. She realized she couldn't avoid telling me the rest.

"I have to deliver handguns to other members of the underground."

"Guns!" I cried.

She nodded. "I don't want you to be afraid. Everything is going to be all right. I promise."

"When?" I asked, almost inaudibly. "When are we going?"

"Probably in a few days. There's one more thing and it's very important for you to remember. Should anyone ask you where you're going, all you tell them is that you're going to visit your grandmother."

It all sounded very familiar. Kees had told us the same thing, when we had visited Mama and Papa.

"I'll tell the other children that I'm taking you with me on an errand. They know better than to ask questions."

"What about Rosie? What shall I tell her?"

"Don't worry about it, I'll think of something," she had said.

"We'd better get going or we'll miss our train." Tante Mien's voice broke into my thoughts. I looked at her. She seemed so calm.

Shortly afterward we were on our way to the train station—the handguns neatly wrapped inside the suitcase.

There weren't very many people on the train this early in the morning, and we didn't have any trouble finding an empty compartment. I took one of the window seats. After she had carefully put the suitcase in the luggage rack above our heads, Tante Mien sat down beside me. Quietly, I stared out of the window. A few people stood patiently waiting on the platform. Occasionally, my eyes met theirs. At last the train pulled out of the station. As it turned out, we were riding a "milk train." It stopped at every village and hamlet along the way. Most of the time nobody was getting off or on. The conductor came to collect our fares, followed by a German soldier who checked Tante Mien's I.D. He returned it and smiled politely.

"*Gute Reise.*" he commented. Tante Mien returned his smile.

"He's nice," I whispered when the German was out of ear shot.

"Yes," she nodded.

The next stop was at a larger town. Quite a few people were getting on. An SS officer walked by. He threw a glance in our direction. Tante Mien and I exchanged glances. I knew what she was thinking: "Just remember, you're going to visit grandmother."

Moments later the officer returned. This time he entered our compartment and seated himself across from Tante Mien. He nodded politely.

"*Gute Morgen.*"

"*Gute Morgen,*" Tante Mien replied, equally polite.

I looked at her from the corner of my eye. She didn't seem a bit worried. The officer had placed his leather gloves neatly beside him on the seat. He carefully removed a speck of dust from his shiny black boots before turning his attention back on his fellow travelers.

"*Auf Ferien?*" he asked. He looked like the type that would try to start a conversation, I thought.

Tante Mien nodded. "My daughter is going to visit her grandmother."

"Sehr schoen," the German smiled, his narrow eyes fixed on mine.

I looked at Tante Mien. Her eyes met mine. We smiled at each other and she gently patted my hand.

"Do you think Grandmother will be up this early?" she asked.

I shrugged. "Probably not," I said.

For a while we kept the small talk going between us, giving the German little chance to converse. Suddenly it occurred to me that he might not get off before we did. In that case, he would probably help us with our suitcase. My heart began to race. I looked sideways at Tante Mien. I wondered if she had thought about it, too.

Then, with the greatest of care, the officer began putting his gloves back on. Getting up, he brushed down his immaculate-fitted uniform, bowed, clicked his heels together, and bid us, *"Auf Wiedersehen."*

"Auf Wiedersehen," Tante Mien replied, smiling gently. The moment he was gone, we looked at each other. Tante Mien let out a soft sigh of relief, while raising her eyebrows.

"What would we have done if he had stayed?" I whispered.

"We would have stayed on, too. I'm sure he would have gotten off sooner or later," she replied in a hushed voice.

When we reached our destination, a new day had begun. It was midday when we returned home from our dangerous mission. The guns were safely delivered. I had a sudden feeling of importance, of having grown up. I no longer was the scared little girl of earlier that day.

Chapter 11

De Zwaan

n August of 1943, the time had come to move once again. I cried when Tante Mien brought me the news. For once, I liked where I was. It reminded me a lot of home—our own home.

"Is Rosie coming?" I sobbed.

Taking my hands between hers, Tante Mien seemed to think about it for a moment. I looked up at her, probing for an answer.

Then, speaking quietly, she said, "I'm afraid Rosie will be staying here, with us, for a while."

"Why? Why me?" I wondered. Maybe they liked Rosie better than me!

Then I noticed the tears in Tante Mien's eyes and I knew I was wrong.

"When am I leaving?"

"Probably the day after tomorrow."

"So soon?"

She nodded. "Would it make you feel any better if I told you that you were going to stay with Kees and Lieske?"

"Kees and Lieske?" I cried. I couldn't believe I had heard her right.

Again she nodded, smiling this time. "Oom Twan asked me not to tell you until you were ready to leave, but I can't stand seeing you so unhappy."

I stopped crying instantly, wiping my eyes with the back of my hand. Tante Mien handed me her handkerchief. "Here! Wipe those tears and blow your nose!"

"You mean I will be staying on their houseboat?"

"Yes, you will be living on the houseboat," she chuckled. "You seem to have heard all about it already, eh?"

I nodded. "Janneke, Kees's sister, told us."

Suddenly, I felt much better. I would miss everybody, of course—especially Rosie, but I couldn't help feeling excited.

Two days later, seated on the rack of Tante Mien's bicycle, I traveled the ten kilometers to the houseboat. When we reached a narrow path on the top a dike, I knew we were getting close.

It was a beautiful, quiet summer's day. Nothing seemed to move—the grass, the leaves on the trees, even the deep, dark waters of the *Juliana Kanaal*—except for some light ripples caused by a barge as it lazily inched its way towards the harbor. I watched a woman taking down her laundry from a clothesline strung across the deck. The skipper, a cigarette pressed between his lips, stood behind the steering wheel, his eyes fixed straight ahead.

"I know how to steer a barge," I thought, with a surge of pride. On the other side of the path hundreds and hundreds of colorful wildflowers covered the grassy, gently sloping dike, unfolding into a vast, golden carpet of corn fields.

When we had reached a sharp curve in the road, Tante Mien stopped pedaling. She turned her head to talk to me. "Watch! In just a moment, you'll see *De Zwaan.*"

Slowly we coasted around the bend, and there she was, in all her majestic glory, like a castle glistening in the afternoon sunlight. She was even more beautiful than I had imagined. "She even *looks* like a *Zwaan* [swan]," I thought, as she lay in harbor surrounded by the barges which were securely anchored—like watchmen.

"This is it!" Tante Mien said, bringing her bicycle to a halt. We got off. Carrying my bag, I followed Tante Mien up the broad gangplank. When we reached the deck, she leaned her bicycle against the metal guard rail. An elderly man stood near the bow. He had momentarily interrupted his chores to wave to us.

"Dag, Leen!*"* Tante Mien greeted, smilingly. "Beautiful day, isn't it?"

"Sure is!" the man replied.

I uttered an inaudible *"Dag."* He waved once more before he continued with his chores. We turned left into the gangway. I noticed that it was a lot wider than the one on the barge.

"This is their store," Tante Mien remarked, pointing at a white, metal structure.

I tried to glance inside, but all I could see was darkness. We had reached the living quarters. The sliding door to the kitchen was open. Lieske had been waiting for us. When she saw us, she threw out her arms. She embraced Tante Mien warmly. "Good to see you again, Mien."

Then she turned to me. She held me at arm's length, her warm, dark brown eyes glued to mine. *"Welkom to De Zwaan,"* she whispered. She hugged me tightly as Tante Mien watched quietly. "Let's go to the dining room," Lieske said, as she took my bag from Tante Mien and put it on the counter. "I'll bet you're thirsty after that long trip."

We followed her through the narrow kitchen into the dining room. "I smell applecake," Tante Mien commented.

"You sure do," Lieske laughed.

"Lieske makes the best applecake you have ever eaten," Tante Mien remarked while seating herself at the dining room table.

Lieske laughed again. "Nonsense, Mien. Yours is just as good."

161

"Not according to Twan."

"Well, let me go and get us all something to drink, and to eat," she winked at Tante Mien.

The dining room was large, just like the ones in regular houses. The deep red carpet dominated the room. The furniture was simple, but elegant. Adjacent to the dining room, separated by sparkling glass in lead sliding doors, was yet another room, equally large. Four huge, very comfortable-looking overstuffed chairs surrounding a round coffee table took up most of the space. Short draperies on shining brass rods covered the windows along both sides of the rooms. They matched the color of the carpet perfectly. The rooms were very bright, with an uninterrupted view of the narrow road and the dike beyond on one side, and the harbor on the other.

Meanwhile, Lieske returned from the kitchen carrying a tray loaded with applecake and drinks.

"Where's Kees?" Tante Mien inquired.

"He should be in the store. I'm surprised he didn't see you come aboard. I'm sure he'll be in shortly."

Lieske was right, the trip had made me thirsty. In no time at all, I had gulped down my lemonade. "Want some more?" She chuckled as she watched me from across the table.

I shook my head. "No, thank you."

Clack, clack, clack. "There's Kees now," Lieske said. A moment later, he emerged from the kitchen, his lips curled at the corners into a broad smile.

"So here's where all my girls are hiding," he laughed. I had slipped off my chair to greet him. Like Lieske, he put his arms around me, his cheek touching mine. *"Welkom aboard,"* he said.

Suddenly, I felt very safe, as if no one would ever be able to harm me, not ever. Kees was not like anyone else I had ever known. He was very special.

He went over to Tante Mien and kissed her on the cheek. "How's Twan?"

"Just fine. He just got off night shift. He'll probably be up to see you sometime soon."

He sat down and looked around the table. "I see you saved me a piece of cake," he teased.

"Let's put it this way, you're just in time," Lieske retorted, while she poured him a cup of coffee. "Mien, do you want yours heated up?"

"No, thank you. I've had plenty."

I watched Kees as he washed the cake down with his coffee. After he had picked up the last crumbs with the tiny cake fork, he wiped his mouth and asked, "How was your trip?"

"Very nice," Tante Mien replied. "And totally uneventful," she quickly added.

Kees half-smiled. He looked at me.

"Well, do you think you're going to like it here?"

I nodded.

"Good! There's lots to do out here."

I felt an immediate sense of belonging. Quietly, I listened as they turned their conversation to people and things I didn't know anything about. After a while, Kees pushed his chair back. He briefly gazed out of the window, across the harbor. Then he turned his attention back to us.

"You'll have to excuse me, but I have to get back to the store." Slowly he rose from his chair, crushing his cigarette butt in the glass ash tray.

"It was good seeing you again, Mien," he said, as he kissed her goodbye. "Have a safe trip home and say 'hello' to Twan and the children."

"Thank you, I will," she smiled, raising her eyebrows as usual.

"What a peculiar habit," I thought. Kees patted me gently on the head. "I'll see you later." He threw Lieske a kiss and left the room.

Clack, clack, clack. I listened to the sound of his clogs as it slowly faded away.

163

After Tante Mien left, Lieske showed me the rest of the interior. Across from the kitchen, on the opposite side of the boat, facing the road, was yet another kitchen; however, it was not as nice. "This is my *bijkeuken* (kitchen annex). I use it when frying fish and other greasy foods," she explained. "Let me get your bag and I'll show you your bedroom."

She hurried back to the other kitchen. When she returned, we went down a very wide staircase located halfway down the hallway and connecting the two kitchens to the floor below. The usual handrails were replaced by thick, velvet ropes that matched the wine-colored carpet. At the foot of the stairs was a large, central corridor.

"This is it," she said, opening the first door to the right. I followed her inside. I couldn't help letting out a little cry of excitement.

"Do you like it?"

"I do, I do!"

Lieske smiled at my obvious approval. The room was small, but very tastefully decorated. In one corner stood the bed. Its ruffled bedspread matched the brightly printed muslins that draped the tiny portholes. Against the wall, underneath the portholes, was a table and a chair. On the opposite wall stood a chest of drawers.

"I have never had a room of my own," I remarked.

"You haven't?"

I shook my head. "Rosie and I always had to share one."

"This one is all yours," she said smilingly. She put my bag on the table and walked over to the closet. "This is where you can put your clothes and your shoes." It sounded funny.

"I only have one pair of shoes," I laughed.

"Maybe we'll be able to get you another pair one of these days."

The closet was big enough to hold a wardrobe ten times the size of mine.

"May I look outside?"

"Of course. You'll probably have to stand on a chair." She pulled a chair beneath the porthole and pulled the tiny curtain aside.

"Go ahead."

Like a painting, the tranquil harbor unfolded before my eyes. It looked so peaceful on this warm summer afternoon. Just below the porthole was the water. "I'll be sleeping right next to it," I thought, feeling a little frightened.

"What's that?" I asked, pointing to my right.

Lieske put her head close to mine in order to see. "Those buckets over there?" She laughed heartily. "Those 'buckets' are called *kiepers*. They are used to load and unload the barges."

I still felt a little uncomfortable about the water being so close. I wondered if it could ever come inside.

"Let's go," Lieske said. "I'll show you the rest."

Next to my room was the bathroom. Across, were two more bedrooms, one similar to mine; the other much larger. It had two single beds. At the end of the corridor was Lieske and Kees's bedroom. It was huge. It had a large bed in the center with a couch on either side. Both couches were built into the wall, and upholstered in a soft, green velvet. The walls were covered with a warm, dark panelling, as were all the other rooms.

Lieske smilingly watched me, as I tried to absorb it all. "We better go back upstairs," she said, slowly walking out of the room. "I should start dinner shortly. The men are always so hungry. They don't like to wait."

"Men? Are there other men?"

Lieske nodded. "Two," she said, holding up two of her fingers. "They are helping Oom Kees in the store. They're staying in the large guest room."

I had noticed that she kept referring to Kees as *"Oom Kees."* She probably would like me to call them *Oom* and *Tante*, as I had all the others before them. I rather liked it myself.

A little later, Kees came to get me to show me the "outside." "Careful, Kees!" Lieske warned, as we walked out the kitchen door. "Remember, she is not used to being near water."

He nodded without turning his head. "Don't worry," he called back. *Clack, clack, clack.* Oom Kees's clogs sounded loudly against the steel surface of the gangway. I would soon learn that the only time Oom Kees did not wear his clogs was when he went to church. I followed him into the store. Rows and rows of shelves were stacked with all sorts of merchandise—paint, tar, flags, tools and many other supplies.

I was introduced to a couple of men who were busy unpacking boxes and replenishing the shelves. One of them had hair so light it was almost white. His name was Geert. He acted very bashful. "We call him *"de Witte"* ("Whitey")," Oom Kees whispered when we got out of earshot. "He doesn't like it." I almost told Oom Kees that Corrie and Nan used to call me "white goat" because of my blond hair, and that I didn't like that either, but I quickly changed my mind. I wondered if these were the two men Tante Lieske had talked about earlier.

"This is my office," said Kees. We entered a small room with windows alongside and to the back. From this unobstructed view of the harbor and the bow of the ship, anyone coming aboard would be immediately noticed.

"Let me show you something," he said. He reached underneath the desk and moved his hand lightly across the carpet.

"Put your hand here," he pointed. A little reluctantly, I touched the carpet and felt a slight bump. I looked at him quizzically.

"That's a buzzer," he explained. "Our hidden warning system, just in case. If I step on it, an alarm will go off everywhere—in the store, the house, *Het Achteronder, Het Vooronder*, everywhere. "Let's hope we'll never have to use it."

I was dumbfounded at all the things Oom Kees had thought of. Obviously, I had yet to be introduced to *Het Vooronder* and *Het Achteronder*.

"Let's go," he said, and I followed him out of the office. I hadn't realized how dark it was inside the store until we stepped into the blinding sunlight.

We started to walk towards the bow. Close to the tip stood a small, metal building. I didn't remember having seen it when I first walked aboard.

The old man who had waved to Tante Mien and me was still there, busily sweeping the deck. I noticed his very bad limp. The moment he spotted us, he interrupted his chores.

"Leen, I want you to meet Manda," Oom Kees said, raising his voice. "He not only limps, but he's deaf to boot," he laughed. I didn't think it was very funny. The man laid down his broom and came walking toward us. His broad smile exposed his brown-stained teeth, several of which were missing. I shook his rough, calloused hand.

"Nice to meet you," he said.

"She'll be visiting with us for a while," Oom Kees explained.

"I see," the man replied. "Well, I'm sure we will be seeing quite a bit of each other then." I smiled awkwardly.

Then he looked at Oom Kees. "Are you giving her a tour of *De Zwaan?*"

Oom Kees nodded. "We're on our way to *Het Vooronder.*"

I didn't miss the surprised look in Leen's eyes. "Well, I guess I'll see you later." He briefly raised his hand. "It's really nice to have you aboard," he added.

"Thank you," I whispered softly, watching him as he limped away and picked up his broom. "What's wrong with his leg?"

"It's artificial."

"Wood, you mean?"

"That's right," Oom Kees laughed.

I couldn't understand why Oom Kees thought it was so funny. Maybe he was used to it. Grownups looked at things so differently sometimes.

"He lost his real leg in an accident many years ago, but he doesn't want anyone to feel sorry for him. As a matter of fact, he always jokes about it." I couldn't help feeling sorry for Leen anyway, as I watched him hobble behind his broom. Oom Kees began searching for his key. "He gets around just as well as you and me," he added, throwing a sympathetic glance in Leen's direction.

When Oom Kees found his keys, he opened the door to the little building. I couldn't believe my eyes. "A toilet!" I cried.

Oom Kees seemed highly amused. "Not really. Watch this." He turned on the light and closed the door behind us. He took the stool and slowly turned it aside. Underneath was a gaping hole. A narrow staircase led to the area below. Oom Kees noted my bewilderment. "Do you want to see what's downstairs?"

I nodded excitedly.

"All right. But be careful—the stairs are very steep," he warned, as he led the way. It reminded me very much of the barge. When I had reached the floor, I found myself standing in a room about five meters deep by four meters wide. Behind the staircase, on either side, were beds. In the middle of the room was a table with benches on both sides, fastened to the walls. A ray of sunshine had entered through the porthole and brightened up the center of the room, making the rest look and feel even more dismal and cold. A short step led to yet another room—so small, I would rather have called it a "space." To the right was a small counter with a sink and a hot plate; to the left, a couple of shelves stacked with pots and pans, dishes, and a few towels. Halfway, a curtain was hung all the way across. "Now, this is the real toilet," Kees smiled, as he pulled the curtain aside. Tucked away in the bow was an old stool. I gasped, amazed by the small living quarters, but seemingly with all the necessary conveniences. Just like a doll house, I thought.

"Who lives here?" I asked.

"No one," he replied, as we walked back to the 'living room.' "At least, not for the moment," he added. He seated himself on one of the benches and pointed at the bench across from him. "Sit down."

Although friendly, it had the definite sound of an order. He rested his arms on the table. The sunlight shone on his folded hands. They were lean, strong hands.

"This is *Het Vooronder*," he said, lighting up a cigarette. "How do you like it?"

I shrugged. "Nice, I guess."

He smiled gently. But as easily as the smile had appeared, it had faded. As he continued to speak, his bright blue eyes became unusually serious.

"I don't have to tell you that what I have shown you and told you thus far is highly confidential—secret," he clarified. "You're not to talk about any of this to anyone! No one!" he emphasized.

I sensed mixed feelings of fear and excitement. I shivered. The room suddenly seemed to have turned a lot colder. "You'll be seeing and hearing a lot of things while you're staying with us. Whatever it is, nothing—absolutely nothing—may ever leave this boat. Do you understand?"

I nodded, my eyes fixed. He put out his cigarette and leaned back against the steel wall. His hands had dropped in his lap. Staring down at them, he became silent. At last he raised his head, his eyes unchanged.

"If you would tell, you would endanger not only your own life but also those of other people, numerous other people, including Lieske's and mine. Do you realize all that?"

I nodded again. I wanted to tell him about the train ride with the handguns, but I didn't. I hadn't told anyone. Not even Rosie. Again I shivered. He noticed. His face broke into a tiny smile and his eyes became soft, filled with gentleness.

"Any questions?"

I shrugged. "I promise with all my heart never to say anything to anyone."

He reached across the table and took my hands between his.

"I know you won't." He paused for a moment, his eyes fixed on mine. Then he said, "Let's go upstairs and finish our tour, shall we?"

What was it about him that made him so different from all the others? Many years later I came to realize that having known Oom Kees had been a rare and precious experience, known only to a few. How fortunate I was to have been one of them.

I slowly got up and followed him up the stairs. When we returned to the deck, the sun felt bright and warm. Leen was gone. "Does he live on the boat?"

"Who?"

"Leen."

He shook his head. "He lives on the other side, in Buchten."

He stretched out his arm and pointed across the harbor. I walked over to the guard rail on the starboard side and peered over the edge. Below me the water was dirty. All kinds of garbage was floating around. *De Zwaan* lay somewhat tucked away in a corner, which was probably one of the reasons for the waste—it simply had no place else to go. Oom Kees joined me.

"What are those colored splotches on the water?" I pointed at the constantly changing pattern of bright colors.

"Those are oil spills."

"They're pretty," I noted.

"Only when the sun shines on them," he replied.

We watched silently for a while. A small tug boat called *Het Zwaantje* and painted in the same colors of *De Zwaan*, lay moored alongside.

"Do you know how to swim?"

"No, but my older sister and my brother do. Papa taught them. He's a real good swimmer, and a good soccer player, too," I added.

Oom Kees smiled. "I know."

I was surprised. "How do you know?"

"Because everybody who likes soccer knows," he laughed. "Maybe next summer I'll teach you how to swim, but for now, let's go and I'll show you my animals."

"Animals?" I cried.

"Why, don't you like them?"

"I love them. Where are they?"

"In that building, over there." He pointed at a large metal pole barn at the foot of the dike. I followed him down the gangplank, across the narrow path and down the dike. The grass was tall and thick. "These are my chickens," he said. Several plump little chickens were picking away in the dirt around the building.

"How many are there?"

"A dozen or so. Oh, and of course, there is a rooster, too. But let me warn you he's mean."

"Why? What does he do?"

"He'll try to pick your legs. He does it with Tante Lieske all the time. I don't think he likes women very well," he laughed.

Immediately my eyes began searching for the rooster. Kees laughed even more loudly. "Don't worry about him. Just shoo him away."

Behind the building, in the cool, dark shade, lay two small billy goats. At the sound of our voices, they raised their sleepy heads to watch us curiously. "Meet Jack and Roger," Oom Kees said.

They were so cute. "Can I pet them?"

"Of course, go ahead."

At my touch, they raised their pink noses to sniff my hand. "Which one is Roger?"

"The one you're petting."

"How can you tell the difference?"

"Roger has a bit of gray around his mouth."

"Do all the animals have names?"

He nodded. "Jack and Roger were named after a couple of English pilots who stayed with us for a day or so after they were shot down." He didn't elaborate any further.

Watching us from a distance was a goat. She appeared to be tied up. "What's her name?"

"Lieske."

"Lieske?" I laughed.

"That's right, just like Tante Lieske." I started walking towards her.

"Be careful. She's mean, too," Oom Kees called.

I stopped instantly. "What does she do?"

"She boxes."

I could hardly stop laughing. "Goats don't box."

"This one does. She'll knock you right off your feet with her head, but I'm sure she'll be all right, once she gets to know you."

I decided that, for the moment, I was not going to try to get better acquainted, and turned around.

"Let's find Jan."

"Who is he?"

"Jan is our sheep. He's called after my brother."

I remembered Oom Kees's brother. He and his wife Almy had visited Oosterhout once or twice. He was the one who was living near Oom Kees.

Stretched out lazily under a big tree was Jan. "He's hot," I commented.

"I'm sure he is. He needs shearing badly," he added apologetically. I petted the sheep's soft curls.

Oom Kees lit up another cigarette. "We'd better get back to the house. Tante Lieske is probably wondering what happened to us."

There were rabbits, too, but he'd forgotten to show them to me. Since it was my first day, I wondered if he had felt uneasy to tell me that I would now be responsible for feeding them and picking the clover for them.

Seated with us at the dinner table that night were Geert and Willem, the two men I had met earlier in the store. Evidently, they were in hiding, too, trying to avoid the forced labor camps in Germany.

After dinner, I met Kapelaan Verhoeven, the priest of a small parish in Buchten and a regular visitor of *De Zwaan.* He was of slight build and wore wire-rimmed glasses. Although he was dressed like a priest in his long, black frock, he didn't seem to act quite the part, at least not like the ones I had met in Oldenzaal or Oosterhout. He seemed much more jovial, human-like. "Kapelaan Verhoeven teaches catechism at the *Schippers School* (Skippers' School)," Oom Kees explained.

The priest took a sip of his tea, looking from Oom Kees to Tante Lieske over the rim of his cup.

"Will she be going to school?" he asked, carefully putting his cup down.

Tante Lieske sought her husband's eyes. "We really haven't thought about it, have we?" There was a long pause. Everybody was waiting for Oom Kees's decision. I felt strangely uncomfortable when people talked about me in my presence, as if I didn't exist.

At last I was let in on the conversation. "Would you like to go to school?" Oom Kees asked.

"I don't know, I haven't been to school in such a long time."

"Are you afraid you're too far behind?"

I nodded. "A little."

"Well, don't be. This school is different. It is especially for children who travel on barges. They don't go to school very often either—just like you." He put out his cigarette. "Everybody works at his own pace," he continued. "Nobody will make fun of you. I promise."

I could feel the penetration of three pairs of eyes. "Well, what do you think?" Oom Kees asked.

I shrugged. He had not sold me on the idea just yet, which was strange. I remembered the times when I had cried myself to sleep because I wasn't able to go to school.

Tante Lieske placed her sewing on the table in front of her. "Wouldn't you like to make new friends?" she asked casually.

I looked at her. I thought about it for a moment. I had been without friends for so long that the chance of making new ones had never even occurred to me.

"All right. I'll go."

Oom Kees's face broke into a broad, curly smile. A twinkle appeared in his eyes. I could tell he was pleased.

"I know you'll fit in just fine," the priest reassured me, while he consumed the last bite of his applecake. "Excellent cake, Lieske, as usual, of course."

Tante Lieske smiled proudly. "Thank you, Mijnheer Kapelaan."

"I think I'll take a walk out to the school tomorrow and have a chat with the principal," Oom Kees said, and his eyes met those of the priest as he continued, "I have heard he is a good man."

The priest nodded, "And very faithful to his country."

Maybe my life would be getting back to normal after all, I thought.

A week later, wearing a new skirt and a new blouse, I started my first day in school. The bow in my hair had been starched and ironed to perfection. My scuffed shoes were polished and my nails never looked cleaner. Tante Lieske accompanied me.

The way to school led halfway around the harbor to where the road branched off into another road leading to town. From there it was another half a kilometer.

The first few days were a bit frightening, but soon it was as if I hadn't missed any school at all. My best subject was catechism, which didn't come as a complete surprise.

During his nightly visits, Kapelaan Verhoeven patiently went over the lessons with me until I had all the answers right. Our relationship was indeed a somewhat "unusual" one. Of course, none of the other students were aware of that.

In class, Kapelaan Verhoeven was just another teacher and I was just another student. With each perfect grade, I was presented with a beautiful picture of Jesus. Pretty soon my bedroom walls were covered with religious 8 x 10 glossies.

If it hadn't been for the "undercurrents" on *De Zwaan,* life could have been considered fairly normal. On Sundays, the three of us attended church in Born. Afterwards, we visited Tante Lieske's parents for Sunday dinner. They owned a small farm house surrounded by fruit trees and a large vegetable garden, right on the edge of town. They were wonderful old people who seemed to enjoy their home and each other with a noticeable contentment. They never allowed us to go home empty-handed, and we usually carried enough fruits and vegetables home with us to last the rest of the week.

More than anything else, I liked to browse through their library. Both of them loved to read and they had books galore. One book especially caught my interest. It was called *De Martelgang van Kromme Leendert* (The Struggle of Crippled Leendert), a Dutch best seller. I didn't know exactly why I was so anxious to read it. Maybe the title reminded me of Leen. Leafing through the pages, I soon discovered that the book was an absolute "no, no," at least for a girl eleven years old. I could have put it back on the shelf, of course, but my curiosity won out. It took me about five Sundays to finish it, back in the barn behind the house.

Summer quickly passed and autumn arrived with its brisk, cold winds and dark, threatening clouds. Even the harbor had changed, exchanging its tranquil little ripples for dark, choppy waters. The smell of tar, which I liked so well and which had penetrated the air on hot summer days, was gone. The last of the flowers alongside the dike had withered away, and the animals were staying inside the metal building most of the time.

I had made several new friends, but I only got to see them when their barges returned to the harbor. Even then, it was only for a few days, which was just as well. In those days, it wasn't such a good idea to become close with anyone.

I kept myself busy knitting pot holders from scraps of wool. While I did that, from across the room came the squeaking sound of the sewing machine as Tante Lieske pushed the pedal continuously back and forth, back and forth. She was trying to alter one of her old dresses into a new one for me. I hadn't really liked it when she first showed it to me. The dress was brown and I didn't particularly care for brown. She had guessed, as usual, and said, "I'll liven it up with a white Peter Pan collar." I had to admit it was turning out quite pretty.

Life on *De Zwaan* was by no means boring. Besides Kapelaan Verhoeven, came other frequent visitors such as "Lange Wim" ("Tall Bill"), "Bolle Frits" ("Chubby Frits"), "De Baron" ("The Baron"), known only by their nicknames, and, of course, Oom Twan. They usually visited the ship at night, after dark. It didn't take me very long to realize that *De Zwaan* was not only a haven for refugees but a center of at least one group of the resistance. They were men from all walks of life: a cigar salesman, a businessman, a supervisor, a priest, and, of course, the skippers who, under the disguise of hauling cargo, transported Jews and other fugitives across the country and even across the border into Belgium, if that was necessary to keep them out of the "claws" of the Germans.

At first, Oom Kees had acted quite cautiously as he invited his guests into the living room, closing the sliding doors behind him. But as the weeks passed, he became less mindful. He knew he could trust me.

Seated on a footstool beside Tante Lieske's chair, I knitted and listened at the same time to the men gathered around the table. More and better hiding places and more ration coupons to feed everyone seemed to be their most pressing problems. At times, when they had something "top-secret" to discuss, Oom Kees would say, *"Kleine potjes hebben grote oren"* (small jugs have big ears). Following that announcement, they all would get up and follow Oom Kees into the adjoining room, closing the doors behind them.

Tante Lieske would watch her husband through the glass, her eyes filled with concern. What could she do? This was her husband's whole life. She loved him too much to stand in his way. Letting out a deep sigh, she'd return to her mending.

Her worries were not unfounded. On one such night, a raid on a distribution office had been planned. Several of the men were to participate. When it was all over, "The Baron," a father of eight, was no longer among them. One of my cherished memories about him was his manner of speech—somewhat pompous, hence his nickname. Tante Lieske and I would laugh and laugh trying to imitate him: "Zand, Zeep and Zoda" ("Sand, Soap and Soda"), each time greatly exaggerating the "Z."

With my legs curled beneath me, I watched Tante Lieske slowly move the iron across the sparkling clean bed sheet. I wanted to ask her what had happened to my cousin Lida, but I was a little hesitant. Tante Mien's words that evening on the barge when she had tried to console Tante Greta kept ringing in my ears. "She's in good hands with Kees and Lieske," she had said, or something like that.

Tante Lieske glanced at me from the corner of her eyes. "What are you thinking about?"

I shrugged.

"You must be thinking of something," she insisted.

"I would like to ask you something, but I don't know if you want to tell me."

She smiled, "Ask."

What happened to Lida?"

She stopped ironing. The question had caught her off guard. I guess it wasn't what she had expected, and she looked at me quizzically. "How did you know about Lida?"

I told her what Tante Mien had said.

She went back to her ironing. "She was a beautiful baby. A very good baby." Her voice was filled with tenderness and her face broke into a smile. "She wouldn't go to bed unless she had that old flannel receiving blanket. She'd suck on it until she'd fall asleep."

"How long did she stay with you?"

"About a year. She was almost two and a half when she left."

"Where is she now?

"In Belgium, with her parents."

"You mean Oom Ies and Tante Greta are hiding in Belgium?"

She nodded. "They left the barge not long after you and Rosie did." There was a long silence as she meticulously pressed the lace edges of a pillow case. "I miss Lida, myself," she said.

It was obvious that she had liked her very much. Maybe she and Oom Kees would have a baby of their own someday.

Tante Lieske glanced at the clock. "All this talk! Do you realize it's past your bedtime?"

I grimaced. "Just a little while longer?" I begged.

She looked at me from beneath her thick, dark eyebrows. "Fifteen minutes. That's all."

It was one of those rare, quiet evenings, when everybody else was gone. It seemed nice to be alone with Tante Lieske once in a while.

"Tell me about the pilots," I said.

She smiled. She knew exactly what I was up to. I was trying to stretch fifteen minutes into half an hour or more.

"What do you want to know about them?" The iron sizzled as she spat lightly against the sole plate.

I shrugged. "Oom Kees told me the billy goats are called after them."

"That's right. He thought it would be a nice way to remember them. At one time, we had several pilots come through here, but not any more, not since we lost our contact in Belgium."

"What happened?"

She seemed to hesitate, searching her mind whether to tell me or not. As she relived the past, she told me. "After they had been shot down, the underground would bring them to us. They usually stayed for only a day or so until Oom Twan arranged for their false I.D.'s. After that, Oom Kees would take them with *Het Zwaantje* across the Maas River into Belgium. They'd stay there with a farm couple until they were ready to be taken back to England."

She smiled gently. "They used to send us back coded messages via "Radio Orange" from London to let us know that they had arrived safely."

My head resting on my arms, I had become deeply engrossed in her story as she continued. "Then one day the Germans raided the farm. Someone had betrayed them. They found some of the pilots. They were taken captive." Her voice seemed to waver. She looked at me from across the ironing board. Her eyes had a distant look. "The farmer and his wife were shot, right in front of their home."

I slowly raised my head as I uttered an almost inaudible, "No!"

"I'm afraid it's true," she whispered.

She grunted, as she picked up the basket with the freshly ironed laundry. "I'm afraid that's the risk we take," she added.

That night I prayed to God not to have anyone ever betray us.

✡

Oom Kees kept his word. He was going to teach me how to swim. A few times he had shown me the breast stroke and at last the time had come to put it into practice. With a rope tied around my waist I was to jump off *Het Zwaantje* and "swim"—just that simple. I didn't quite see it that way, but as long as I was in Oom Kees's hands, what could possibly go wrong? Besides, it wouldn't be much of a jump. *Het Zwaantje* was not very high.

Tante Lieske shared my mixed feelings, and from the *bijkeuken* she anxiously watched my first swimming lesson. "Kees, be careful!" she called.

"Don't worry. She'll be all right!" he hollered back.

Then I felt myself go under, deeper and deeper, terrified. Bubbles where rising alongside me. I was drowning. Just then, I felt a tug on the rope. Moments later I was back aboard the tugboat, shaking like a leaf.

"Bring her in! Right now!" Tante Lieske yelled.

"I will, I will! "

That day I discovered Oom Kees's one imperfection. He was a terrible swimming instructor.

✡

Papa, Mama and Nan's hiding place in Helmond turned out very troublesome. Surely, they were grateful to their benefactors for their shelter. Nevertheless, it didn't seem fair that many a night they went to bed hungry. Papa not only felt that he paid enough, but he was aware that enough food was available, and that knowledge got him even more upset. When Papa's gums became severely infected it was the straw that broke the camel's back. He blamed his problem mainly on the lack of proper nutrition. Since he wasn't able to see a dentist, he had to rely totally on pain killers. After a while, the lack of sleep due to the constant pain just about depleted all of his strength and endurance.

One morning, after another measly little breakfast, Mama watched him in bewilderment as he pushed his plate aside, jumped up from his chair, grabbed his overcoat, and stomped out of the room.

"Where are you going?" she cried. He never answered her. Instead, he headed for the stairs. She wanted to run after him, but Nan held her back.

"Nan, you have to stop him! He's gone mad!" she cried.

Nan shook his head. "He hasn't gone mad, Mama. Just let him go."

"What do you mean, let him go? Wasn't Vught enough for you?"

Meanwhile, downstairs, Papa and the old man were embroiled in an argument.

"Where do you think you're going?"

"SS Headquarters!" Papa shouted. "And you'd better get your coats, because you and your wife are coming along."

Mama had grabbed Nan's arm. "Please, stop him."

The wife joined her husband in the hallway. "What's going on?"

"He's gone insane! He says he's going to turn us in!" the man cried.

The woman became hysterical. "But why? What have we done?"

"You're starving us to death, that's what. I know that there is a food shortage, but not in this house. I know that you are receiving liters of milk and dozens of eggs, fresh from the farm each week." Then he paused for a moment, his whole body shaking. "Your own son told us that when he sneaked some food up to us when he came to visit you. Imagine, your own son!" Papa sneered.

181

The old man stood motionless, his wife grasped Papa's sleeve.

"Please, Manus, please don't," she begged.

Without the slightest sign of sympathy, Papa pulled his arm free and walked toward the door. But with his hand resting on the door knob, he couldn't deny the pleas and cries any longer. What had come over him? After all, weren't they trying to save his life and that of his wife and son? His hand shook so badly, he wasn't able to turn the door knob.

"Manus! Don't!" came Mama's voice from upstairs.

Slowly, he turned around, his dark, penetrating eyes fixed on the elderly couple. His throat felt parched. It seemed like an eternity before he was able to speak; but his voice had lost its earlier strength.

"For my wife and son's sakes, I'll give you another chance."

"Thank you, Manus. Thank you," the woman wept, her hands pressed against her face.

He ignored her words of gratitude. "I expect milk and enough food so we don't have to go to bed hungry any more." He wearily started up the stairs. He felt he had aged a hundred years.

It didn't take very long for Oom Kees to find out what had happened. A few weeks later, he boarded *Het Zwaantje* for Helmond. Two days later, he returned, bringing Papa, Mama and Nan back with him, hidden beneath the deck, an area not even high enough to be considered a crawl space.

After dark, Papa and Mama were quickly moved into *Het Vooronder*, while Nan was taken to the *Nikki,* one of the barges owned by Jan and Nikki Hornick—also members of the underground. There he stayed for several weeks before joining Mama and Papa on *De Zwaan.*

Although we were now staying in the same place, I still got to visit Papa and Mama only once a month and on special occasions, such as birthdays and Sinterklaas. Somehow, I didn't mind it all that much. Was it because I knew they were within reach, or had I grown that much more independent?

One thing I was sure of, I was very happy and content to stay with Oom Kees and Tante Lieske. Sometimes I wondered what it would be like without them—especially Oom Kees. I'm sure that the threesome in *Het Vooronder* often must have wondered the same thing. Oom Kees's frequent visits after dark, either to deliver groceries, pick up dirty laundry or tell his latest jokes, brought new zest to their lives. And whenever their cabin fever became unbearable, Oom Kees would think of something to release the pressure, such as the "after dark" fishing contest through the portholes between Papa and Nan. When Papa thought he'd finally caught something, he was not totally surprised to find an old, rusty wash basin tied to the end of the line.

"You know who you hear laughing out there, don't you?" Mama would say.

"I know very well who he is," Papa would reply.

One day I couldn't wait to go to school. I wanted to show my girlfriends my new poem album. Oom Kees had bought it for me because all the girls had one. He was the first one to write in it. His was a beautiful poem he composed by himself, especially for me. On the page next to it, he put a sticker of a tiny, white dove. The poem goes:

> Your "happy childhood" surely hasn't been
> all that nice.

> It has been a time of slander and scorn, of
> fighting and struggling for your earthly
> existence, although, in your innocence, you
> have done nothing wrong.

> However, I want you to take this lesson for-
> ever to heart, whenever you're bent under
> worries or grief.

Even though your life didn't have a pleasant start, behind the clouds there is always the sun.

May this tiny dove bring peace soon.

That's my profoundest prayer for my "little Manda."

I think it's so beautiful, it makes me cry each time I read it.

Once again the air was filled with signs of spring. Buttercups and daisies large and small blanketed the dike. The animals came out of their shelter and the billy goats especially were kicking up their heels. I spent a lot of my free time making wreaths out of daisies. It was too bad they wilted so quickly. The harbor had a totally different look now that the dreariness of winter was gone.

Seated on their scaffolds, a few early-bird skippers started to restore their barges after the wear and tear of the last few months. The smell of tar permeated the air. I loved that smell. It will always remind me of *De Zwaan* in the spring. Everything looked and felt so new. Could it be because I thought I was in love? Could that be the reason why everything felt so wonderful?

His name was Hans. He was very handsome and at least four years older than I. Truthfully, I didn't think he had noticed me. I also had a feeling that Tante Lieske knew how I felt. Each time I mentioned his name, she'd look knowingly at me from the corner of her eyes. I seemed to be talking about him a lot, although I really tried not to. One day, I joined her in the kitchen. As I watched a barge being towed into the harbor, I casually mentioned that I liked red and white trim best of all. She never looked up, but she asked, "Why? Are those the colors of Hans's boat?" I could feel myself turn as red as a beet. I wondered how she knew.

Awful news reached us. Oom Philip and Tante Nettie were arrested. Their two children, Rose and Herman, were able to escape. They were quickly taken to Belgium.

Mama was very upset and so was Papa. Oom Philip was one of Papa's best friends. Suddenly, memories came rushing back to me, things that otherwise probably would never have been all that important or all that funny. There was one time, for instance, when Mama had taken us back to Sittard on a vacation. We had all stayed at Oom Philip and Tante Nettie's house. Tante Nettie not only was quite orthodox but also liked to sleep late, a wonderful combination for the rest of us who wanted to get up early to enjoy a breakfast which included crisp, fried bacon. Seated around the table, the frying pan placed in the center, Oom Philip used to get the biggest charge out of watching us quietly sop up the bacon grease with the freshly baked bread. Afterwards, we'd all pitch in to help clean up the "unkosher" evidence before Tante Nettie called for her early morning tea.

At least there would always be the memories to last us a lifetime.

Suddenly, Rosie joined me. The neighbors where she was had begun to gossip, wondering about her true identity, which meant it was high time to move on. Papa and Mama were so happy to see her. It had been at least a year. *De Zwaan* was getting pretty crowded, but there always seemed to be room for one more.

The next Sunday, after church, we visited Tante Lieske's parents as usual. The trees in their orchard were heavily weighed down with cherries. We picked almost all afternoon.

I love cherries, especially the big, black ones. Tante Lieske canned most of them. The rest we'd have for dessert.

It was while we were enjoying our cherries one evening that Oom Kees told us to put all our pits in an empty vegetable dish in the center of the table. "When we're through, I want you to guess how many pits there are in that bowl. The one who comes closest will win the pot."

"What pot?" Tante Lieske asked.

"A *stuiver* (nickel) each."

All eyes went immediately to the bowl.

"You can't count now," he warned. "That's dishonest."

Tante Lieske got up to get her change purse. She took a nickel out for herself and one each for Rosie and me. Oom Kees had begun writing down our bets on the edge of a newspaper.

"Lieske, you count," he said.

Using her spoon, she methodically moved the pits aside, two at a time. "117!"

Kees glanced at the paper. "I won!" he cried. His blue eyes crinkled at the corners.

"Beginner's luck," Tante Lieske teased.

For the next three nights, we played our *stuivers,* and each time Oom Kees won. The following night, as I set the table and was just about to carry the cherries inside, Tante Lieske stopped me. "Wait a minute," she said, and without further explanation, she dug her hand into the cherries, removing a handful of them.

"What are you doing?"

"We'll teach him a lesson," she giggled, as she neatly straightened the remaining cherries. I wasn't quite sure if I knew what she was up to, but I thought I had a fairly good idea.

The time came once again for counting pits. "104!" Tante Lieske announced, and a faint smile crossed her lips. Oom Kees didn't immediately check the paper; instead, he looked visibly surprised.

"Well, who won?" Tante Lieske asked. This time it was her eyes that sparkled.

Oom Kees slowly turned to the paper. "Geert, you won!" he said, but without quite the enthusiasm he had shown previously.

"Good!" Tante Lieske replied, and her mischievous little smile didn't escape me when she and Oom Kees exchanged quick glances.

Sunday, when we were at church, I was watching the collection plate being passed from row to row. A chubby man with a shiny, round face, seated a few rows ahead of us with his equally chubby wife, always seemed to put in a guilder, because his contribution never made any noise when he dropped it on the plate. I leaned over to Oom Kees. "Is he rich?" I whispered behind my hand.

Oom Kees looked surprised by the sudden question. "Who?"

"That fat man." I motioned my head toward the rows in front of us.

He chuckled. "I don't think so, why?"

"I think he gives guilders. His money never makes any noise."

I could tell Oom Kees had a difficult time keeping himself from laughing out loud, but he successfully controlled himself. "You can't see it from here, but he takes out the change," he grinned.

I shook my head. Oom Kees! He was so funny. I loved him so much. I couldn't quite imagine life without him. One day, he was overjoyed when he read the news bulletin from England—the Americans had landed in Normandie. "It won't be much longer now," he said, his eyes glistening.

Suddenly, there was that gnawing thought again. It made me actually feel a little ashamed. "What will happen to me when the war is over someday? Maybe they'll let me stay on *De Zwaan!*"

I leaned over. "Can I stay with you when the war is over?" I whispered.

Oom Kees looked startled.

"I can become Catholic!" I hastened to add.

He slowly shook his head. His eyes had a penetrating look, without the usual sparkle, when he said, "You'll go back to your Papa and Mama. They love you as much as I do, and you always stay what you are."

I bowed my head. I thought of Papa and Mama in *Het Vooronder* and felt ashamed. Then I felt the touch of Oom Kees's hand on mine.

My arms resting on the kitchen counter, I watched quietly, but not without abhorrence, as Tante Lieske prepared our weekly meal of *kunstgehakt* (artificial hamburger) made with oatmeal instead of meat. It always stuck to the roof of my mouth, if not in my throat. I absolutely loathed it.

"What's for dessert?" I asked.

"Vanilla pudding with cherry sauce, but only if you eat your *kunstgehakt*," she laughed.

"I will. I promise." No one made pudding like Tante Lieske. Its texture was so creamy and smooth, it tasted almost like ice cream. Feeling somewhat less antagonistic toward "the main course," I continued watching her as she tried to neatly shape the gooey mass into patties. Suddenly, my attention was distracted when Oom Twan's thunderous voice came from the dining room. "We have to get them out, Kees. I don't think we have an alternative."

Tante Lieske and I exchanged quick glances. You could really tell when Oom Twan became upset.

"What makes you believe the matter is so pressing?" Oom Kees inquired.

"For one thing, there's the lack of food. For another, he seems to have become unusually interested in one of them—a pretty, young girl. She's afraid of him. She has threatened to run away. He's also got a large picture of Hitler hanging in his vestibule."

"I wouldn't worry too much about the picture. That may be his way of diverting attention," Oom Kees replied.

"That may well be, but I'm telling you, Kees, the situation is very critical."

The long, heavy silence was interrupted only by the squeaking sound of the *Kiepers*, floating in from across the harbor.

"How many of them are there?"

"Fourteen."

"Fourteen!" Oom Kees repeated. His voice revealed concern. "Where in the world are we going to place all of them?"

Oom Twan was seated in the armchair by the window. I was able to watch him from where I was standing. He had begun rolling a cigarette. "Unless we come up with a sound answer, I don't think he'll release them. Don't forget, for some they are a good source of income." The tip of his tongue slowly moved along the edge of the flimsy cigarette paper. He briefly inspected his creation, put it in his mouth and lit it.

I was quite sure I knew whom they were talking about. Only one family kept that many Jews hidden. They were living across the harbor. I had heard Oom Kees talk about them once or twice.

"I suggest we tell him that he's under suspicion. As a matter of fact, I'll tell him myself," Oom Kees said.

Oom Twan blew soft circles of smoke toward the ceiling. "And then what are we going to do?"

"I'll take them," Oom Kees replied. He sounded as determined as always. "We'll put them in *Het Achteronder* until we can place them."

Oom Twan slowly rose from his chair and turned toward the window. "How do you plan to bring them aboard?" he asked, looking out across the water.

"With *Het Zwaantje*, a few at a time." The reply was calm and deliberate.

Tante Lieske had reached into the cupboard to take out the dinner plates. They clattered so loudly, I thought she was going to drop them.

In the days that followed, everyone on *De Zwaan*, at least those above deck, worked alongside each other to prepare *Het Achteronder*, the dark, cold, steel-walled hiding place beneath the rear deck, for its guests. Someone delivered a pot, so big it could hold enough soup to feed an entire army.

At last the "14" arrived, exactly according to plan—a few at a time. Poor Tante Lieske, she worked harder than ever. Besides the six of us and the three in *Het Vooronder,* she now had to take care of an additional fourteen. When she wasn't cooking meals or baking bread, she'd be washing clothes. Still, she never once complained. Meanwhile, Oom Kees and his men worked equally hard trying to find hiding places. Unlike at the beginning of the war, fewer and fewer people were eager to take the risk. Eventually, after about three weeks, *Het Achteronder* was once again "for rent." All but one, an elderly gentleman, had left. He had joined Papa and Mama in *Het Vooronder*, where cabin fever was becoming progressively worse.

Returning home from school one day, Rosie was walking quietly beside me. She had never liked school too well, but she seemed to like "mine"—probably because she didn't feel threatened by a class full of children her own age, and no one was poking fun at her. Thus far, she had only one year of school, including our "education" at the one-room, Jewish school house, and she was already nine years old. I had at least been able to complete the first grade and part of the second. Although it didn't come easy, I had been doing some fourth-grade work. I had to admit it was nice to be together again, even though at first I hadn't been too enthusiastic about sharing my "number-one spot."

"Don't you like that smell?" I asked.

She sniffed a couple of times. "It's all right, I guess. What is it anyway?"

"It's tar. I love it," I said, inhaling a burst of the smell of tar mixed with the sweet, delicate fragrance of wild flowers. The harbor was one of my favorite places. *De Zwaan,* gently touched by the silver ripples of the water shimmering beneath the blue sky, looked unusually peaceful. The sliding doors to the kitchen and the dining room were wide open, inviting the sounds of summer.

I noticed that Oom Kees had a guest.

He looked up when he heard us enter. Surprised, he glanced at his watch. "Is it that time already?" Then he turned to his guest.

"Doctor, these are my *Rotterdammertjes,*" he explained. "Girls, this is Dr. de Jong." We shook hands politely. The man had a sympathetic look in his eyes. He was of average build, probably somewhere in his forties. His dark brown hair was slicked back, making his round, smooth-shaven face appear even rounder. "Doctor de Jong will be staying with us until tomorrow."

I wasn't surprised. Through the year, I had seen many people come and go on very quick notice and sometimes without any notice at all.

My eyes fell on the man's heavily-bandaged left hand. Oom Kees blinked as he tried to intercept my curious glance. I knew I was not to ask any questions.

"Where's Tante Lieske?"

"She had to run an errand in town. She should be back shortly," Oom Kees replied. Then he quickly added, "Why don't you go and feed the rabbits. You may have to pick some clover. I think we're almost out."

"All right," I said. Together, Rosie and I left the room to tend to our animal friends.

The atmosphere at the dinner table that evening was unusually strained. Perhaps everybody felt intimidated because our guest was a doctor. From what I had gathered from Tante Lieske, he had been arrested by the SS and had later escaped during transport to the Dutch concentration camp of *Westerbork*. That's when he had hurt his hand. Some nearby hospital had bandaged it. From there, he had gotten in touch with Oom Twan, who in turn had delivered him to *De Zwaan*. He would be leaving for Belgium in the morning.

I didn't care much for the doctor, and I didn't think Tante Lieske liked him very much either. I especially didn't like his narrow eyes. They moved constantly. I watched him as he reached into his pocket and pulled out a bunch of papers. He studied them quietly for a moment. Then he shook his head slowly and with apparent amazement. "I can't get over the tremendous job they did in falsifying these papers," he said. "You can't tell them from real ones."

Proudly, Oom Kees agreed.

The doctor began putting the papers back in his pocket. "I don't think I'll have any trouble crossing the border with them. Do you?"

Oom Kees shook his head. "I wouldn't worry about it for a moment," he assured him, and he slowly rose from his chair. He looked at Tante Lieske. "I promised the doctor to show him *Het Vooronder.*" She didn't answer. Instead, she gave him a peculiar glance. Then the two men left the room.

After we had washed the dishes, it was time, once again, to get our nails cleaned—a weekly ritual. Rosie watched intently. I hated the way Tante Lieske dug way beneath my nails with the sharp little tool. Occasionally, I tried to pull my hand back, but she kept a tight grip on it. "Just a few more," she said. Tante Lieske seemed very quiet—her thoughts far, far away. We heard someone enter the kitchen. It was Oom Kees and the doctor.

"Ouch!" I promptly pulled my hand back. This time she let go. "I'm sorry," she said ruefully, as she watched me put the injured finger into my mouth. "Let me see."

I showed it to her. She put a quick kiss on it.

"You have a wonderful setup down below, Mevrouw Zwaans. Very ingenious," the doctor complimented, as he entered the dining room.

Tante Lieske looked at him briefly. She smiled politely. "Thank you."

The man did not sit down again, but glanced at the clock.

"I lost my watch during the fall. It's truly a nuisance," he commented.

"Here, why don't you take mine?" Oom Kees had already begun to take off his watch.

"Thank you, Kees. That's very nice, but I'll buy one myself."

"Consider it a souvenir," Oom Kees insisted, as he handed the doctor his watch, who looked at it for a moment.

"I'll always treasure it," he said. "Well, I hope you'll forgive me, but I think I'm going to turn in. I have a big day ahead of me."

Oom Kees rested his hand on his guest's shoulder. "No apologies necessary. We understand. Let me show you your room." The man shook Tante Lieske's hand. "Thank you again for your hospitality, Mevrouw Zwaans."

"You're welcome," she replied. Once again I recognized that peculiar expression I had noticed at the dinner table.

"Good night." The doctor waved once more, before he followed Oom Kees out of the room.

"I have to go back to *Het Vooronder* for a minute," Oom Kees said when he returned.

Tante Lieske looked at him, obviously distressed. "Why?"

"Manus wants to talk to me about something. When I walked up the stairs, he pulled my pant leg. When I turned to looked at him, he motioned me to come back."

"What do you think he wants?"

Oom Kees shrugged. "I have no idea. Maybe he would like to go fishing again," he joked.

She shook her head. "Don't be late."

193

"I won't."

When he entered *Het Vooronder,* Papa and Mama were sitting at the table, waiting for him. The room had grown dark. Nan and the old man had gone to bed already. Kees knew something was wrong the moment he sat down.

"Would you like a cup of tea?" Mama asked.

"No, thank you. I promised Lieske not to stay long. Well, what is it that you want to talk to me about, Maan?"

Papa put out his cigarette. "It's that doctor, Kees. I wish I didn't feel the way I do, but I don't trust him."

Oom Kees lit a cigarette. For a moment he studied the glowing tip. "May I ask why?"

Papa paused for a moment before he continued. "I don't know. There's just something about him. As a matter of fact, I had that feeling the moment I watched him walk aboard with Twan this morning."

He turned to Mama. "Didn't I tell you, Elsa?" Mama nodded affirmatively.

Oom Kees was listening quietly, his back resting against the wall. When he leaned forward to flip the ashes from his cigarette, his hand seemed to shake lightly.

He looked straight at Papa. "We had him checked out thoroughly. I'm sure your suspicion is unfounded."

Papa shrugged with a sense of hopelessness. "I hope you're right."

"I know I am." There was a hint of irritability in his voice. "Do you think I would have brought him down here if I wasn't?"

"I guess not," Papa replied, unconvinced.

"I guess I'd better get back." Oom Kees stood up slowly and headed for the stairs. He hesitated. "Remember what I have been telling you. *He who trusts in God, builds on a strong foundation.*"

"Again, I hope you're right," Papa replied.

"By the way, Lieske was wondering why you wanted to see me. I guess I'd better think of something quick. No need to worry her needlessly." He raised his hand, "Good night."

For the second time that night, he began climbing the narrow stairs. Papa and Mama listened silently as the stool was moved back in place.

Using one of Oom Kees's bicycles, the doctor left before daybreak. Besides the watch, he also wore one of Oom Kees's best shirts. At the foot of the gangplank, the two men shook hands.

"Thank you. I'll be in touch," the doctor said.

"Good luck," Oom Kees replied.

Then they waved goodbye one last time. Behind the tiny window of the porthole, Papa let out a deep sigh as he watched the doctor ride away into the darkness.

An hour or so had passed when the phone rang. Oom Kees answered. As he listened to the voice at the other end of the line, his face turned ashen, his hands shook. He hung up. "Dear God. Dear God, what now?" he whispered, his head bent, his hand still touching the telephone. Moments later he staggered into the kitchen where Tante Lieske was preparing breakfast.

"Lieske!" he cried.

She looked up. "What happened?" She looked at him in horror. She had never seen him this way. She seized his arm. "Kees, what happened? Who called?"

"Van den Berg!"

"Van den Berg? What did he want?"

"Not to let him leave the house. He is not a doctor. He's wanted by the underground!"

"My God!" she screamed, horrified. She buried her head against his chest, but for once Oom Kees was unable to give comfort.

With strict orders "to kill," the underground tried to track the imposter down, but Dr. de Jong had long since disappeared.

The Betrayal

Two days had passed since the doctor had left. Rosie and I were on our way home from school when a woman came running along the dike toward us. Her hands kept signaling us to go back. When she came closer, I recognized her. It was Nikki. We stopped walking. "Go back!" she cried breathlessly. "There's a raid on *De Zwaan*," she said, when at last she had reached us. My legs became like rubber. "Go back, Manda. Go to town. S ee Jan, but whatever you do, don't come back!" She turned around and ran back, leaving us standing.

Rosie started to cry. Scared and confused, I stamped my foot. "Don't! Stop your crying!" I yelled. I tried to think, but everything in my head seemed scrambled and fuzzy. At last we turned around and started back to town.

I was gripped by fear. Would they shoot everybody on *De Zwaan*, just like they had the farm couple in Belgium? Rosie kept looking at me. I knew she wanted me to tell her that everything was going to be all right, but I didn't want to talk to her. I had to think—think.

When we reached Jan's house, I rang the door bell. The apartment was located above the store. I could hear someone

197

come running down the stairs. The door opened. It was Almy. Her eyes were red from crying.

"What are you doing here?" she snarled.

"There's a raid on *De Zwaan*. We don't know where to go!"

"I'm sorry, but I can't let you come in. They're looking for Jan. They've found radios that belonged to you—Jews, I mean. Go and see my parents. You know where they live, don't you?"

I nodded. She quickly closed the door. Once again, we were left standing—all alone. A small green car pulled up behind us. When we turned around, four Germans jumped out. Three of them were soldiers, the other an SS officer. The soldiers pushed us back until our backs were against the store window. Then they raised their rifles. I could look right into them.

"*Nahme!*" the officer yelled. Suddenly Amama's picture appeared in front of me. Because of her we understood German and now she had come to help us.

"De Boer."

"Where do you live?"

"On a barge." The German was visibly surprised as the words kept coming.

"What are you doing here?"

I didn't know. What were we doing here?

The German's expression became quizzical.

"We're here to check for mail," I blurted.

There was a pause. "No more questions, please no more," I prayed.

The officer raised his hand. "*Raus!*" Did it mean we were free to go? "*Raus!*" The officer repeated—louder this time. With our hands welded together, we slowly moved away from the barrels. The green of the trees and the blue of the sky ran together into an huge blur.

Almy must have called because her parents were already waiting for us.

Gradually, I regained some of my composure. I knew that I didn't want to stay where we were. I had to get back to the harbor, one way or another. I wanted to know what had happened.

"You really should stay here until they come to get you," Almy's mother pleaded.

I shook my head. "I'm all right. I'm not going near *De Zwaan.* I promise."

I tried to talk Rosie into staying, but she begged me not to leave her. "All right. But promise not to cry."

"I won't. I promise."

"Make sure you come back if you can't find a place to stay," Almy's mother said.

"We will."

Soon after, we were on our way back to the harbor.

When we reached Jan's house, the same Germans were still patrolling. "What if they recognize us?" I thought. "Just keep walking—don't draw their attention."

What followed, happened so quickly, I hardly had time to gather my thoughts. The moment Rosie recognized the soldiers, she turned around and walked back.

"Don't!" I hissed. "Look, you lost something." I pointed at the road a little ways back. She looked at me as if I'd gone mad. "Bend over and pick it up. Pick it up . . . something . . . anything." Slowly she followed my orders.

"Give it to me."

She held out her empty hand, her eyes brimming with tears.

I took "it." "Let's go . . . don't look at them . . . don't cry. . . . Laugh. Yes, let's laugh."

The rest of the way, we walked in almost complete silence. At last we reached the harbor with its late-afternoon tranquility. The long shadows and the golden sparkles of the parting sunlight sprinkled across the surface of the dark waters.

"Where are we going?" Rosie asked.

"The *Nikki*."

"What's the *Nikki*?"

"Remember that lady this morning . . . who came to warn us about *De Zwaan*?"

She nodded.

"Her barge is called *Nikki*, also. There she is," I pointed. "The one with the white and green trim."

We began to walk a little faster. Carefully, we climbed the narrow, wobbly plank. How much easier it seemed, compared to that first time in Amsterdam. Of course, it had been dark and slippery that night. We walked across the deck to the cabin. I knocked. Nikki opened the door. When she saw us, her eyes grew large in disbelief.

"What are you doing here?" she cried. "Didn't I tell you to stay in town?"

"Never mind, Nikki. Have them come in," her husband broke in when he noticed us standing in the doorway.

I suddenly felt uncomfortable. All my self-assuredness had suddenly left me. Nikki was right. Maybe we shouldn't have come.

"Sit down," Jan said. I noticed he didn't look well. He suffered from some kind of a disease. Tante Lieske called it diabetes. He had only one leg. I looked around the small room with the plain furniture. From one of the other rooms came the sound of children. A couple of them were crying. Jan and Nikki had quite a few children—five or six. I wasn't quite sure.

"What happened on *De Zwaan*?" I asked.

"We don't know yet," Nikki replied softly. She didn't seem upset with us any longer. "The Germans have sealed off the whole area around the boat. No one can go near it," she continued.

Instantly, the story of the couple in Belgium flashed through my mind again. I was scared. Nikki noticed. She opened a small tin of cookies. "Have some," she said. "I'm sure we'll be hearing from them before long."

Jan agreed.

200

"Tell me. Did you go to Jan and Almy Zwaans's house?" Nikki asked.

I nodded. "We couldn't stay, though."

"How come?

"The Germans were looking for Jan."

Nikki stole a glance at her husband. "Why? What, for heaven's sake, would they want him for?"

"Almy mentioned something about radios that belonged to Jewish people . . . I don't know." I suddenly felt very tired. I didn't really feel like talking anymore. I looked at Rosie. She sat quietly munching at her cookie.

"So then where did you go?" Jan prodded.

"Almy told us to go to her parents. Just when we were leaving, some Germans stopped us."

Clapping her hand over her mouth, Nikki looked as if she had suddenly been struck by lightning. Her face had turned very pale.

Jan looked equally concerned."Did they ask any questions?"

I nodded. "They wanted to know our names and why we were at the Zwaans's place."

Nikki and Jan glanced at each other. Nicki's hands, now resting on the table, were clenched into tiny fists, her knuckles bloodless white. "What did you tell them?" she asked, afraid to learn the answer.

"I told them that we had been sent to check if there was any mail for us, something like that."

Her eyes were wide, filled with a mixture of amazement and doubt. "Did he understand you?"

I nodded. "I know how to speak German; Amama taught us."

"Amama?" She choked back a laugh. "Who's Amama?"

"My grandmother. She is dead now."

Then she broke out into hysterical laughter. Jan smiled broadly, shaking his head slowly. "How did you think of it?" he asked.

I shrugged. "I don't know (I would never know), it was the only thing I could think of."

Still shaking his head, he kept staring at me. "Incredible," he whispered. Then he said, "You're staying with us tonight."

We waited up for a while longer, but there was no further news from *De Zwaan*. Finlly, too exhausted to stay awake any longer, we went to bed.

"I'm so proud of you . . . so very proud . . . we could very well all have been dead . . . I mean all of us." The voice—it came from somewhere far away. Then I recognized it. It was Papa's voice.

I had told him what had happened. I could feel his hands touching my face. There was a light—not a very bright light. I rubbed my eyes. I had been dreaming—or had I? A big black blur was sitting on the edge of my bed. I squinted. It became gradually clearer, the outlines sharper. I raised myself up on my elbows. Papa? "Papa!" I cried, as I fell sobbing into his arms.

"You're all right . . . everyone is all right," he whispered, stroking my head. Then I saw Mama and Nan, watching quietly. Rosie was beginning to wake up, too.

"Where are Oom Kees and Tante Lieske?" I wanted to know.

"Still on *De Zwaan*." Papa answered.

"Are you sure they're all right."

Papa nodded.

I started to cry again.

"Only De Witte was arrested."

"De Witte?" I cried. "How come?"

"He gave himself away. He didn't answer their questions properly. Willem was smarter. He grabbed a bunch of supplies and walked off the boat posing as a customer the moment he saw them arrive."

"That was smart," I thought, but I couldn't help feeling sorry for De Witte, and so close to the end. They probably would be sending him to a work camp somewhere in Germany.

"What did you do?" I asked. "Didn't they find *Het Vooronder?*"

"Oh, yes, they did."

"So, how did you get away?"

"Through the trapdoor underneath the table."

Oom Kees had never told me about a trap door. I must have looked puzzled for Papa continued, "Underneath the floor is the oil storage tank, and that's where we have been hiding all day."

"In the oil?"

He nodded. "Up to our knees," Nan clarified. He laughed nervously.

"I can't believe you're here," I said, hugging Papa tightly. I was so glad he was proud of me. I would always remember that moment.

The following day, before dawn, Oom Kees and Tante Lieske got on their bicycles and pedaled to the tiny village of Stein, near Geleen. There they boarded a barge belonging to Tante Lieske's uncle. They traveled for several weeks, until they decided to drop anchor in Andel to await freedom.

Allied troops were moving rapidly towards the Dutch border. Then came September 5, 1944, *Dolle Dinsdag* (Mad Tuesday). An erroneous news bulletin came from England that the Americans had crossed the border at Breda. Wild rumors were flying from every direction, causing mass confusion among the German troops. Many of them began fleeing back to Germany—by car, by foot, and by stolen bicycles. The Dutch people thought that, at last, the war was over. There was dancing in the streets. But Hitler put a quick end to the bedlam and ordered his high command to restore order immediately.

Once again, the Dutch people retreated to the safety of their homes, but many were left lying dead in the streets— shot during the melee. It was on this "Mad Tuesday" that

Oom Kees and Tante Lieske disembarked and rode their bicycles to Oosterhout—Oom Kees's home town, twenty miles away. Tied on the rack of their bicycles, they carried a bit of luggage and a large wheel of cheese. By the time they reached Oosterhout, "Mad Tuesday" was history. Reluctant to stay with Oom Kees's parents, they found refuge at a small bakery in town. Less than two weeks later, Oosterhout was liberated.

Mama, Papa, and Nan stayed aboard the *Nikki* until the liberation forces moved into their area on September 21, Mama's birthday.

Corrie never did return to Breda. After leaving De Zwaans family, she had been taken to Tilburg, twenty kilometers southeast of Oosterhout. It was not yet liberated, and hiding places were getting more expensive and harder to come by.

The family which had offered to give Corrie shelter had nine children of their own; one more wouldn't make that much difference. Besides, Corrie could be of great help in their dime store.

Corrie hated it. Not only did she have to work twelve to fifteen hours a day, but when she returned home after a long day's work, she'd find very little left to eat. And for that, Papa had to pay one hundred and fifty guilders per week. She was liberated on October 26 by the Canadians.

Rosie and I were not quite as fortunate. The day following the raid, Oom Twan came to take us home with him, but only for a couple of days. Then we were taken to Vlodrop, a small town on the German border. For us, the worst part of the war was yet to come.

None of us would ever set foot on *De Zwaan* again. On September 18, not long after everybody had abandoned her, the Allies bombed the locks, causing the harbor to be laid dry. As a result, *De Zwaan* tipped over on its side.

Chapter 13

Almost There. . . .

I welcomed the shade of the big old oak trees that lined the streets. It was one of those very rare, hot Sunday afternoons. Not a leaf was stirring. A little earlier we had left Rosie at her new hiding place. She surely was lucky—a brand new house and two little girls to play with. She even had her own bedroom. I felt homesick for *De Zwaan*. No matter where I'd end up, nothing would ever compare with *De Zwaan*.

"Are we almost there?" I asked.

"Almost," Oom Twan replied and he gently squeezed my hand.

Although the village seemed asleep, I had a strange feeling that hundreds of curious eyes were watching us from behind the neat, lacy curtains. A couple of old men were sitting on a bench beneath one of the trees. They were talking quietly, as if they did not want to disturb the stillness surrounding them.

We had reached the sun-drenched village square and I could feel the unevenness of its cobblestones against the soles of my feet. Across from the square Oom Twan stopped in front of a small building, which had "CAFE" written in bold white letters all across its large front window.

"This is it," Oom Twan said. I felt disappointed. He noticed. "I'm sure you are going to like it here," he added, trying to raise my sunken spirits.

When he opened the door, the sound of a bell rang through the establishment. It reminded me of Mijnheer De Dood's candy store at home, and suddenly I could smell the sweet fragrances of gum drops, jaw breakers, and licorice sticks in the large glass containers sitting on the counter.

Occasionally moving a chair or a table, Oom Twan led the way. He knocked on the milk-glass window of yet another door. There was no answer. He slowly opened it and stuck his head inside.

"Anyone home?" he roared. I winced. His thunderous voice embarrassed me.

A man in a wheelchair appeared in the doorway across the room. When he recognized his visitor, his face lit up and he quickly wheeled himself inside.

"Dag, Twan. Sorry to keep you waiting. I was in the back of the house." he apologized.

"That's all right," Oom Twan assured him, shaking the man's frail hand. "How are you, Willie? You're looking very well."

"Thank you. I've been feeling pretty good lately. The beautiful weather is agreeing with me, I guess." Then he cocked his head to try to get a better look at me. More intimidated by the wheelchair than the man himself, I'd hid behind Oom Twan's towering height. "And you must be Manda."

"Yes, she is." Oom Twan answered for me, stepping aside and putting his arm around my shoulders. The man reached out his hand. I politely shook it.

"Welkom!" His dark brown eyes, deep in the pale, heavily-lined face, smiled warmly. I was sure he meant it. Then, still holding my hand, "I hope you're going to like it

here." Not totally convinced that I would, I returned his smile. He let go of my hand.

"Sit down, Twan. You too, Manda, sit down."

Oom Twan lit a cigarette. "Where is everybody? I've never seen this place this quiet."

Willie laughed. "They have all gone to watch the soccer game. It's Sunday, remember?"

Oom Twan tapped himself lightly against the forehead. "Of course. How could I possibly forget?"

"That's right. How could you?" Again Willie laughed. "How about a cup of coffee and a piece of *vlaai*?"

"A cup of coffee sounds good, but forget the *vlaai*. We had a big dinner just before we left the house."

Willie looked at me from the corner of his eye. "I'm sure you could eat a piece."

I wasn't all that hungry, but I felt sorry for him. He was trying so hard to make me feel at ease. I nodded, "Thank you."

"Would you like a glass of milk to wash it down?"

"All right."

"I'm warning you, Willie," and Oom Twan's big hand ruffled my hair, "this kid is going to eat you out of house and home!"

I felt embarrassed. Why did he have to say those things? It wasn't even true.

"No problem," Willie said. "We still have plenty to eat, some of it is from our garden and some of it is *ersatz*." He pushed his chair away from the table. "I'll be right back." Quickly he turned his chair around and wheeled himself into the adjoining room, which I assumed was the kitchen.

Glancing around the room, I noticed how small it was. It barely accommodated the large dining table and the six chairs. Behind me was a window, its heavy brown woolen curtains tightly drawn. A small ceiling fixture spread a circle of light over the table. "Do they always keep it this dark?" I wondered. Maybe he didn't like the sun to come in.

In a corner, next to the window, was a large overstuffed chair. The room was probably being used as both living room and dining room.

I glanced at the carpet that covered the hardwood floor. It obviously had seen better days. It was wrinkled and its colors had faded. Across from me, on the wall, was a large oval portrait of a middle-aged couple. The man, sporting a huge handlebar mustache, was seated on a straight chair with the woman standing behind him, her slender hand resting on his shoulder. She was sort of pretty. I liked her beautiful lace gown. I wondered who they were. Willie's parents, maybe? My thoughts were interrupted as Willie returned to the room carrying a tray in his lap. Oom Twan quickly got up from his chair. "Let me give you a hand."

"Sit down," Willie motioned. "I'm an expert at this," and he placed the tray on the table, carefully pushing it toward the center. "Go ahead. Help yourself." He straightened his thin, bony shoulders and settled back in his chair, folding his pale hands in his lap. "How are Mien and the children?" he asked, as he watched us help ourselves to the food and drinks.

"Fine. Just fine," Oom Twan replied, slowly stirring his coffee. "Mien complains a lot that she doesn't see much of me these days, but there is not much I can do about that. And how is your father?"

Willie seemed to hesitate for a moment. "Pap is fine. He has his own room at the other side of the house. He keeps pretty much to himself. He even does his own cooking. The boys and Pap have never been able to get along, but I guess I told you about that. It became worse after Mam died, and so he decided it best to withdraw to his own room."

"That's really too bad."

"Yes, it is." He shrugged his shoulders as if to emphasize his helplessness. "How is the *vlaai*?" he continued, trying to change the unpleasant subject.

"Delicious!" I loved Limburger pie, which the locals called *vlaai*. Single crusted, covered with fruit, it was not only twice as large as a regular pie, but the crust was much thinner as well.

While the two men became engaged in conversation, I felt myself staring at the thin man in the wheelchair. He couldn't be very old, "not as old as Papa," I thought. His strawberry blond hair was neatly parted in the middle. I remembered having seen some real old pictures of Papa, when he had his hair just that way. With Willie barely able to take care of himself, I wondered how he was ever going to take care of me. Not that it mattered that much. By now, I had learned pretty well how to take care of myself. Although for different reasons, I too, had become independent, just like Willie, and I felt a certain affinity with my new "uncle."

My thoughts returned to the present as bits and pieces of the men's conversation began to penetrate. They were discussing the progress of the war. Everyone thought that it would soon be over. It had been quite a while since D-Day.

The war had started more than four years ago, and for more than half of that time I had been wandering across the country from one place to another. New faces—always new faces. My earlier anxieties had turned into acceptance of some sort. I had almost forgotten what it was like to live in a home with a father and mother, brother and sisters, and I very rarely thought about it anymore. In a sense, even Papa and Mama had become distant—out of reach.

"The neighbors across the street are anxious to meet you," Willie said. "They have two girls, just about your age." Impolitely licking some pie crumbs off my fingers, I listened with interest. "They were very excited when I told them that we were going to have a *Rotterdammertje* stay with us, at least for a little while. I won't be surprised to see them over here before the day is out."

"That's great!" Oom Twan retorted, glancing at his watch. "Here you were worried about not having any friends!" Again, he ruffled my hair. He always did. I didn't like it because it made my bow crooked.

"I'd better get going or Mien won't be talking to me for the rest of the week," he said. Willie chuckled.

Oom Twan put out his cigarette and rose from his chair. He shook Willie's hand. "Thank you. Remember to call if there are any problems. You know where to get hold of me."

Willie nodded, "I don't anticipate any. She looks just like a *Rotterdammertje*." He winked at me.

"Fortunately, she does," Oom Twan replied. "Do I get a *moel* before I go?" Oom Twan often talked dialect, which nobody understood, except the people who were born and reared in the province of Limburg. Mama used to speak it whenever she got together with her relatives and, as a result, we were able to understand most of it. I got on my toes and put my arms around his neck.

Then my eyes followed him as he hurriedly walked out of the room, never looking back. The door bell rang, he was gone, and I was left alone again with my "new uncle"—one of the many I had acquired over the last couple of years.

There was an uneasy silence. Oom Willie was the first one to speak. "Everything is going to be just fine," he said, leaning across the table, softly patting my arm.

There was another pause, as if he had run out of things to say. I don't think I'd ever felt so awkward. He looked at his watch. "The boys should be home soon," he muttered, and he began talking about his brothers, whom he affectionately called "the boys." "Wim is married. He lives in Posterholt. The other three, Frits, Hans and Joop, are all still living at home. Joop is the youngest."

"Where is Posterholt?" I asked, feeling the need to say something.

"About four kilometers south of here. Wim owns a bakery. We usually go out there on Fridays to pick up enough bread to last us all week. Good bread, I mean. He bakes it especially for us. My stomach doesn't tolerate that *ersatz* bread too well." He shuddered thinking of it.

From what I had learned thus far, I had a sneaking suspicion that there were no women around. "We also have a housekeeper," he continued.

"He has read my mind," I thought, listening intently, my elbows resting on the table, my head cupped in my hands. "Her name is Lenie. I'm sure the two of you will be getting along just fine."

"Where is she?" I asked.

"She went home for the weekend. She always does. During the week, she stays overnight. You and she will be sharing a bedroom. I hope you don't mind?"

I shook my head between my hands, as scenes of Oom Frans's barge and its dirty bed flashed in front of my eyes.

Just as I began to feel a little more comfortable, the whole house, or so it seemed, suddenly became filled with voices as Oom Willie's brothers barged into the room.

"Who do we have here? Let me guess. You're our *Rotterdammertje*," one of them said.

"That's right," Oom Willie said. They had hardly allowed him the time to introduce me. Stiffly I shook their hands.

Then, just as quickly as they had come in, they disappeared into the kitchen. "What's there to eat?" one of them yelled.

Oom Willie shook his head, smilingly. "There's lots of *vlaai* left in the cupboard," he called back.

Soon afterward, everybody was seated around the dining room table, eating, drinking and talking soccer. Joop, the youngest, looked a lot like Oom Willie, except for his hair. It was a lot redder. He had more freckles, too. But he had the same smile. The other two were very blond. All three of them were quite tall. Their presence made me feel uncomfortable. Oom Willie seemed to notice. "Why don't I take you to meet our father?" he said. Quickly, I got up and followed him through the kitchen into a long corridor. He knocked on one of the doors.

"Come in."

211

The voice didn't sound particularly friendly. At a table, cluttered with dishes and junk, sat an old man with an expressionless face. His bushy mustache held small particles of food. It was hard to tell how long they had been there. His brown threadbare suit was stained, and the pants showed the bulges of his knees. I got a distinct feeling that he never wore anything else, maybe even slept in it. The room looked very messy. There was junk all over. His expression never changed when I shook his hand. I didn't know whether he was happy or sad to see me. "I'm glad I won't have much to do with you," I thought, trying to push away the depressing thoughts that were beginning to surface.

After dinner the neighbor girls came over to meet me, just as Oom Willie had predicted. Their names were Anneke and Tineke Van Zuilen. They seemed very nice, and they looked very pretty, too, in their stiffly starched Sunday dresses and with their hair all done in rigid ringlets. Tante Lieske had tried to do my hair that way, but it never lasted no matter how much sugar she put in the water. My hair was just too straight for any kind of curl. The girls didn't stay very long, but promised to be back the next day.

That night I slept alone upstairs in Lenie's room. There was only one bed, and I assumed that it wasn't just the room that I would be sharing with her. In the fading evening light, I noticed how the flowered, badly water-stained wallpaper was coming loose in the corners. The gray painted floor was worn and was beginning to reveal some of the rust-colored undercoat. The paint on the window frame was peeling and the ceiling had large areas where the plaster was cracked and about ready to fall down. The house was definitely in need of repair. With my eyes resting on the yellow-stained sink and the splattered wallpaper above it, I thought of my pretty room on *De Zwaan,* with its bright curtains and the thick blue carpet that had felt so warm under my feet when I had gotten up in the morning. I quickly brushed at an itching tear that ran across the bridge of my nose and onto my pillow.

Before I knew it, I awoke to another beautiful day. At first I had trouble remembering where I was, but it soon all came back to me ... Vlodrop ... Oom Willie ... Pap. I glanced at the alarm clock on the night stand. Almost nine o'clock! I jumped out of bed. I couldn't believe I had slept this late. When I looked out of the window on the narrow cobblestone street below and the square to the right, it looked almost as peaceful as the day before. The narrow row houses which framed the square lay tucked away in the coolness of the shade of huge, age-old oak trees. A couple of women were sweeping their sidewalks. The rhythmic strokes of their large straw brooms seemed to be the only distraction.

It was going to be another hot day, I could tell, and suddenly I was eager to go outside. I pulled my white dress with the red pin dots out of the shopping bag and held it up in front of me. It was wrinkled. I reconsidered. I shrugged my shoulders. So what! Everything else was probably wrinkled, too. Maybe I should unpack? No, I would do it later. There wasn't all that much anyway. I walked over to the sink. The tap turned hard, but when the water finally came, it felt good against my skin. I used the thin towel which hung from a hook next to the sink to dry myself and got dressed. For a while I struggled, trying to put the bow in my hair. I hated to have to do it myself. It always looked crooked. I quickly made the bed and went down stairs.

A young woman turned around the moment I entered the kitchen. Wiping her hands on her calico apron, she reached out her hand.

"I am Lenie, and you must be Manda," she said, smiling broadly.

I nodded, shaking her slender hand, which still felt slightly damp. I wondered how much she already knew about me.

She was very pretty. I especially noticed her hair. It was a beautiful auburn color with large waves that fell halfway down her back.

She pulled one of the chairs away from the table. "Sit down and have some breakfast," she said, putting a large brown egg in the egg cup next to my plate. Then she pointed at the small basket filled with large slices of brown bread. "Try some of that. It's delicious. Willie's brother bakes it especially for us."

"I know. He told me."

"He did, did he?" she chuckled.

Momentarily she returned to her dishes, while I helped myself to the bread. I took a large bite. Lenie was right. It tasted very good, especially with the apple butter. I had gotten so used to the *ersatz*, I quite honestly didn't remember what "real" bread tasted like.

"Where is Oom Willie?" I asked.

"Puttering around in his garden," she replied, carefully placing some of the clean dishes in the cupboard above the sink, "and the boys have all gone to work," she added. Then she turned around and took the chair across from me. Her arms folded on the table, she asked, "Did you sleep well?"

I nodded.

"Willie wanted you to sleep in. He thought you might be tired from the trip and all."

"I'm all right."

She pointed at the egg, still untouched in the small cup. "Don't you want your egg?"

"Yes, but I'm not very hungry."

"I'm sure you'll do better tomorrow," and she threw me a slight wink. "Did Willie tell you that you and I'll be sharing a bed?"

I nodded, "He did."

Willie must have told you everything," she laughed.

I didn't want to tell her that he had only mentioned the room—not the bed.

Suddenly, her dark brown eyes became serious. "Do you kick a lot?"

214

I could feel my heart begin to beat faster. "I don't know!" I lied. Everybody who had ever slept with me had complained about my kicking. My uneasiness must have shown, as she tried to wave away my concern.

"Don't fret about it. If it gets too bad, I'll put you out on the floor." The laugh that followed sounded so clear—almost like the little doorbell. I managed a sheepish grin.

Lenie got up and brushed the front of her apron. "I'd better get busy or Willie will fire me!" She began clearing away some of the remaining dishes, while I finished the last of my bread. As I glanced around the kitchen, my eyes fell on the brown woolen curtain that seemed to divide the kitchen. It was similar to the ones in the dining room. For some reason it had captured my curiosity, maybe because it reminded me of *Het Vooronder*. "What's behind that curtain?" I asked.

"The bathroom," Lenie retorted casually.

"The bathroom?"

"That's right." I must have sounded quite surprised; so in order to prove it, she suddenly dropped what she was doing, walked over to the curtain, and pulled it aside, unveiling a huge galvanized tub. "You see?"

"Does everyone take their bath in there?"

"Of course!" Again she sounded her clear laugh. "This isn't a fancy house, you know."

I felt my face turn red and I wished I had never said it. Lenie had returned to her chores. "This kitchen is a busy place on Friday and Saturday nights," she chuckled. "That's why Willie takes his bath on Friday afternoon." Standing with her back toward me, she motioned her thumb across her shoulder. "He usually fills the tub for himself. But I'll bet you he'll have you do it from now on." She was obviously referring to Pap, and I was beginning to get the impression that Pap wasn't very well liked.

I yearned for *De Zwaan*. Everything here was so different—gloomy almost. On *De Zwaan*, everybody had liked everybody else. There had always been so much laughter and fun.

A sound came from the hall. "There's Willie now!" Lenie said, putting an abrupt end to my depressing thoughts. Moments later, Oom Willie appeared in the kitchen doorway. "Good morning, young lady!" His warm eyes smiled at me. "Did you sleep well?"

I nodded.

"Did Lenie give you your breakfast?"

"She didn't eat her egg," Lenie broke in before I had a chance to answer.

Again I heard myself apologizing for not being hungry. Oom Willie ran a hand through his hair. "Don't worry about it. Let's go. I'll show you my garden." Carefully he backed out of the kitchen, and I admired the skill with which he maneuvered his chair. Although I didn't care much about gardens, I was thankful for the opportunity to get out of the house. I jumped off my chair and followed him down the red-tiled hallway to the patio. When we passed the closed door of Pap's' room, I tried to sharpen my hearing, but there wasn't a sound. I couldn't help wondering what he was doing all day in that room. I had never met such a strange person.

The patio was piled up with junk, and most of the yard was overgrown with weeds, but Oom Willie seemed completely oblivious to it all as he pointed at a small section of neatly planted rows of green.

"That's my vegetable garden," he gloated.

We never had grown our own vegetables. Mama had always bought them from a man who came to the door and I couldn't tell one green from another.

Oom Willie looked at me. "Do you like it?"

I nodded politely, but he must have sensed my ignorance, because in very plain terms he explained the various vegetables to me, when he had planted them, and how soon we would be able to eat them. A few times he used an odd-looking short-handled rake to remove a few stub-

216

born weeds from the otherwise meticulously kept garden. All the time I tried to listen with at least some interest.

Suddenly, he turned his chair around. "Let me show you something else." We went to the edge of the yard where Oom Willie opened a small gate. It squeaked badly and I could feel ripples run down my spine. I noticed that a couple of slats were missing. Like everything else, it, too, needed fixing.

Oom Willie rolled his chair halfway across the alley which ran between the backyards of the houses on our street and those on the street behind us. "Let me show you a shortcut," he said, wheeling his chair slightly further into the alley. "Right next door is a courtyard." He pointed his chalky white hand to the left. "Cross that, and you'll get right back to the square." He followed my glance to make sure I understood. "The other way leads straight to the school." I could feel my excitement soar the moment he mentioned the word "school." "It's vacation time, right now," he emphasized.

"When does school start?"

"In about three weeks, I believe. You have to ask Anneke or Tineke. They'll be able to tell you better than I." He moved his chair back into the yard and closed the gate.

As we strolled back to the house, my mind was filled with happy thoughts about school, and suddenly the place didn't look quite as somber.

I gulped down my milk and jumped up from the table, leaving half of my breakfast untouched. "Am I excused?"

Oom Willie, who had been quietly watching me from across the table, shook his head and laughed. "I've never seen anyone so happy to go to school. I sure never was."

"Me neither," Lenie joined in wryly, as she clattered the dishes in the sink.

Oom Willie looked at his watch. "You're much too early!"

"I promised Anneke and Tineke that I'd be at their house early. Just the first day? Please?"

"All right, go ahead."

"Thank you. Bye, Lenie."

"Bye. Have a good day."

I could hear their laughter as I ran across the cafe floor and out the door.

After school, Oom Willie was usually waiting for me with a large piece of *vlaai* and a glass of milk, and this particular afternoon was no exception.

"How was school?" he inquired, while I attacked the pastry—boysenberry, my favorite.

"Good," I mumbled, with my mouth full.

Oom Willie laughed. "Don't eat so fast. You'll choke."

When I had washed down the final crumb with my milk, I quickly got up. I wanted to change my clothes and go outside.

"Don't go yet. I want to talk to you for a minute." I slowly sat down again.

"Is it bad?" I asked.

Oom Willie smiled, slowly shaking his head. "No, not really. Pap told me he had seen you in church last Sunday with Anneke and Tineke van Zuilen. He was very pleased."

I sensed something was up.

"He wants you to go more often."

"More often? Why?"

"He feels that if people see you in church more often, they'll become less suspicious."

"When I lived on *De Zwaan,* I only went on Sunday mornings and nobody ever asked any questions," I ventured to protest.

218

"I know, but Pap is an old man. He is afraid that people might find out that you're not a real *Rotterdammertje*."

I could feel myself getting angry. "Pap, what business is it of his anyway?" I thought. I had only seen him a few times. He hardly ever spoke a word to me.

Afraid for the answer, I asked, "How often does he want me to go?"

Oom Willie rubbed his hands, nervously. "Before school, and on Sunday afternoons."

"Anneke and Tineke never have to go in the mornings," I opposed in one last effort.

Oom Willie acted as if he hadn't heard. "I'll tell Lenie to get you up at a quarter after six. That's plenty early. I'll have breakfast with you when you get back."

I slowly got up. "Can I go now?"

Oom Willie nodded.

Swallowing hard, I ran upstairs to change my clothes. I wanted to go across the street and talk to Mevrouw van Zuilen, but I couldn't. I couldn't tell anyone. After all, no one was to know why I had to act more like a Catholic than a Catholic.

Suddenly my world became very small. I felt very lonesome, just like that time in Oosterhout. That evening, I lay awake for the longest time and for the first time, the noise of the drunks in the cafe below bothered me. I wanted to go home. I just wanted to go home.

The youngest brother of the lady who was caring for Rosie had entered the priesthood. Now he was ready to serve his first Holy Mass. As was customary, the whole town would receive him in grand style. For the past couple of weeks, some of the leading townspeople had been planning the procession. Most of the women and children had been working feverishly on hundreds of light blue and white crepe paper flowers that would be used to decorate the

219

church and the carriage in which the new priest would ride. Both Rosie and I would be taking part in the procession. I was excited and scared at the same time. The church, with its deep red carpet and many flowers, had looked just beautiful the night before when we had gone for our final rehearsal.

I grinned at myself in the mirror as I hurriedly tried to untangle the fraying strips of cotton—the remains of an old bed sheet. "You're going to look beautiful," Mevrouw van Zuilen had predicted, as I had watched her, with some uncertainty, wet my hair with plenty of sugar water, winding each small strand of hair skillfully around the cotton strips.

I smelled coffee. Oom Willie must be up already. My last curl—finally. I gently shook my head. I shook it again, this time a little harder. The curls didn't move. I carefully touched them. They felt like rock. Too much sugar. Mevrouw van Zuilen's words echoed through my mind. "You're going to look beautiful."

"You look stupid," I thought to myself, feeling slightly disillusioned. Quickly, however, I decided to put all negative thoughts aside. Mevrouw van Zuilen would know what to do with it. Anneke and Tineke's hair always looked nice. I glanced at the white dress which lay carefully draped across the chair. It was so pretty. I gently touched it. It felt soft and new. Mevrouw van Zuilen had sewn it for me. She had also made the headpiece—a circle of small white daisies. I picked it up and laid it on top of my stiff curls. Yes, I was going to look beautiful, just as Mevrouw van Zuilen had promised.

I quickly washed my face and started to get dressed. Oom Willie had bought me a pair of new white knee socks. They felt nice and tight around my legs—not like the old woolen ones. Those had been washed so many times, I had to put a rubber band around them to make them stay up. Carefully, I pulled the dress over my head and smoothed it down. Oom Willie would have to help me with the buttons in the back. I looked at myself in the mirror and twirled around. I had not looked this pretty in years. I wished I had a tall mirror so I could really have a good look at myself. When I picked my old shoes off the floor, I felt a pang of disappointment. Oom Willie had polished them as well as he could to cover the scuff marks, but they still looked ugly. Well, I was not going to let them spoil my day. I picked up the headpiece and ran downstairs.

Oom Willie looked up when I walked in. As usual, on Sunday, the others were still sleeping. "Let me have a look at you. How pretty! You're going to be the most beautiful girl in the procession." He made me feel embarrassed.

"I don't think so. Tineke and Anneke are much prettier than I."

He shook his head and grimaced, "I don't think so."

I stooped beside his chair. "Could you please do my buttons?"

"Sure." Gently he fastened the tiny buttons. "Now sit down and have some breakfast." He pushed the bread basket toward me.

I turned up my nose. "I'm not very hungry."

"You have to eat something. It's going to be a while before your next meal." I took a slice of bread and spread some butter on it. "Don't get it on your dress."

"I won't."

He watched me silently as I washed down the bread with the milk he had poured for me. My mouth still full, I got up. "I'd better go. Mevrouw van Zuilen has to brush my hair yet. We have to be at the church at nine. What time is it, anyway?" I asked.

He glanced at his watch. "Almost eight. You have plenty of time."

I headed for the dining room. When I reached the door, I hesitated and turned around. "I wish you could come."

"Me too." His voice shook.

I ran toward him and put my arms around him. "I love Oom Willie a lot," I thought as I hurried out the door.

When we reached the church, the lineup had already started. First were two priests dressed in festive-colored garments. Next came the altar boys, one of whom was carrying a huge cross. Then came the carriage drawn by two shiny brown horses decked out with white and blue crepe paper flowers, and finally, the children.

Rosie stood beside me. She looked very pretty. Her dress had a large bow in the back. She looked at my shoes and grinned. "Yours aren't any better," I whispered. A lady handed each of us a few long-stemmed lilies. I looked at Rosie from the corner of my eye. Did she feel as out-of-place as I? After all, neither one of us had ever walked in a procession before. Jews didn't do things like that.

At last the long train of people began to set itself slowly in motion. I wished Papa and Mama could have watched us. Papa's nostrils, undoubtedly, would have quivered.

At the edge of town, the apples in the orchards were ripening quickly. One of those small orchards belonged to Oom Willie. During supper one night, the question was raised concerning who would pick the apples.

Previously, the boys had done it, but this year they didn't show much enthusiasm. "I think we should just leave them," Frits said, his eyes focused on his plate.

Joop agreed. "He's right, Willie. It's too dangerous out there. God knows, until now this town has been lucky. All around us they have been picking up guys whenever the mood strikes them."

Willie wiped his mouth and put his napkin down. "You're absolutely right. I wouldn't want you to take any unnecessary risks. Still, I would like to have some to put in the cellar before winter. I'll find a way." Then he added, "I plan to store some potatoes and carrots as well. After all, nobody really knows how much longer this war is going to last."

When I looked up from my plate, I noticed three pair of eyes staring at me. Seeing the sudden look of misgiving on my face, Lenie started her hearty laugh. Willie knew immediately what the boys were up to. He slowly turned his head toward me. Our eyes met briefly. Then he looked back at his brothers. Leaning back in his chair, his fingers resting on the edge of the table, he shook his head. "I will not let her climb those trees, if that's what you're thinking."

"She won't have to!" It sounded like a chorus.

"There are enough apples on the lower branches to fill two cellars," Hans said, slowly stirring his coffee.

"She can use a crate to stand on if she has to," Joop suggested. I looked from one to the other. I had never picked apples in my life, but there was no sense in protesting.

Oom Willie put his hand gently on mine. "What do you say? Do you think you could do it?"

I nodded. "I guess so."

"Good!" Hans said. As far as he was concerned, the matter was settled. He moved his chair back, ready to leave the table.

"Wait a moment," Oom Willie said, motioning him to stay. "How is she getting them home?" Suddenly, one could have cut the silence with a knife. Obviously, it was something they hadn't thought about. I felt a glimmer of hope. Maybe there wasn't a way to get them home! Maybe we would have to leave them, just as Joop had suggested.

But a plan was already taking shape in Joop's head. I could tell by the look on his face. "How about a goat cart?" he blurted.

They all started laughing, except Oom Willie. First, I thought he was joking, but I quickly realized that he was serious about his plan.

"A goat cart!" I cried. "I hate goats!"

"They don't hurt you!" Fritz commented.

"Yes, they do! They box."

223

Again, they burst out laughing, including Oom Willie this time.

"They box, eh?" Hans teased. "When this one does, call me. I'd like to watch it!"

I didn't think it was very funny. Nevertheless, Joop's idea was accepted, and he was appointed to build the cart. They all knew someone who would loan them a goat for a week or so.

"You'll need a pair of wooden shoes," Oom Willie prompted.

"No problem. We'll get her a pair," Fritz answered, and the subject was closed.

All this time, Lenie had sat quietly, watching me from across the table. She hadn't joined in their laughter. Occasionally, she had smiled, but there was no amusement in it. She knew the teasing had gotten to me. She began gathering some of the empty plates.

"Why don't you help me with the dishes?" she said, as she got up from her chair. Grateful for an excuse to leave the table, I followed her into the kitchen. It was sometime before the laughter in the other room finally died down.

Draped in a blue and white apron several sizes too big and carrying a bucket and a brush, I stood quietly in front of Pap's room. How I'd dreaded this moment. Reluctantly, I knocked at the door. I thought what I heard was a mumble, or something, but I wasn't quite sure. I slowly turned the door knob and walked into the room.

Surrounded by dirty dishes and stained coffee cups, the old man was sitting at the table, a newspaper spread out in front of him. He looked up. His glasses had slipped halfway down his nose. With a slight nod, he acknowledged my presence, but his face never changed expression. Then he turned back to the paper.

My eyes moved across the room. "The same mess as always," I thought. Dirty pots and pans everywhere were staring me. The one clean thing I noticed was his window and that was only because Lenie washed it once a week.

I began gathering the dishes and the silverware. After I finished washing them, I put them away and began focusing my attention on the small hot plate. The baked-on grease was so thick, I could hardly get it off. Some of it probably never would come off.

I turned up my nose as I glanced at the floor around me. A mischievous voice inside me tried to persuade me to forget it, but I knew I couldn't do that, so I went down on my hands and knees. Dipping the brush in the bucket, I began scrubbing the grimy planks. I heard Pap move his chair back. Automatically, I looked up. He had turned himself halfway around, facing me. Stunned, I watched as he pressed his index finger against one side of his nose and blew it in the direction of the floor. I gagged. Something terrible happened to my stomach. I swallowed hard to keep down the juices that had gathered in my mouth. When I reached the spot, I took a deep breath, closed my eyes, and vehemently scrubbed the brush across the floor. I could feel the tears pricking my closed eyelids. I was almost finished. Just a little more. Then I quickly left the room without a word.

Lenie had already left for the weekend, so I went into the kitchen to prepare Oom Willie's bath. It took about eight buckets of water to fill it to where he liked it. I could hear him talking to someone in the dining room. I didn't feel like going in.

"Your bath is ready!" I hollered.

"Thank you, Manda," came the answer from the other room. Oom Willie always sounded so nice.

I ran upstairs and fell across the bed. Then tears came freely. After a while, I turned around, staring at the cracked ceiling. I wondered what it would be like to be back home again. Would I ever get used to my old name again? Strangely, de Boer had become very much a part of me.

Then, in my mind's eye, I saw *de Zwaan* again. She was so beautiful. She had lifted her anchor and begun slowly drifting away—farther and farther, until she finally disappeared for good behind the horizon.

Intently I watched Oom Willie as he painstakingly tried to divide the small piece of meat into equal portions. Our meals had gradually become less fancy, and meat, no matter how small a piece, was a luxury to be enjoyed only on Sundays. Still, we had many reasons to be grateful. We had the fresh vegetables from Oom Willie's garden, for instance. I had to admit my views regarding Oom Willie's "greens" had changed considerably since that day he had first introduced me to them. And, of course, there was still the "good bread" from Wim, Oom Willie's brother. Seated on the back of Lenie's bicycle, I usually went with her to Posterholt to get a fresh batch.

Dinner had been unusually quiet. The few words that had been spoken were mainly about the war. I shivered. It was cold in the house; probably because it was getting colder outside. The telephone rang. Nobody seemed anxious to answer it. It rang again.

"Wonder who that is," Frits mumbled. He put down his fork and knife and slowly got up. "Hello, Frits Willems. . . . What? How many?"

I watched his face turn pale, his hand reach for his head. "Yes, thank you." He almost dropped the receiver. "Annie, Karel's wife. . . . The S.A.—they're on their way," he stammered. "She says at least three trucks are coming this way. They're picking up guys everywhere." With a jerk of his head, he said, "Let's go!"

The others jumped to their feet and followed him into the kitchen. Moments later, we heard the door to the patio slam shut. Evidently, one of them had tried to escape via the roof because we suddenly saw someone fly by the window. It was Hans. He must have hurt himself because we could see him limping away.

Oom Willie's face was ashen. He hated the S.A. in their mustard-colored uniforms. They couldn't be that far away. Annie and Karel—good friends of the boys—were living only a few kilometers outside of town.

"Take the plates to the kitchen—quickly. Put them under the sink in the cupboards any place, just so they won't see them!" Oom Willie's voice was agitated. He helped gather some of the dishes and silverware that were within his reach and handed them to me. His hands were shaking terribly. It was the first time I had seen Oom Willie frustrated with his disability.

I thought of Putten. Could they possibly do the same to Vlodrop? One day the S.S. had rolled into town taking captive every man and boy over sixteen. Those who resisted were shot immediately. The rest were sent to labor camps. Very few returned. Among those who didn't were the father and son of the family with whom we'd stayed during our last vacation in 1940. And what about Oom Willie? What would they do to him?

"Are you done with the dishes?" Willie called impatiently from the dining room. I ran back into the room. "Everything has been put away," I said.

"Go outside and let me know when you see them coming!" he ordered.

Seated on the sidewalk, with my back against the cafe wall, I looked up at the sky. Low, gray clouds were moving rapidly. The street and the square were deserted. I had finally come to appreciate my blonde hair that allowed me to pass for a non-Jew.

There they were! I'd recognize that sound anywhere. It was ominous, and it reminded me of that terrible winter night in Oldenzaal.

Moments later, I saw the first truck come down the street, closely followed by a second one. They stopped. Soldiers jumped off and broke into some of the houses.

They banged their rifles against the doors of others. I ran inside. "They're here! They're here," I cried.

Oom Willie tensed. I noticed the swollen veins in his hands as he grabbed the side of his wheel chair. Then I heard him pray softly, "Dear God, help the boys get away."

"Pap! We forgot to tell him!" I shouted.

"I already did. When you were outside."

I had totally forgotten about the old recluse.

One of the trucks rumbled by, but the next one came to a screeching halt. The soldiers burst into the cafe. The little bell over the door jingled wildly, almost angrily. We heard shouts as they ran through another door leading toward the back of the house and up the stairs. Then the dining room door flew open. A large mustard-colored figure planted himself in the doorway, his rifle pointed right at us. A contemptuous smile crossed his lips as he looked at the crippled man in the wheel chair. Cries for help from outside filled the room. I didn't dare look at Oom Willie. Instead, I kept my eyes glued on the rifle, just like that other time, only a few months ago. All the time we could hear them moving over our heads, from one room to the next. Finally they came bolting down the stairs. One of the soldiers walked up to the figure in the doorway. "*Nur einer alte Mann* (Just an old man)," he reported. They couldn't do much with Pap, nor with Oom Willie, for that matter. The figure turned around and, as abruptly as he had appeared, he also disappeared, following the others out the door, slamming it angrily behind him.

I slowly turned my head. Oom Willie revealed his nervousness by rubbing one hand over the other, over and over again. There were tears in his eyes. Closing them for a moment, he sounded a sigh of relief.

"They're desperate, very desperate," he said. I thought I detected a note of satisfaction. He looked at me. He looked tired—older—but a smile appeared in his tear-filled eyes.

Very late that night Oom Willie received a phone call from Wim's wife. The boys were safe, but she wouldn't tell him where they were. They wouldn't return home, at least not for a while.

I wondered what would have happened if Annie hadn't called.

Meanwhile, the war continued to rage. The secret bulletins of "Radio Orange," which were still delivered to Oom Willie regularly, were very encouraging. "It can't last much longer!" he kept saying each time he finished reading them.

Apparently, he wasn't the only one who thought so. Wild rumors began going around that the city of Breda had been liberated, and that the war could end at any time. Disillusioned German soldiers began scrambling for the border to return home. It was September 4, 1944—*Dolle Dinsdag.* But the euphoria was not meant to last. The Germans returned once again with a final burst of energy and a burning desire to win.

I slept very little that night as I listened to the sounds of men and equipment moving into town. By dawn, the town square had been turned into a small fortress. Tanks, trucks and soup kitchens were parked alongside each other with soldiers and officers milling about. By mid-day, most buildings had been taken over, including the school and our cafe. I watched them from my bedroom window, as they carried in mattresses, tables, chairs and desks. I felt somewhat relieved to see that our new houseguests were just members of the *Wehrmacht*—ordinary soldiers—and not the despised *Gruene Polizei.*

Deflated by the sudden turn of events, I went downstairs. I found Oom Willie sitting idly at the table, his eyes fixed on the door leading to the cafe. I sat down beside him. "Did you see all the stuff they're moving in?" I asked.

He shook his head. "I haven't seen it, but I have definitely heard it—all morning long." There was a pause. "They've brought Russians with them, too."

"Russians?" I cried.

229

He nodded, his eyes still on the door. "Prisoners of war. Mostly women."

"How did you find that out?"

"Lenie. Someone told her about it this morning."

"Where are they?"

He shrugged his shoulders. "I don't know."

I had never seen Oom Willie so passive.

"How long do you think they'll stay? In the cafe, I mean."

Again he shrugged his shoulders. "Probably until the end."

"The end?" I blurted.

He turned his head toward me. "Don't worry. The Americans are not very far away. They'll be here soon." I thought I noticed a spark return to his eyes.

Glancing at the door, he pulled a neatly folded piece of paper out of his coat pocket and waved it in front of me. I recognized the bulletin from "Radio Orange."

"Good news," he whispered. Then, without saying any more about it, he quickly stuck it back in his pocket.

Since the boys had left, Pap had made himself a little more accessible. He probably realized that Oom Willie needed his help. This morning he had even helped Lenie and me hitch the goat to the cart. It would be my first trip alone to pick apples, and I was scared to death.

"Don't be afraid," Oom Willie laughed, as he watched me finish my breakfast. "That goat won't go anywhere."

I didn't care if it did or didn't. It still worried me. I stepped into my wooden shoes. "You'd better wear your coat," Oom Willie warned. "It's getting quite chilly."

Wearing my coat over a long blue-striped apron, a kerchief tied around my head, and my new wooden shoes, I at last climbed into the cart. As I slowly rolled out of town toward the orchards, I wondered what I would do if any of my old friends suddenly showed up and saw me like this.

Standing on a crate, I picked apples only from the low-hanging branches. I had been strictly forbidden to climb the trees. A few times I felt tempted, but on second thought, changed my mind. It only took me a couple of hours to fill the cart, leaving just enough room for myself. Looking at the bright red apples, I felt very pleased with myself and my fear for the goat had all but disappeared.

Buoyantly, I stepped on one of the spokes to get into the cart. As the wheel began to turn, the goat got the wrong message. I hadn't *told* her to go yet, but the wheels' turning started her off. Suddenly, there was a loud *craaaack*! My wooden shoe was caught in the turning spoke. "Dumb animal!" I cursed. But she didn't seem to care. She was only too glad to return home.

As we rolled toward town, I examined the shoe a little closer. It was split in half. I was so afraid Oom Willie might be angry, but he wasn't. Actually, he thought it was quite funny. That evening, Pap put a metal strip around the cracked shoe and I was all set to go again. Next time, I was a little wiser.

The shopping bag filled with freshly baked bread swung gently back and forth on the handlebar each time my knee touched it.

Ever since that Sunday when the boys had left home, my chores had increased considerably. One of them was the weekly eight kilometer bicycle ride to Posterholt and back on Lenie's bicycle. It was definitely one of the more pleasurable chores. The next day would be Friday, which meant that I had to clean Pap's room again. I shuddered. I didn't want to think about it. Not now at least. It was such a beautiful fall day. The sky was very clear with only a few clouds drifting by. I liked fall almost as much as I did spring—except that there was some sadness about it. I didn't know exactly why, I just felt that way about it.

In the fields, farmers were busy harvesting their crops. A few looked up and waved at me. "They must remember me from my last trip," I thought. Carefully, I let go of my handlebar to return their greeting, but the bicycle pulled sharply to the right where the shopping bag was hanging. Lenie's bicycle was actually too big for me. Even with the seat lowered as far as it would go, I could hardly reach the pedals and moving sideways across the saddle became quite uncomfortable after a while, so I'd try riding in an upright position. Sometimes, when the wind was at my back, I would pedal very fast, plop myself down on the seat, and with my legs stretched out straight in front of me, my wooden shoes dangling from my feet, I'd coast along until I'd run out of momentum.

All at once I heard the distant sound of a plane. I scanned the sky but didn't see anything. Suddenly, anti-aircraft guns shattered the serenity. I dropped my bicycle and threw myself behind some beanstalks. The shooting was coming from behind me. I could hear the shells whistle over my head only to watch them explode in the sky ahead of me.

My heart raced. I dug myself deeper into the weeds. Slowly, I raised my eyes toward the sky. It was sprinkled with small black puffs caused by the flak.

Then I watched in horror as the sky suddenly opened up and dropped a burning plane to the earth, turning and turning, engulfed in flames, until at last it hit the ground in a cloud of black smoke. Against the clear autumn sky, on the ripples of the wind, four silhouettes appeared. Tied to their wide-open parachutes, they sailed slowly above the trees.

"How beautiful! Thank God, they're alive!" I whispered. I watched until they disappeared from my view. Meanwhile, the shooting had stopped and the little black clouds had blended with the sky. Everything graduaally returned to normal. I slowly got up and brushed myself off. I walked over to my bicycle and rode home as fast as my wooden shoes would allow me. The noise of the shells still rang in my ears.

There was laughter from some of the soldiers when I barged into the cafe and into the living room.

"Oom Willie!" I called.

"We're in the kitchen!" he called back.

Seated with Lenie at the kitchen table, he reached out and grabbed my hands.

"I saw them!" I cried. "I saw the plane get shot down!"

"I'm so glad you're home. We were very worried. We hoped you were still in Posterholt, but when Lenie called they said you had already left."

"There were four parachutes!" I panted, ignoring his words of concern.

Willie had let go of my hands. He nodded. "I've heard. They were Americans. They were trying to take pictures of the German reinforcements."

"Did anyone see them land?" I asked.

Lenie nodded. "They have come down in Germany," she said in a small voice.

I sat down at the table and rested my head on my arms. Suddenly I felt exhausted. For years and years to come, I would remember the stark contrast of the burning plane and the four silhouettes as they peacefully drifted along the sky.

Thursday night was catechism night. After supper, Tineke, Anneke and I would walk to church together. We hated catechism under the direction of the old, absent-minded priest, who, since he was too old to serve Mass, was given the responsibility of the catechism class.

As we read aloud the questions and answers, he paced back and forth between the pews, his hands folded behind his back, his eyes glued to the carpet, quietly mumbling to himself. He never wanted to have anyone sit farther than the fifth row and the three of us made sure we never sat any closer. We hardly paid any attention. The class was extremely boring—especially for me, since I had learned all that stuff already when I was on *De Zwaan.*

One night I learned something very important, something I had not known before. One of the other girls, who occasionally sat with us, told me that if someone entered church service just before the priest carried the missal from one side of the altar to the other for the last time, it would still count as having attended Mass. If you came in afterward, then you were in serious trouble. Since she had been a Catholic much longer than I, I never questioned the validity of her belief. I used my newly acquired knowledge the very next morning.

I had never gotten used to getting up early in the morning to go to church, and now that it had become a lot colder, I really dreaded it. I usually stopped off at the little bakery and sat down on the stoop for a while. The steam escaping through the vents felt warm as my thoughts would drift off to another time, long, long ago and another bakery—beneath *Grootmoeder's* apartment. The smell of freshly baked bread had floated up the stairs and had made us ravenously hungry. I wondered what had happened to her. Then my thoughts returned to the present. I had to get to Mass in time.

I pulled the heavy church door open just far enough to be able to peek inside. Father Verbeek was conducting Mass as usual. I watched him closely. Now he was picking up the huge missal, with its colorful streamers hanging down from between its pages. He was ready to walk toward the other end of the altar. I quickly slipped inside, quietly taking my seat in the last pew underneath the balcony, feeling satisfied that I had fulfilled my spiritual duties and that everything was still all right between God and me.

For many who no longer owned a clandestine radio, the "Radio Orange" bulletin was the only source of news. After Oom Willie had read it, one of the boys would take it and circulate it among a few local members of the underground. It was always to be returned to Oom Willie who immediately destroyed it. Now, with the boys gone, there was no one to pass the bulletins around.

While having breakfast one day, Oom Willie said, "I wonder if you would be able to run a very special errand for me."

I looked at him curiously. "What kind of special errand?"

He reached into his pocket and pulled out the familiar-looking bulletin.

"I need to get this out," he said, holding up the news release.

"Me?" I pointed at myself. I didn't believe he was serious. He nodded. "Don't be afraid. The Germans are less suspicious of a man in a wheel chair and a young girl than they are of anyone else. I guess that's why the underground picked me for this job to begin with," he chuckled. He made it all sound too casual. "You know who gets them, don't you?" he continued.

I nodded. I had become pretty well acquainted with Oom Willie's "illegal" operations, just as I had with Oom Kees's when I was living on *De Zwaan.*

"You can't make any mistakes; you realize that, don't you?"

"I do."

"Remember, you cannot leave it anywhere. As soon as one person has read it, you take it to the next. But you always return it to me. Understand?"

I nodded.

"Good." He pointed to my knee sock. "I think we'll just stick it in there, on the inside, right there, where it's rolled up. No one will ever notice."

That night, sleep didn't come easily. I was going to be a courier. I had met several couriers on *De Zwaan,* but I had never dreamed I would be one myself someday.

"Quit your tossin' and turnin'," Lenie grumbled. "I'll put you out on the floor in a minute. Remember?" I did remember her threat, but it didn't frighten me in the least. The Americans and the English were on their way. I felt bold and defiant.

Finally, the day came for what was to become my weekly run. With the bulletin tucked away in my knee sock, I walked into the cafe where the soldiers were sitting around the tables talking and, really, not doing much of anything.

I had come to the conclusion that I didn't mind them very much. I thought they even liked me. A few days before, one of them, a very young soldier, had shared with me some of the cookies his mother had sent. I could tell that he was very homesick and I felt sorry for him.

As I walked by one of the tables, one of the men suddenly grabbed my arm. He startled me. He was fat and too old to be a soldier. "Don't be afraid, *Liebchen*," he said smilingly, as he pulled me onto his lap.

I watched with terror as his fleshy hand reached for my leg and gently patted it just below the knee—not far from the bulky hem of my knee sock. I swallowed hard. My heart pounded, as my eyes stayed fixed on the man's hand.

"You look just like my granddaughter," he commented. The others at the table laughed, making fun of him, thinking he was an old softy. He ignored them.

"She's blond, just like you," he continued. His hand moved from my leg to my hair, and he softly stroked it. I decided not to wait for his hand to move again, and I quickly jumped off his lap.

"I have to run an errand. I have to hurry!"

The German chuckled. "*Auf Wiedersehen!*" he waved.

"*Auf Wiedersehen*," I replied, running out the door. I sounded a sigh of relief as I began my rounds. I knew all the names and addresses by heart. The first two stops were easy because no one was home. I knocked softly on the kitchen door of the next one.

"Come in!" When I opened the door, I noticed my contact sitting at the kitchen table having a cup of coffee.

Seated across from him was a German soldier. I was bewildered. I had to think of a fast way out.

"How are you, Manda?" the contact asked.

"I'm fine," I lied, my eyes fixed on the soldier. For a moment I wanted to turn around and run, but I quickly regained my composure. "The potatoes you ordered are in the barn," I stammered.

He smiled and got up. He turned to the German. "I'll be right back," he said. Silently we walked toward the barn. Inside, I handed him the bulletin.

"Wonderful news!" he said when he finished reading. He patted my head. "By the way, you don't have to worry about that German. He and I got to talking, and I invited him in for a cup of coffee."

I smiled awkwardly, "I see."

While he walked back into the kitchen, I skipped to my next contact, feeling ten pounds lighter.

I recognized Father Verbeek's bicycle as it stood leaned against the cafe window. The young priest was a frequent visitor, and Oom Willie truly enjoyed his company. Both men looked up as I entered the dining room.

"*Dag,* Manda," the priest said. He was a tall thin man wearing metal-rimmed glasses.

"*Dag, Vader,*" I answered, shaking his hand politely.

"Did you have a good time?" Oom Willie inquired.

I nodded. Oom Willie smiled. "Since school has been closed, she spends more time at the van Zuilen's than with us."

I knew he was just teasing, but I couldn't help feeling a bit guilty. The priest noticed and he quickly came to my rescue. "They're very nice girls and a wonderful family."

Oom Willie agreed.

Then Father Verbeek turned to me. "We were just talking about you."

I looked from one to the other and could feel my heart begin to beat more rapidly. I had been late for church a couple of mornings. Had he come to tell Oom Willie?

"Don't look so worried," the priest laughed. "I have come to tell Willie all about our nightly prayer services which we will be starting next Monday at the little chapel behind the church."

I felt relieved. He probably wanted me to go to the meetings. His elbows resting on the arms of his chair, and his hands folded as if in prayer, the priest seemed to think for a moment before he continued.

"The war will soon be over. There's a lot of fighting going on, especially in this area. Many courageous men have come from far away to free us, and many will lose their lives doing it. We want to ask the Lord to protect them and us, and to pray for a quick end to the battle." He paused for a moment. Then abruptly, "I came to ask Willie if he'd agree to have you lead us in prayer."

Me? My heart leaped in my chest. I looked at Oom Willie for help. There had to be a way to get out of this invitation, but all I saw on Oom Willie was a proud smile.

"But I'm afraid! I don't know how!" I blurted.

"You don't have to be afraid," the priest said. "All we do is pray the rosary together. I'll show you exactly how." He tried to sound comforting. I guessed the matter was settled; to protest would be a waste of time.

Shortly after, he got up and pushed his chair back to the table to end his visit. "Stop by the parsonage tomorrow and we'll talk about it."

I was right, the matter was settled. I wondered who I had to thank for this assignment. The underground? Probably.

Still in a state of shock, I felt my hand resting between those of the priest's. "Thank you, Manda. I know you'll do just fine."

Oom Willie's smile never left his face. He was obviously proud of the "honor" bestowed upon me.

The following Saturday, carrying a bucket of water in one hand and a couple of rags in the other, I slowly started down the steep hill behind the church. Although Father Verbeek had not mentioned it at the time of his visit, besides leading the congregation in prayer, I was also responsible for cleaning the chapel once a week.

When I reached the bottom of the hill, my feet and socks were soaking wet and only half of the water was left in the bucket. There stood the tiny chapel at the crossing of two narrow, deeply rutted country roads, embraced by lofty, old willow trees. At that moment, even though winter was upon us, it seemed to be the most peaceful spot on earth. A light breeze gently swayed the branches back and forth.

I ran my hand across the small lacquered altar. It was covered with a thick layer of dust. The chapel obviously hadn't been cleaned in a long, long time. I picked up the statue of St. Joseph. I noticed one of his arms was missing and his face looked weather-beaten. I put the statue back in place and began wetting one of the rags. I worked until I satisfied myself that the chapel was clean, except for some stubborn scratches on the low, wooden bench in front of the altar. Overall, it looked pretty good. It would look even better with the flowers. I turned and began to climb the hill to the parsonage.

Somewhat reluctantly, I pressed the doorbell. I could hear the shuffle of footsteps and I visualized someone old, wearing huge slippers. Juffrouw Vermolen, the house-keeper, opened the door. She was a heavy-set woman with pleasant features. She was wearing a black dress and a crisp white apron.

When she saw me, she smiled broadly. *"Dag,* Manda! Father told me I could expect you. Please come in."

When I stepped into the vestibule, I became aware of the strange smell. I had noticed it also just the other day when Father Verbeek had received me in his office to explain to me all about the nightly prayers. It was an old smell, probably from the wood. Suddenly I remembered—Tante Annie's apartment! It had smelled exactly the same.

"Let me show you the garden." I was brought back to reality by Juffrouw Vermolen's voice. I followed her down the long, carpeted hall into the kitchen. "She walks like a duck," I thought, trying not to laugh. She opened the door to the back yard.

"So many flowers!" I cried.

She threw her head back and laughed. "Aren't they beautiful?"

I nodded. "Very beautiful!"

"Pick whatever you need." For a moment, I didn't even know where to begin. There were dahlias and mums of every imaginable color. I began to pick a few here and a few there. Soon I had my arms full. It reminded me of *De Zwaan* when I had picked daisies and yellow buttercups for Tante Lieske.

I went back into the kitchen. Juffrouw Vermolen looked up. "Do you think you have enough?"

I nodded. "I'm sure."

"You can always come back for more," she said as she took the flowers from me and began wrapping them in newspaper. "They need fresh water," she explained.

"I know."

"Good! They won't last, otherwise." She handed the neatly wrapped flowers back to me.

"Thank you!"

"You're welcome. I'll have to walk down to the chapel to see for myself how well you did," she said. I smiled shyly.

"I'll see you next Saturday. Oh, no, I almost forgot," she corrected herself. "I'll see you next Monday and Sunday, of course, at services." Why did she have to remind me? Moments later, the heavy oak door closed softly behind me.

Back at the chapel, I filled the vases and placed them strategically on the altar. The larger vase would easily cover the spot where some of the paint was chipped off. One of the other ones would go right beside the statue of St. Joseph to hide its broken arm. I stepped back for a final look. I was pleased.

Putting the dirty, wet rags in the bucket, I started back home. I drew a deep breath. I was tired. Monday would be the first night that I would lead the prayer. Silently, I wished Monday would never come. Maybe the war would be over by then. Who knew?

Monday, however, came very quickly. Standing in front of the chapel, dressed in my Sunday best, I frantically watched the crowd grow larger and larger. It was a beautiful fall evening as twilight streaked the sky. Father Verbeek stood next to me. Occasionally he would put a hand on my shoulder—to assure me, I guess.

"It looks very nice—the chapel, I mean." His voice sounded gentle.

"Thank you, Father." I had to admit it did look pretty, even though some of the flowers had already started to wilt.

Not very far back, stood Mevrouw van Zuilen. Anneke and Tineke were with her. They waved at me, giggling. I shot them a dirty look. I wished they were standing up front instead of me. I watched Mevrouw van Zuilen talk to them, and quickly their faces became serious.

The priest turned toward the crowd and raised his hand. Everyone was silent, and only the sounds of the birds and the whispering wind could be heard. There was a long pause. I could feel the eyes of the crowd pierce my back. I trembled, as the light blue beads of my rosary stuck to my sweaty palms. "Go ahead! You may start now," the voice next to me whispered.

And I heard my shaky voice begin to pray, "Our Father, who is in Heaven. . . ."

Lately, as often as two to three times a week, we were awakened by the wailing of the sirens. This was one of those nights. I groped for Lenie's hand. I felt her fingers tighten around mine so I knew she was awake. Lying motionless, side by side, we listened to the swelling sound of the approaching airplanes—swarms of them on their bombing missions to Germany. All the time, the searchlights wildly criss-crossed the sky, making our faces appear ghost-like as they lit up the room.

"Don't you think we should go to the cellar?" I whispered.

"Let's wait a bit longer," Lenie replied almost inaudibly. "It sounds as if they're flying pretty high tonight." Lenie had developed a sensitive ear for altitude. When they flew "high," it usually meant they were going deep into Germany, but when they flew "low," their targets, as a rule, were closer by, sometimes right across the border. This time, Lenie's theory proved wrong. Suddenly the shrill sound of a plane breaking away startled us. The next thing I knew, I was in the cellar. Pap and our neighbors were there already. They had helped carry Oom Willie down. The cellar smelled musty. The walls were dripping wet. They shook with each explosion. The dim light flickered. Softly I prayed until the monotonous sound of the siren finally told us we were free to come out.

The airplanes were gone, leaving a gaping hole across the square, where only hours ago, the shoe repairman and his wife had lived—now both dead. In one of the farmhouses near the little chapel, a young boy from our school was killed. I went to see him. It wasn't quite as scary as that time in Oosterhout. I was learning quickly.

Early one morning, I awoke to the sound of someone moaning, then a piercing cry. I jumped out of bed and ran toward the window. Horror stricken, I watched as a small, wretched caravan of Russian prisoners moved slowly through our street toward town under the grey, wintry sky.

Many of the women, their feet wrapped in rags, too weak to go on, clung to each other for support. Their faces under the large scarves were barely visible. The cry came from one of the men. Like a snake, he moved across the icy cobblestones, his hands and feet wrapped. Chained to the leg of one of the other prisoners, he tried to push himself slowly ahead, using his knees and his elbows. Irritated with the slow pace, the German guard, from time to time, would kick the defenseless body, and a cry would escape from the man's mouth.

I slowly turned away from the window and went back to bed tears stinging my eyes. I shivered. It was very cold in the house. We were running dangerously low on coal and on food. In fact, we were running low on just about everything, even electricity. A couple of times a week, I'd pedal the bicycle in the living room to generate some badly needed power, but it was hardly enough.

I shivered again and crawled deeper under the blankets. It seemed strange to have the whole bed to myself. Lenie had gotten married a month ago, and the only ones left in the house were Oom Willie, Pap and me. I missed Lenie.

I wasn't able to sleep any more that morning. The sound of the man's cries had grown weaker and weaker, but I could still hear it ringing in my ears. I stared at the cracked ceiling. I wondered what would happen to Oom Willie when I left. Would Pap take care of him? He seemed quite a bit nicer lately. I didn't even have to go to church in the morning any longer. It was too cold. No one would be in church anyway. My trips to Posterholt also had come to a halt. The last time I'd gone, I had been stopped by German patrols on my way home. First, they'd refused to let me go through. Then I started to cry. "How will I be able to get home?" I asked. At last they'd decided to let me go.

We'd eaten most of the apples I had picked, but we still had some potatoes and carrots. Until just a few weeks earlier, we had shared some of the little we had with a few of the Russian women prisoners. Hunched behind the tiny gate at the end of our backyard, I carried a sack filled with sandwiches as I waited for them to come by on their nightly walk down the alley. They knew I was there. As they neared the gate, they slowed down their step as I slipped the bread through the gap where the slats were gone. Stealthily, they took the bread and quickly ate it before they reached the German guard at the other end of the alley.

Many of the towns around us, some less than 20 kilometers away, were already liberated. It was our bad luck to be caught in a small, but strategic corner. Not only did the Ruhr River flow through the town, but just across the German border, factories were still producing weapons for their country's last hurrah—a battle that would go down in history books as the Ruhr Offensive.

In some of the nearby towns, the *Gruene Polizei* drove the people from their homes with only the clothes on their backs. They pushed wheelbarrows and baby carriages filled with potatoes and other edibles they had been able to save. It was a sad mixture of people and cattle that walked aimlessly across the snow-covered roads.

Vlodrop, by and large, had been spared except for the raids by the S.A. The only men left in town were either handicapped or old. The Russian prisoners were too weak to work. As a result, many of the Dutch women and children, myself included, were enlisted to help the Germans prepare for their final battle. We dug trenches in exchange for a bowl of *Nudel Suppe* from the army soup kitchen. In general, life had come to a virtual standstill as we waited and waited through one of the longest, coldest winters in Holland's history.

The bulletins from "Radio Orange" had been stopped for quite some time. Our hope was kept alive by rumors that the English would be coming soon, but when?

On January 24, 1945, the rumors suddenly grew stronger. "The English are near Posterholt," some said. People began leaving town to meet them, carrying only a few of their belongings. I decided I was not going to stay behind. I went to get Rosie, but she didn't want to come.

She was afraid. I felt I had a chance to be free—maybe tomorrow—and for once, I'd be leaving without her.

Pushing Oom Willie's chair, I joined the long stream of people across the icy roads and snow-covered fields toward Posterholt.

"Get down!" someone called. Out of nowhere a plane seemed to drop out of the sky and shear over our heads. Someone helped me lift Oom Willie out of his chair and onto the ground. As we lay on the frozen ground, the plane returned once more, then it disappeared into the thick winter sky. We continued our way to freedom. Late that afternoon, we arrived at the bakery in Posterholt. Together with Oom Willie's brother and his family, we spent the night in the small, musty cellar. No one was able to sleep as the town was shelled all through the night. Sometimes, the whole house would shake from the heavy artillery fire, and I could hear small pieces of cement and rubble hit the floor. Shortly before dawn, the shooting seemed to quiet down. Suddenly, it stopped altogether. Uncertain of what was going on, we decided to wait a while longer.

"Listen!" Wim said. "Do you hear that noise?"

We all tried to listen. It became deadly quiet in the tiny cellar. Outside, the sound became increasingly stronger.

"Tanks!" Oom Willie said.

"I'll bet you're right!" his brother yelled, and he jumped up and ran for the stairs. There was hysterical confusion as we all tried to follow him at once. Someone had thought of Oom Willie and carried him to the living room.

The narrow street alongside the bakery was already lined with people. The bitter cold was forgotten. "The Tommies! . . . the Tommies are here!" someone cried.

This time, it was for real. People were laughing and wiping their tears at the same time. Squeezed between them at the edge of the sidewalk, I looked down the cobblestone street. I felt confused. What was I looking for? Then, as out of nowhere, they appeared—tired, weary soldiers, but smiling nonetheless. People cheered and pulled at their uniforms. Through a blur I watched them as their eyes moved along the crowd. They seemed to me to be looking for someone. I was sure it could only be me—to my childish mind this whole army had come just to rescue me. I wiped my tears. It was January 25, 1945. I was free.

In mid-afternoon, a jeep pulled into the driveway of the bakery. Seated next to the uniformed driver was an officer.

"Tommies," someone in the room commented. "Wonder what they want?"

A moment later, the doorbell rang. Surprised by the unexpected visit, Wim's wife got up to answer. When she returned with the officer right on her heels, she looked straight at me. "He's looking for you. Manda Wijnperle," she said, smiling gently. Just then, I realized that Manda de Boer was gone—she no longer existed. She had left early that morning when the soldiers had marched into the street. "He's come to take you to Sittard to your parents."

I felt a jolt. My eyes searched for those of Oom Willie's.

"I'm not going!" I cried.

The officer, who had entered the room, tried to talk to me, reassure me, but I didn't understand a word he was saying. Again I looked at Oom Willie, vehemently shaking my head. "I'm not going! I don't know him!"

Everyone in the room, including the Englishman, broke into laughter. I didn't think it was very funny at all.

"Will you go if I go along?" one of the girls in her early twenties asked. She was one of Oom Willie's relatives. "I know people in Sittard where I can stay," she added.

Shortly after, I was seated in the back of the jeep. I kept asking myself how they'd known where to find me. Probably someone in the house had called the underground. After all, they always knew where to find each other. But why the English soldiers?

Finally, I stopped trying to make sense of it all, and I thought of Oom Willie. He had cried. I felt so sorry for him.

Then I settled back. I was finally going home—for good.

Scenes from "The Hiding"

Oom Piet and Tante Annie

Kees on his motorbike

Left to right: Harry, Oom Kees, Janneke, and Tonnie

The little synagogue "around the corner" which later served as
our one-room school house

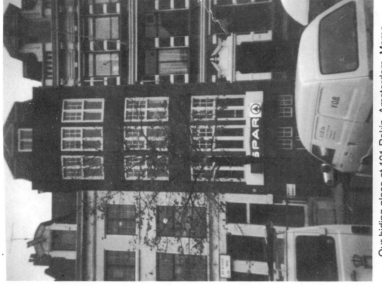

Our hiding place at 101 Rokin, Amsterdam. Mama and Nan were arrested here.

The Zwaans girls, left to right: top—Corrie, Moeke, and Annie; bottom—Tante Lieske with Lida, Therese, Tonnie, and Janneke

Kees

Oom Twan

The little chapel in Vlodrop

Left to right: Anneke, myself, Tineke, and their dog in Vlodrop

Kees and Lieske enjoying afternoon tea on the rear deck of *De Zwaan* with a relative. To the right is the hatch which gave access to *Het Achteronder*.

Chapter 14

The Final Curtain Call

apa and Mama were living in a big house. It was given to them by the city of Sittard, rent-free, if they'd agree to take in fourteen service men of the English Field Security. Among them was Captain Lutzius, the officer who had come to take me home that day. Suddenly, all the pieces seemed to fit. Tommy and Jack, who had tried to get Rosie and me out of the battle zone several weeks earlier, were there also. Their jeep, however, had hit a land mine, leaving Jack deaf and Tommy blind in one eye. Actually, there were fifteen soldiers. Because of his excellent command of English language, the Field Security had asked Nan to join them and to serve as their interpretor.

If Mama's hands had been idle for the last four or so years, she was making up for it now. She daily prepared breakfast, lunch and dinner for her fourteen houseguests, with the assistance of Corrie and some of Corrie's friends.

The first day, when the fourteen servicemen had carried their mess kits into the kitchen, Mama had asked, "What's that?" They'd looked at each other and laughed. "Didn't this woman know anything?"

"I've set the table for you," she remarked, as she flipped over the pancakes.

They'd laughed even louder when they'd entered the dining room and seen the long table set—complete with white tablecloth, china and silverware. Amazing, how quickly they adjusted!

Others were there, too—Leon Blum from New York, who would give me wild jeep rides to school; and, of course, Gordon Guard (Gordie) from Detroit, whom Mama had nursed back to health after he suffered shell shock. He became our "adopted G.I. brother" for the rest of our lives.

The days that followed were truly a whirlwind of delicious white bread, marmalade, thick chunky "ration" chocolate bars, and a new dress made out of a parachute. They were times of laughter, happiness, emotion and tears.

Who, for instance, could forget the tank that didn't quite make it down our narrow street and ended halfway in our living room, while in the room right above it, Nan was trying to recuperate from a shrapnel wound in his leg? (He had received the wound during one of his missions with the Field Security people.)

Or the bitter-sweet escapade of "Hitler's" official visit to the city? The whole town was ready for the reception. Early on the morning of the visit, Nan and one of his friends visited their barber, who did an outstanding make-up job. Nan looked unmistakably like the "resurrected" Hitler. His friend, as Goering, didn't look bad either. At noon, a German staff car (seized earlier by the Americans) arrived at city hall, located at the town square. A large crowd had gathered. Slowly "Hitler" followed by "Goering," climbed the stairs to the balcony where he greeted a cheering crowd.

"Hitler" delivered what was probably his most memorable speech, and the crowd responded in unison, *"Sieg Heil."*

Then there were the nightly trains carrying returning Jews, survivors of Auschwitz, Buchenwald, Bergen Belsen, Treblinka—only a handful compared to the many that had left. Searching for a loved one, a relative, a friend, anyone, they walked through the streets, calling out names.

And there were many reunions. One day, while I was shopping with Mama, she ran into a friend whom she hadn't seen in years. Both women became engrossed in sharing their memories. Bored, I looked at the goings-on around me. I noticed three women at the far end of the street. They came walking slowly toward us. They looked awful—dirty and tired, just like the ones on the trains, I thought. One of them had long black hair. Uncombed, it hung loose around her shoulders. I suddenly felt myself staring at her. It couldn't be! No, it couldn't be! I seized Mama's arm. "Tante Sophie, Mama, look!"

For a moment, Mama's face seemed to show an expression of annoyance as she quickly pulled her arm back. She must have thought I was joking.

"Really, Look!"

"Elsa!" cried the woman's weak voice.

The next moment we were all in each others arms. Poor Tante Sophie! She had lost her husband to tuberculosis while in hiding, and all she had left now where her two daughters. They had walked all the way from Rotterdam, hoping to find someone, anyone they knew—someone still alive.

Yet, the war was not over for everybody. Five weeks had passed since I had returned home. The day after I had escaped from Vlodrop, *the Gruenen* had stormed the town, chasing the people out of their homes and across the Ruhr River. While *the Gruenen* were doing their work well, the Allies did theirs, and bombed the town, killing tens of people and injuring many. At last, *the Gruenen* left town in a rain of grenade fire and Vlodrop, or what was left of it, became "No Man's Land." The approximately 800 people that were left behind had to wait another five weeks until February 28—their freedom.

On that day, from beneath the rubble of what once had been a neat, little house, twenty-four people emerged. One of them was Rosie. The surrounding area was infested with land mines, and it wasn't until March 12 that Oom Kees and Mijnheer Schragen, a fellow-underground worker, were able to set out on Oom Kees's motorcycle to bring her home. As we waited, the hands of the clock hardly seemed to move, but at last the kitchen door flew open and Oom Kees walked in. In his arms, he carried a thin, pale little girl with no lustre left in her eyes.

Rosie had come home at last.

Carefully, he handed her over to Mama, who could barely see through her tears. Kees looked around the room, and his blue eyes briefly rested on each and every one of us. Then he turned to Papa and took his hand. "I can't believe it, all six of you." His voice broke, "I've got all of you back together. Maan, let's drop the curtain for the last time." Then they embraced. Papa's nostrils quivered more than ever before. He wasn't able to speak. But there was no need for words. Oom Kees understood.

Standing near the door, Mijnheer Schragen watched silently. Oom Kees was the first one to speak. Clearing his throat, he said, "Well, we'd better get going." He began walking toward the door, but before he walked out, he turned around one last time to remind Papa of their trip to Belgium the following day. They would be going to get Oom Philip and Tante Nettie's children—now orphans. "I'll be picking you up at seven o'clock!"

"All right!" Papa replied. "I'll be ready!"

Then the door shut.

It couldn't have been more than a couple of hours later that the doorbell rang. Its piercing sound made all of us jump. Papa went to answer. On the stoop stood Harry, Oom Kees's youngest brother, trembling, his face ashen.

"Harry! What's wrong? What's happened?" Papa pulled Harry inside.

"Kees! It's Kees!" Putting his head against Papa's shoulder, he broke down. We had all gathered in the hall.

"Has something happened to Kees?" Papa asked. Harry nodded.

"After he left here, his motorcycle was hit by a truck—an American army truck. Schragen is dead. Kees is very seriously injured," he cried.

Papa staggered against the wall.

A strange feeling came over me. I heard what they were saying, but I felt as if I wasn't really there. Then I saw Papa grab his coat and follow Harry out the door.

A short time later, Papa quietly entered the hospital room. Tante Lieske was sitting at her husband's bed side, holding his hand. Her eyes were red and swollen. She briefly looked up to acknowledge Papa's presence. Then her eyes went back to the chalk-white face in the bed. The heavy bandages on his head left only a small part of his face visible. The sharp, thin nose seemed even more prominent.

Papa pulled a chair near the other side of the bed. "Kees! Kees—this is Maan," he whispered. "I'm here with you."

No response. Papa and Tante Lieske exchanged quick glances. She slowly shook her head.

Putting his mouth closer to Oom Kees's ear, Papa repeated, "Kees! This is Maan. Can you hear me?"

Oom Kees's eyelids quivered. His lips moved ever so slightly. Papa put his ear close to Oom Kees's mouth. Faintly the words came, "Belgium . . . you go . . . . "

Choking away his tears, Papa replied, "Yes, I'll go to Belgium. Don't worry," and he softly patted the transparent white hand.

Even then, Oom Kees's thoughts were still with those who needed him.

He died the following day.

Not comprehending, I stared down into the gaping black hole at my feet. People, wearing black clothes, were standing all around it. Then Papa's voice speaking beautiful words, seemed to break all around me.

Next, I stood in the small living room of Tante Lieske's parents' house. The heavy curtains were closed. I hardly recognized it. More people were lined against the walls. My throat was so dry, it hurt. Tante Lieske held me. I felt her tears.

Outside, it was almost spring, my favorite season. Soon the sweet scent of hundreds of wild flowers blended with the smell of tar would permeate the air; bright-colored oil spills would shimmer in the late afternoon sunlight and slowly drift away across the water.

Chapter 15

Re-entry

When, at last, the tears had subsided, the war had officially ended, and our soldier houseguests had left, the time came to return home.

Papa decided to go first. The Americans were happy to offer him a "ride" and soon he began moving north with the troops, back to Amsterdam—a city now ravaged by hunger and starvation.

Even if our house in Amstelveen had still been available, it would never have accommodated the large number of people that Papa was planning to bring back.

The mayor of Amstelveen was very sympathetic to Papa's dilemma and offered him a large home at a minimal rent. Ironically, the owner had been a member of the N.S.B. and was safely behind bars. For a time, he had used part of the house to conduct meetings for the *Jeugd Storm* (Hitler Youth).

Excited about the fruitful result of his trip, Papa returned to Sittard immediately. He bought a used truck and we were ready to depart. The truck was large enough to hold all of us, including our "furniture"—a number of mattresses (the only furniture left to our name)—as well as some blankets.

Seated on a yellow kitchen chair, Mama had a ring side seat. The rest of us were gathered around her. When I say the rest of us, I mean: Papa, Corrie, Nan, Rosie and me; Tante Sophie and her two daughters; two friends of one of Tante Sophie's daughters who had survived the camps; the two children of Oom Philip and Tante Nettie; and two other young men we had picked up along the way. One of them had been in hiding in a chicken coop for two years; the other was a survivor of the camps. Fifteen of us altogether.

With Papa behind the wheel, we were finally on our way, singing: *"Wij zijn Sittard moe. Wij gaan naar Mokum toe."* (We're tired of Sittard, we are going back to Mokum [Amsterdam]). This time we were leaving Sittard for good.

Our truck was not closed completely in. All it had were side panels. Nervously, I watched Nan and a couple of our cousins. They were sitting at the back of the truck, dangling their feet, waving at some military trucks parked alongside the road. Meanwhile, I kept holding on to Mama's chair, afraid she might fly over the side.

It was a long and agonizing trip. Our progress was greatly hampered by military convoys and Bailey bridges. After about ten hours, just when we'd entered the Amsterdam city limits, one of the mattresses came loose. It barely missed our heads, landing in the middle of the road. We yelled for Papa to stop, but he apparently didn't hear us. He just kept on trucking. Since a military convoy was right behind us, it really wouldn't have made any difference.

At last we arrived at the house. It was quite nice and it didn't take us very long to get settled. All we had to do was drop the mattresses.

For the next few weeks, three times a day, we took full advantage of the "take out" service offered by the soup kitchen parked down the street. We took turns picking up our breakfast, lunch and dinner.

"How many?"

"Fifteen."

"Fifteen?"

"Yes." Fifteen scoops of "delicious" porridge, prepared from some kind of cookie, were sloppily dumped in our pot.

"There you go."

The same was repeated for lunch and dinner, except instead of "cookie porridge," we were treated to a watery soup.

Slowly, life improved, and before long we were almost back to normal. It was time to return to school.

I had my mind set on attending the Amsterdam Lyceum and maybe joining some of the children with whom I had started first grade. I hoped so. But it was not meant to be. I failed my entrance exam. I spent that year in a different, slightly easier school. It gave me an opportunity to catch up, which I did. The following year, I entered the Lyceum.

Unfortunately my dreams of a wonderful time turned into a nightmare. The war had finally caught up with me. The extrovert had turned into an introvert. I no longer had anything in common with my peers. As a result, I endured a lot of teasing, even injury, but I decided to fight it out by myself.

During one of our school outings, as I was leaving a campfire sing-along, I was roughed up by some of the boys.

Later that night, one of the girls, who later became my best friend, heard me crying in my sleeping bag. She asked me what had happened. I told her, "Nothing." But she had noticed the bruises on my face and decided to report it.

The teacher who had been selected to supervise our three-day trip was Juffrouw van Geldermalsen, a physical education instructor—a wonderful grey-haired lady with a gentle demeanor, as well as a great regard for fairness. When she learned about the incident, she quickly called a meeting—that very night. I can still remember the room with the ironing board sitting in the middle "like a judge's bench"—the accused on one side and I on the other.

As the teacher began talking about my experiences, of which she was very much aware, the room became notably quiet. She never seemed to blame anyone or make anyone feel guilty. She handled it very wisely, and when she was finally finished, we parted, quietly, without so much as a glance at each other.

The following morning was a new day, the beginning of a new dawn. The best years of my life were just about to begin.

A Reward for Tante Leiske

As I was leaving for work early on the morning of December 3, 1980, I lingered a while to absorb the quiet of the new spring day. By now, I was married to an American and living and working in Michigan. On this particular morning the sky was a clear, cloudless blue that only comes with spring. The air smelled clean and fresh. In the corn fields across the road, the first signs of the new crop had already begun to show. The usual sounds surrounded me—the singing of the birds, the engine of a lonesome tractor far away out in the fields somewhere—but rather than distracting, they seemed to add to the peacefulness.

Slowly I began driving along the lonely, narrow country road. Suddenly I realized that the precious moment of just seconds ago had already become a part of the past—a mere memory to join the many others that had gone before.

Along the way I passed isolated homes and farms interrupted only by a single orchard, some abandoned fields, a small church, and a small country gas station where the regulars congregated daily. I felt a sense of appreciation for being alive. I thought of the people living inside some of those houses and pictures began to emerge of a familiar scene of a different time, long ago. I saw my grandmother playing hide-and-seek with my younger sister and me while Mama did her daily household chores. As evening came I saw Mama and Papa sitting, as usual, on either side of the hearth—Mama forever mending our socks and Papa consuming every inch of the evening newspaper. At the dining room table my older brother and sister tried unsuccessfully to concentrate on their homework as Rosie and I kept the family entertained with our home-made theatrical acts.

All that seemed so very long ago and yet so very near. I often wondered why I clung so to my memories. Could it possibly be because the early, carefree years were taken away before I had been given a chance to enjoy them? I discovered that the bad memories were much easier for me to explain and to deal with if I held on to the little time I had consciously enjoyed. I wanted to preserve those good times though I knew that for me they were indelible—they existed in a time that would be earmarked for its greatest crime against humanity.

At a very vulnerable age and because of my Jewish extraction, I had an opportunity to witness both sides of humankind—both unspeakable evil and unparalleled generosity and unselfish love had seemed to evolve to affect and to enrich my life forever. To have survived such a phenomenon and not reflect on it, and on those who had voluntarily offered to exchange their lives for mine, would be unjust.

Before I knew it, I reached the highway and the traffic began to interfere with my thoughts. I turned on the radio and, as was the case each morning, the familiar voice of Wally Phillips of radio station WGN-Chicago joined me the rest of the way. He again mentioned, as he had for the last several weeks, a "Fantasy Contest" sponsored by WGN. Unlike other mornings, however, this time the announcement seemed to jump out at me. The moment he mentioned the word "Fantasy," all I could think of were the words of Tante Lieske's latest letter to me: "Maybe some day I will have a chance to come to the U.S."

Should I try and enter the contest? Could this be the answer to her dream? Wouldn't it be a wonderful way to tell her "Thank you for being there when there was no one else to take care of me. Thank you for drying my tears when at times I became frightened or overcome with homesickness. Thank you for always knowing what to do, and for teaching me the early lessons of childhood. Most of all, thank you for the tremendous price you had to pay in the end. I'll never forget it."

All kinds of thoughts were going through my mind, and I could feel the pressure on the accelerator increasing. When I reached the office, I ran inside, ignoring everyone in my path. Within seconds I was typing away, trying to condense the five years of heroism and bravery of a husband-and-wife team in Nazi-occupied Holland during World War II to less than two full pages. All the while I kept telling myself: "I'm going to win this! I know I'm going to win this?" Why? I'm not quite sure. Perhaps at the time I felt that the story about those, in whose names I had entered the contest, would be difficult to exceed.

Soon the excitement of the moment began to wear off, and after several weeks had gone by, I hardly ever thought about it. Consequently, when I answered the phone one morning and a pleasant woman's voice said: "Mandy, Wally Phillips would like to talk to you," my response was immediate—I hung up! Even though I had been so sure I'd win, I guess I'd convinced myself even more that this couldn't ever happen to me.

Moments later the phone rang again. The same gentle voice said: "Mandy, please don't hang up. You are on the air." I guessed I wasn't dreaming after all. Speechless, and with tears streaming down my face, I listened to Wally's voice as he read my letter over the airwaves, telling his listeners that, from among thousands of entries I had been chosen by an illustrious panel of judges as the winner of the "Fantasy Contest." Tante Lieske was going to have her wish; and I couldn't wait to tell her.

It truly was the beginning of a wonderful fantasy. The Royal Dutch Air Lines would provide Tante Lieske's first-class flight to the United States and back. For the whole month, she and I would travel across the United States, visiting any place we desired. Our hotel accommodations would be provided by the Hilton Hotel Corporation. I read our itinerary over and over again. I could hardly believe all the events planned for us.

Then a thought crept into my mind. Wouldn't it be great if Tante Lieske and President Reagan could meet each other? After all, both had contributed greatly to history—the President as a great political leader who believed in freedom for all, and Lieske as a young, 27-year-old resistance housewife trying to save the lives of innocent people. They definitely had something in common. Maybe I was pushing a little too far. Or was I? "Nothing ventured, nothing gained," I told myself, and thus my mind was made up.

I knew that time was running out and that I couldn't delay my request another minute. But how could I be sure that the President would receive my request? Then it occurred to me that perhaps I should seek the assistance of congressman Guy Vander Jagt. I got in touch with his Michigan office and was advised to direct my request to his Washington office. Once again I sat down to formulate yet another wish to add to our fantasy. As expected, I received a response from the congressman advising me he would do all he could, but the shortness of time would definitely militate against my dream.

A few days later I was surprised by a phone call. This time it was the White House—and this time I was not going to hang up! The call was quite formal, asking for my social security number and Tante Lieske's address. That was it. I felt a pang of disappointment. I guess I had expected a firm time and date to visit the President. How absurd! So the waiting continued.

In early March 1981, Tante Lieske arrived in the United States. A few days later our trip got underway, perfectly orchestrated by John Briska, one of Hilton's public relations directors. Our first stop was Chicago, where for the next four wonderful days, we were guests of the Palmer House. Our suite was one that only the privileged can dream about. Two dozen roses, wine, and an assortment of cheeses and fresh fruits were awaiting us. The following morning, during a press conference, we were finally introduced to Wally Phillips of WGN-Chicago; Mr. Sherin, the Senior Vice President of Hilton Corporation; and many other participants in our "Fantasy." We were presented with several gifts, including a check from WGN. Some of the highlights were: dinner at the Empire Room, two plays, and a tour of Chicago offered by American Limousine. I'll always remember the kind gesture of the chauffeur when, at the end of our tour, he opened the trunk and handed both Lieske and me a beautiful bouquet of flowers. We were wined and dined wherever we wished. We had made instant news, and it was strange watching our faces on the nightly news.

Friday arrived and the next day we would be leaving for Washington, D.C. I still had heard nothing from either Congressman Vander Jagt's office or the White House. I had previously decided not to tell Tante Lieske about my bold undertaking. I wanted it to be a surprise, and at that point I was glad I had.

At 4:00 p.m., the phone rang. That wasn't a total surprise, for the last few days it had rung constantly—radio stations, TV stations, Game Shows. Everyone, it seemed, wanted to meet Tante Lieske.

"Mandy Evans, please?" a woman's voice asked.

"Speaking."

"This is the White House. I'm calling on behalf of the President. He would like to meet you and Mrs. van Kessel next Wednesday at noon. Do you think you can make it?"

"Yes, we will." I blurted out. If any protocol had been called for at that moment, it totally escaped me.

"Of course, if something unexpected arises, such as a war . . . ," the woman continued.

"There is not going to be a war," I assured her.

She laughed gently. "The President will be expecting you then."

When I told Tante Lieske what had just transpired, she seemed excited yet strangely calm. She couldn't quite understand my nervousness.

"The President is just a nice man," she said. I guess she was right about that. After all, Tante Lieske would always be Tante Lieske.

In Washington we stayed at the Washington Hilton, which, incidentally, was the same hotel where the President survived an assassination attempt only two weeks later. I often thought how nearly prophetic the woman's words had been when she had said: "Of course, if something unexpected arises. . . ."

We were treated with the same kindness and hospitality as at the Palmer House—roses and all. Shortly after our arrival, the general manager and his wife, Mr. and Mrs. William L. Smith, kindly invited us to their living quarters. They had us join them for a Sunday brunch—the likes of which I had never seen—and afterwards showed us around Washington, D.C.; and Georgetown.

On Monday morning, we were invited by NBC to appear on Tom Brokow's *Today Show*. The interview with Carol Simpson took place in the Washington studio. In spite of Tante Lieske's limited knowledge of English, she never seemed to lose control—not for a moment, even on national television. Later we did some sightseeing, took a tour through the White House, and attended a session of the Senate. The lines were extremely long, but with our passes from Vice President Bush, we were promptly admitted to the Vice President's Gallery. The following day, St. Patrick's Day, we were the personal guests of Congressman Guy Vander Jagt, who took us on a private tour of the Capitol Building. For a brief moment Tante Lieske was allowed to take the seat of the Speaker of the House. For lunch the congressman invited us to the House of the Republican Party. To be eating corned beef and cabbage among some of the best-known leaders of our country was quite an event in itself. Later that afternoon, we were invited by Judge Webster of the FBI and we visited with him for about fifteen minutes. Our visit was appropriately concluded with a private tour provided by two FBI agents through the FBI building.

Wednesday arrived before we knew it. I was quite nervous, to say the least, but it seemed that even the imminent visit to the President wasn't going to shake Tante Lieske. I could only watch her in wonder. By 11:45 a.m. we were seated in the waiting area of the White House, along with Congressman Vander Jagt and Wally Phillips. At one point, someone walked up to us and apologized that the President was running a little behind schedule. That was all right, we weren't planning to go anywhere else anyway.

The moment arrived. We were to meet the President of the United States. Finally, standing near the doorway of the Oval Office, smiling broadly, his arms stretched out ready to welcome us, was the President. All my anxiety simply vanished. The President, who tried to make us feel very much at ease, inquired about our trip. And, of course, the topic of World War II came up. He talked about his own wartime experiences. "If anyone ever tries to tell you it didn't happen, I can show him some photographs of the atrocities," he said.

After about twenty minutes, one of the security people pointed to his watch as he tried to get the President's attention to alert him to his time schedule. The President nodded his head. "It's all right," he said. The man smiled, and the President continued. Our visit lasted about half an hour. It had been truly wonderful. Before leaving, we were able to visit briefly with Jim Brady, the President's press secretary—moments for which I'll always be grateful.

Even though this was without a doubt the highlight of our trip, the remainder of our "Fantasy" should not be undervalued.

Following our visit to Washington, we spent a few days in Denver where we stayed at the Denver Hilton. We toured Denver's beautiful surroundings with its majestic Rocky Mountains, visited the Capitol Building, and had lunch in one of the city's beautiful parks with the tamest squirrels I had ever encountered. Tante Lieske was elated. She had never been close to these little animals before, let alone have lunch with them. Afterwards, as in Washington, we were interviewed on KWGN-TV. We began to feel like professionals.

In Los Angeles, we stayed at the Beverly Hills Hilton. Lieske was truly "queen for a month." Among the attractions was a tour of Universal City and, of course, Disneyland. When we arrived at the VIP office in the Park, we were greeted by "Willie" Van Der Zwaag, an attractive young woman who addressed Tante Lieske in Dutch. When she noticed the surprise on Tante Lieske's face, she laughed and quickly explained that both her parents were from the Netherlands. Since she spoke Dutch and also happened to be that year's Ambassador for Disneyland, she was chosen to guide us on our tour. First, however, she wanted Tante Lieske to meet another VIP. I had a pretty good idea who she was talking about, but Tante Lieske didn't have a clue. Moments later we watched as the band, led by Mickey Mouse, came marching down Main Street to personally welcome this wonderful lady to Disneyland. It was the only time I cried during the whole trip.

After the official welcome ceremony had ended, we began our tour. We visited nearly every exhibit. Tante Lieske enjoyed herself tremendously. "It's just too much," she kept saying. It all must have seemed like a dream to her. It surely was for me.

Our final stop before returning to Chicago was San Diego. We had made the short trip by Amtrak. Waiting for us at the station was a limousine fully equipped with TV and bar. This time our hotel put two floors at our disposal. We were provided with fresh flowers each day, as well as wine, cheese, and exotic fruits. The general manager of the hotel, William Edwards, Jr., and his assistant Lex Lyon could not have been better hosts. They were quite protective of us since the press was constantly present. They made a car available whenever we wished to go somewhere. Thus, with the exception of one press conference, our time was pretty much our own. We spent a day across the border in Mexico and visited Seaworld, as well as San Diego's beautiful zoo. Seaworld was Tante Lieske's favorite. I had a terrible time tearing her away from the dolphins. For the rest of the time, we just ate, lazed around the pool, and ate some more.

The trip back to Chicago, through the western states, was very beautiful and very impressive, especially for Tante Lieske who was born and raised in a country half the size of Indiana. It was truly a month to remember.

Even though countless others of the resistance movement had put their lives on the line for Jewish families, I am glad that I had the opportunity to express my gratitude to at least one member of that brave group—Tante Lieske—through the kindness of a radio station in Chicago. Although quite some time has elapsed since that fantasy trip took place, I would like to publicly thank everyone who helped make it possible to turn a nightmare into a dream that can only be called a "Fantasy."

For us survivors, there will always be the memories—the good and the bad. *Lest We Forget* any of them, this book has been an attempt to remind us of our past.

Israel Recognizes Some Heroes

Tante Lieske being presented with the "Yad Vashem" ("The Righteous among the Nations") medal by the State of Israel

Gerard Sijmonsma accepts the "Vad Vashem" medal from the state of Israel for his parents, Oom Piet and Tante Annie Sijmonsma

Tante Mien receives the "Yad Vashem" medal from the State of Israel

Tante Lieske's Trip to the United States in 1981

Taken with (left to right) Wally Phillips of WGN Radio in Chicago; Tante Lieske; and Mr. James Sheerin, senior vice president of Hilton Corporation, Central Region

A news conference at the *Palmer House* in chicago

Congressman Vander Jagt introduces Tante Lieske to a bowl of jelly beans

Congressman Vander Jagt introduces Tante Lieske to President Reagan

A visit with the President in the Oval Office

With Tante Lieske and Wally Phillips,

In San Diego with Tante Lieske and
William Edwards, president of the Hilton
Hotel division, during her visit to the
United States in 1981

Tante Lieske with Mickey Mouse
and tour guide

1988—The Past Revisited

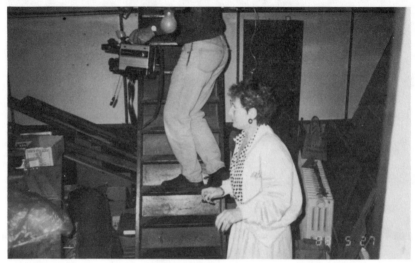

The stairs leading to *Het Vooronder,*
the hiding place

Janneke and me

Tante Sophie and Rosie

Visiting with Harry Zwaans and his wife Tonnie

Left to right: Kee's sisters, Corrie and Annie, and myself (center)

Taken with Jan and Almy Zwaans

Flanked by two other members of the Zwaan family, Tonnie and Jacques

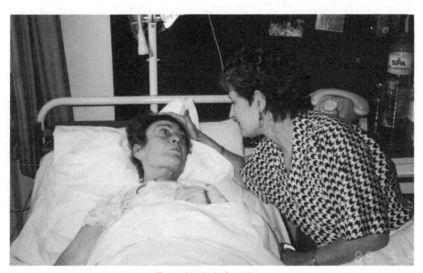

Tante Lieske's final days

The survivors. Left to right: Corrie, Mandy, Mama, Rosie, and Nan

"De Zwaan"

De Zwaan after she had capsized

The "hiding place," brought back into service later, before becoming a pleasure ship

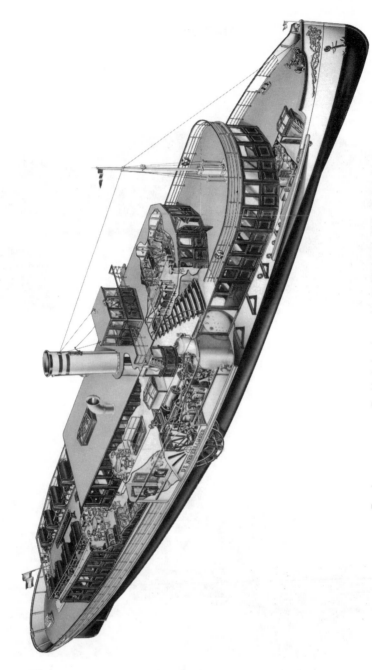

Bearing a new name, *De Nederlander*, and completely refurbished, the old "hiding place" now carries happy tourists instead of its former sad cargo

Epilogue

1991

*T*he following is a list of the main characters of the story—what eventually happened to them, and where those still alive in 1991 are living.

Papa—just when he was getting back on his feet in 1947, was stricken with a heart attack from which he never fully recovered. He died December 12, 1963, while visiting the United States.

Mama—at the age of 90, is living quietly in her own apartment in Toronto, Canada.

Corrie—moved with her husband and family to the United States and is presently living in Minnesota.

Nan—is still living in Amsterdam. His wife is the only survivor of a family of six.

Rosie—is living in Toronto, Canada.

Lieske—remarried a "skipper." For many years she and her new husband travelled on their barge. After their retirement, they lived quietly in the small town of Beneden-Leeuwen. She was presented with a civilian award by the Israeli government and was received by President Ronald Reagan at the White House in 1981. She died in 1988 after a long battle with cancer.

Oom Twan—died on November 19, 1971.

Tante Mien—is still living in Geleen, Holland.

Tante Annie & Oom Piet—both died several years ago.

Zus—died not too long after her parents.

The Zwaans Family—Oom Piet and Moeke died many years ago, but all the children are still living. Most of them are residing in and around Dongen, Holland, except for Jan who is living in Belgium with Almy, and Harry who is residing in Australia with his wife Tonnie.

Oom Willie—I lost contact with Oom Willie, which is one of the things I have regretted most in my life.

Grootmoeder—died in Auschwitz.

Oom Philip & Tante Nettie—both died in Auschwitz.

Guus—died in Mauthausen.

Tante Sophie—and her two daughters returned safely. Her husband died while in hiding. Her oldest daughter preceded her in death in 1972. Her only surviving daughter, Mini, is living in Amsterdam with her husband. Tante Sophie died in 1989 in Amsterdam.

Sarina—married her friend. They moved to Canada where she lives today.

Oom Ies & Tante Greta—have died.

Lida—is living in a suburb of Amsterdam with her family.

Nikki & Jan Hornick—Jan died many years ago, but Nikki is still living in Born, Holland—not far from the harbor.

Gordon Gard—lives in Birmingham, Michigan, with his wife, Lorraine.

De Zwaan—is still in service to this day! Harry, Kees' youngest brother, owned her for a while before selling her. Since that time she transferred hands several times. The last time I saw her was in 1988, just a few days before she was to be taken to the scrap yard. I even visited *Het Vooronder*. She looked awful. I could have wept for her.

Several years later, to my enormous surprise, I received a letter from Harry, along with a colorful brochure which described a brand new "pleasure boat" which now cruises the waterways of the Netherlands. Yes, it was *De Zwaan*. Someone had bought her and turned her into a beautiful ship that everyone can enjoy. Her name has been changed to "The Nederlander"; however, her past will never be forgotten, and I will always remember her as *De Zwaan*. A loose translation of part of the text of the brochure I received reads as follows:

> The past and the present meet in *The Nederlander* [De Zwaan]. Eighty-five years after its conception, it is reborn and travels the important Dutch rivers all year long. Even on the coldest days there seems to be a special warmth aboard the ship. . . .
>
> This royal vessel has a rich history behind it. During the first period of its existence it serviced a number of towns in the province of Zeeland, and once served as the royal yatch for her majesty, Queen Wilhelmina. . . .